the BOY *on the* LAKE

What People Are Saying about Trevor Schaefer,

the BOY *on the* LAKE

"I think Trevor's testimony is something that will be difficult to ignore and, if you witnessed it, impossible to forget."

Daniel Rosenberg

"Meet Trevor Schaefer: Riveting Testimony Anchors Strong Senate Hearing on Disease Clusters and Environmental Health"

March 29, 2011

"Trevor beat cancer that he got when he was just a child and is inspiring a lot of people to make sure that others do not have to go through the same thing. Trevor has come out of his experience with great purpose. He has decided to devote his life to helping children who also face the frightening reality of having to beat cancer."

U.S. Senator Barbara Boxer (D-CA)

Chairman of Senate Environment and Public Works Committee

March 29, 2011

"Trevor Schaefer has an incredible history that helps us address this issue of cancer clusters in children. Through raising awareness and research funds and providing mentoring services for young cancer survivors, Trevor Schaefer and his mother are shining examples of how the selfless actions of individuals can make a real difference in the lives of those in need."

U.S. Senator Mike Crapo (R-ID)

March 29, 2011

BOY *the* on *the* LAKE

*He Faced Down the Biggest Bully of
His Life and Inspired* TREVOR'S LAW

A True Story
by SUSAN ROSSER
with Charlie Smith
and Trevor Schaefer

NEW YORK

the BOY on the LAKE
He Faced Down the Biggest Bully of His Life and Inspired TREVOR'S LAW

ISBN 978-1-61448-333-5 paperback
ISBN 978-1-61448-334-2 eBook
Library of Congress Control Number: 2012945361

Morgan James Publishing
The Entrepreneurial Publisher
5 Penn Plaza, 23rd Floor,
New York City, New York 10001
(212) 655-5470 office • (516) 908-4496 fax
www.MorganJamesPublishing.com

Cover Design by:
Rachel Lopez
www.r2cdesign.com

Interior Design by:
Bonnie Bushman
bonnie@caboodlegraphics.com

In an effort to support local communities, raise awareness and funds, Morgan James Publishing donates a percentage of all book sales for the life of each book to Habitat for Humanity Peninsula and Greater Williamsburg.

Get involved today, visit
www.MorganJamesBuilds.com.

Habitat
for Humanity®
Peninsula and
Greater Williamsburg
Building Partner

DEDICATION

To the children:
Like the music of the mountains and the colors of the rainbow,
they're a promise of the future and a blessing for today.

John Denver, "Rhymes and Reasons"

Contents

Note to Readers

This story is true. Even so, some of the events have been compressed and/or the times of their occurrences have been altered for a smoother narrative. In addition, we have changed some names of people who appear in this story and combined characters in certain instances. These will be denoted with an asterisk (*).

The sins of the past cast a long shadow.

Irish Proverb

ACKNOWLEDGMENTS

A project this long in the making can only be accomplished with the enduring support of friends and family. To my husband, Bob Rosser, you kept me grounded and determined. To my son Jon and daughter Julie, your encouragement has always kept me going when the road ahead seemed too steep to climb; your insightful readings and wise suggestions have made the difference along the way. A huge debt of gratitude to my sister Teri Schwartz, whose own perseverance has been a beacon for me to follow and whose understanding of what makes a good story helped shape ours.

To my good friend Bonnie Bruckheimer, who believed in this project almost before it got off the ground; her involvement and encouragement at the earliest stages were paramount. Thanks to Catherine Buckley who pointed me in the right direction. To my friends who generously read, and sometimes reread, the many versions of *The Boy on the Lake* and offered enormously helpful critiques: Barbara Federman, Judy Brodsky, Candy Sindell, Margie Kulp, Bunni Benaron, Barbara Keller, Georgia Fogelson, Patti Massman Neuwirth, Deborah Jacobson, Madeline Redstone, Nancy Schectman, MK Zordani, Trudy Schwartz and Andrea Belzberg. A special thanks to Wendy Gross DeWoskin, a good buddy and editor extraordinaire. Thanks to Dr. Elaine Miller, who helped so much on parts of my research. To Tara Frier, PR maven and cheerleader, who kept us going on her energy and enthusiasm alone. To Amanda Rooker and all the people at Morgan James who have done a remarkable job shepherding this project to a successful conclusion.

To former *L.A. Times* reporter Deniene Husted, to whom we are indebted-- her scientific background was an invaluable aid in turning those parts of our story into a more readable narrative. Thanks to Lori Milisic and Else Fuller for taking me back through the Smiths' lives with honesty and objectivity. To Mike Stewart and the citizens of Valley County who gave of their time and their knowledge, and opened every door into the true history of that breathtaking part of Idaho. To Professors Paul Sheppard and Mark Witten, who generously shared their understanding of the history and science of childhood cancer clusters. Without their input, we never would have been able to fashion Trevor's Law. To U. S. Senator Barbara Boxer, thanks for pushing us farther than we thought we had a right to go. Her steadfast belief in S.76 remains rock hard, and her indomitable spirit and fervent belief that we must make our country safer for all of our children is an inspiration for us all.

Most of all, I want to thank Charlie and Trevor for being so willing to embrace the fight for justice for children with cancer. I know it has been hard for them over these past nine years. So much sacrificed. So many friends lost because they could not accept that Charlie and Trevor were on a different path to fulfillment. They are truly amazing people. They know how much I adore and respect them both. They are part of my family now.

Susan Rosser

There are many individuals to whom I owe a debt of gratitude for helping me overcome so many obstacles in my life. To my mother Charlie Smith: Most of the people I knew and loved fled when the going got tough. But you stayed with me in my darkest hours. You gave me hope and the courage to win my battle against the bully cancer. You taught me respect, integrity, and loyalty. I honestly don't believe I would have made it without you. I love you, Mom.

To Joan Kroc: Even though you weren't my biological grandmother, you were there for me from the day I was born until the day you died. You gave me hope and strength during my cancer treatments. I only wish I had a chance to say goodbye to you. You will always have a special place in my heart, Grandma Joan.

To Susan Rosser: Thank you for hanging in there for so many years while this story developed. I have learned a lot from you, Suzy Q! To Senator Barbara Boxer: You are truly a hero, a true warrior for the protection of our children and communities. Thank you for introducing Bill S.76, Trevor's Law, and for your passion to create a better tomorrow. To Senator Mike Crapo: You are one of the many reasons why I am proud to call myself an Idahoan. Thank you for co-sponsoring Bill S.76, Trevor's Law, and for your continued support. To Erin Brockovich: Thank you for your work with environmental issues, disease clusters, and for your support for Trevor's Law. You are an inspiration to me and to so many others. This world is a much better place with you in it. To Channel 7 Anchorman Mark Johnson: Thank you for your friendship and support for Trevor's Trek Foundation and covering the many stories about children who have battled cancer and environmental issues. To PGA Professional, Jerry Breaux: Thank you for teaching me to be a gentleman both on and off the golf course.

And many thanks to: Make-A-Wish Foundation of Idaho; Camp Rainbow Gold; Dr. Stan Olsen; Doug Oppenheimer; Dr. Cherny; Dr. Chang and everyone at the children's oncology department at St. Luke's Hospital; Mr. Carlton; Dr. John Park; John Bertolero; Lori Milisic; Jean Uranga; Kirk and Hillary Anderson; and Bob Rosen, whose wise counsel, caring ways and support for my story helped boost my resolve from the very beginning of this journey.

A very special shout-out to Bradley Springer and all of the cancer kids who have taught me how precious life is.

And last but not least, to my chemo dog and best friend, Elliot. You were there for me 24/7; a dog is truly a man's best friend.

Trevor Schaefer

To my son Trevor for his strength and courage in beating back the bullies in his life. You gave me the strength and power to fight my own battles. You are my hero; you are truly "the wind beneath MY wings." I love you.

To Joan Kroc for the many pep talks when I needed them the most. Your support and encouragement got me through the toughest time of my life. You always said what doesn't kill you makes you stronger; you were right.

To Mike Stewart: You encouraged me to never give up. Thank you for being my wingman on many adventures.

Thanks to former Idaho governor, Cecil Andrus, for your incredible tenacity and passion on environmental issues in Idaho and throughout our great country. You have paved the path to being non-political in a political world.

To Tona Henderson for the many hours you spent with Susan, Trevor, and me, helping us understand how environmental toxins have affected your family, and for your selfless devotion to get the truth out about what's happening to the Downwinders in our state.

To Julie Hampton: You are my right hand gal, always there when I need you. I know you understand the impact of childhood cancer even more now that your three-year-old grandson has been diagnosed with this dread disease.

To Else Fuller for the thirty-five years of friendship and making me laugh when I wanted to cry.

To Susan Rosser, author and friend, for the incredible job writing this story. You always have been there for us.

I would also like to acknowledge: My niece, Lori Milisic; Dr. Mark Witten; Dr. Paul Sheppard; Paul Woods; Tonya Dombrowski; Leslie Freeman; Floyd Sands; John Bertolero; Deniene Husted; Tara Frier; Dr. John Park; Dr. Scott Harris; Kathy Lovell; Dave Holland; Patti Moran and the Comprehensive Cancer Alliance for Idaho; Bonnie Bruckheimer; Theresa McLeod; Mary Wood; Kirk and Hillary Anderson; Mayor Dave Bieter; and Governor Butch Otter.

And a special thanks to other family and friends who have stood by me all the way. You know who you are.

Charlie Smith

PROLOGUE

Washington, D.C.
March 29, 2011
Environment and Public Works Oversight Hearing
Senate Hearing Room 211

Trevor Schaefer took his seat at the long table reserved for witnesses. His nameplate was first. "You'll be the first to speak," an aide had told him. "You'll set the tone."

Just what I needed to hear! Behind the anxious twenty-one-year-old were rows of occupied chairs, with more people milling in the aisles and lining the back of the room. Senate and congressional aides, officials, and reporters all talking at once sounded like a swarm of cicadas in heat. Added to that, camera operators scurried here and there, adjusting their clunky tripods and turning on their blinding lights.

Overwhelmed, he shook his head to alleviate the constant buzz in his ear. It mixed with the drone of the other noises, elevating his anxiety level. *Can I go through with this?* He looked around for a clear path to a quick exit, just in case. *Don't be ludicrous*, he thought, almost laughing out loud at himself. He could picture the headline in tomorrow's hometown newspaper: "Cancer Kid Plays Hooky."

A female reporter walked over. Asked if he would stay afterwards for an interview. Trevor turned up the bravado. "Sure. Be happy to."

He eyed his watch when she walked away. *Liftoff in less than two minutes.* Another shiver of nerves rippled through him. He took off his glasses and wiped them clean. Wiped them again. In quick tic-like movements he straightened his tie, eyed his pants zipper, undid the button on his blazer. Touched his hair—still slicked back. *All good to go: check, check, check.* At least externally his life was in order. No worries there.

It was the things no one could actually see that still made him so apprehensive. Constant, no-kidding fears: memory loss; double vision; stumbling over his words. Yesterday he'd lost it. Had a meltdown smack in the middle of the bar and grill in the hotel where he was staying. He'd fled the table in the middle of a conversation with a consultant to take cover in a secluded alcove before his mother could even ask him what was wrong. He knew he was descending into another of those frightening, dark moods that swept over him from time to time.

She found him sitting there with his head in his hands. The buzzing in his ear really bothered him. He felt confused and disoriented. He was certain he'd ruin all that they had striven to accomplish over the past eight years. Finally, he managed to fight back his demons and prepare himself for today.

The Environment and Public Works Committee chair, Senator Barbara Boxer, was gaveling the Oversight Hearing to order. He heard the senator calling upon him to speak about S.76—Trevor's Law. He took a deep breath, pushed his glasses up on his nose, and gathered his papers together.

Okay, Trev. This is it. Make eye contact with all the senators. Smile. Take a sip of water. Breathe slowly. Deliberately. Clear your head. Feel the meaning...feel who you are and why you are the one who has to deliver *this important message… **imagine a world without children**…You can do it…*

The metallic, grating noise of his microphone being turned up caused him to pause. All at once, the sound threw him back nine years. He was in a different room in a small hamlet in the mountains of Idaho…

The gift is in the problem.

Teri Schwartz

Dean, UCLA School of Theater, Film, and Television

Part One:

THE WRONG
KIND OF PARADISE

CHAPTER ONE

McCall, Idaho
Pilgrim's Cove
September 28, 2002

The grating noise of the intercom yanked twelve-year-old Trevor out of a restless sleep. He sat bolt upright, head pulsing. He could hear his father's voice through the intercom.

The throbbing in his head increased with every word his father uttered. It wasn't merely the unfamiliar tone of his voice; it was what he was saying: graphic sexual banter with someone on the other end of his cell phone. Trevor Smith was in the great room of the main house but heard everything as though he were right next to his dad. His father must have accidentally pushed the intercom button and now was broadcasting his sexual desires from the two-bedroom guesthouse, where he presently lived.

Since Trevor's mother, Charlie, filed for divorce from his dad a few months earlier, a court order had banished Ballard Smith to the quarters above the garage. It was a pretty pathetic comedown for his father, who used to be a big shot in San Diego. He was the president of the San Diego Padres baseball team in the early 1980s. His dad had been

5

married to Linda, the only daughter of Joan Kroc. Joan's husband was Ray Kroc, the billionaire McDonald's Hamburgers mogul and owner of the ball club. Before his divorce from Linda, his dad enjoyed a life of vast wealth and high drama in the public spotlight.

Even though everyone in McCall knew about his dad's former life, Trevor could tell that the divorce court judge really didn't care who Ballard Smith had been. Right off the bat, he awarded his mom the run of the main house. Trevor lived with her. He preferred it that way. His dad's moods were like a pinball in one of those arcade games—crazily bouncing all over the place. Lately he had felt increasingly uneasy around him.

Right now, Trevor was thinking that if he'd slept in his bed upstairs instead of on the couch in the great room, he wouldn't have heard any of this sordid conversation. With no intercom system installed there, his dad's voice wouldn't have penetrated the thick log walls. But Trevor no longer loved his bedroom. Where once its woody darkness cocooned him, now he merely felt claustrophobic. These days his whole life felt like it was closing in on him.

Once he realized that his parents were really heading toward a divorce, Trevor spent a lot of time thinking about the arc of his life in McCall. Back when he was six and moved there full-time from San Diego, California, his existence was like one big playtime. Every season brought with it another delight.

Each summer, Trevor virtually lived on Payette Lake, honing his skills at water sports. During the winter, he had easy access to snowboarding at Brundage Mountain located a few miles north of his house. In fact, he actually could see the popular recreation area from their kitchen window. A good athlete in a family of athletes, by the age of eight he had won a medal for his Mighty Mite Ski Team.

Not twenty minutes south of his home on Payette Lake near Jug Mountain sprawled the family ranch. Trevor loved his horse and rode as often as possible. Each spring, his family escaped McCall's long winter to spend six weeks at their estate overlooking the deep blue Sea of Cortez in sun-drenched Cabo San Lucas, Mexico.

Although none of the children who lived full-time in McCall enjoyed a larger-than-life-style anywhere comparable to his, Trevor possessed a generous nature and had many friends whom he included in all of the fun activities and vacations provided by his parents. As he got older he came to recognize how much more he had than his classmates, most of whom were the children of the town's support workers.

Trevor often heard the term "late-in-life baby" linked with his name. "Guess they saved the best for last," he frequently joked. Family meant everything to him. His five older half-siblings and his parents used to make him feel wanted. Adored. They were at war now. The pending divorce had split the family into two bitter factions. He feared he was becoming an afterthought.

There were recent signs that the breakup was coming. The beauty of his surroundings turned bleak whenever he walked through the front door of the house. Increasingly fierce arguments. Stony silences. Escalating differences between what his mom and dad wanted to do with their lives often left him bereft, torn between love for both of them and his own buried wishes.

Then last November his mom told him she could not deal with his dad's unconscionable behavior any longer. She was filing for divorce. Hearing this, Trevor felt as if he had skied recklessly out of bounds past the danger signs and suddenly found himself overcome by an unexpected, powerful avalanche. Divorce: a word like a wall of snow that knocked him over and nearly suffocated the life out of him. At first, Trevor felt seething anger at his dad for causing the breakup but almost as much for his mom. She *promised* him they'd always be a family.

His disappointment with his mother faded quickly after that. But his relationship with his dad continued to deteriorate. It seemed nowhere was safe enough to escape his father's Jekyll and Hyde behavior. Certainly not the sunny great room with its massive picture window and its comforting overstuffed sofa, which he had preferred to his room most nights in the past few weeks. Not now with that damned screechy intercom jolting him out of sleep...

No kid should have to wake up to his dad's voice boring into him in such a totally creepy way, Trevor thought. He guessed that the recipient of his father's cell phone sex talk was his latest girlfriend. She was a clerk in his parents' store, Out-A-Idaho, just like the other woman who caused his parents' initial breakup months ago. The clerk his dad had called his "soul-mate."

But why is he sitting there with the intercom on, putting me and my mom in the middle of this? He'd have to be deaf not to have heard that awful sound. He has to know we can hear him.

Trevor felt almost unhinged by the increasingly lewd things his dad was telling his girlfriend he was going to do to her. The pounding in his head increased another notch.

What? Now he's talking to her about **me!** That did it! Trevor leapt off the couch, a growing sense of injustice fueling his charge out the mudroom door. He stormed up the guesthouse stairs two at a time and yanked hard at the door only to find it locked. He banged his fists on it, fighting to control his escalating fury. Suddenly, the door opened, and his father stood there, cell phone a few inches from his ear, looking early-morning disheveled and slightly bewildered to see his son at this hour.

"Trevor, what..."

"I heard every gross thing you said, Dad! You're disgusting."

Trevor whirled around and bounded down the wood stairs, slamming the mudroom door to the house behind him as hard as he could. He wasn't surprised that his father didn't try to follow him. He'd already come to the depressing conclusion that he was unimportant to his dad. And now this morning, his father's own words confirmed Trevor's worst fears: He was an albatross around his dad's neck. In between the man's explicit sexual overtures to this latest woman, already his *third* soul-mate since the divorce proceedings began, Ballard was insisting that he would prefer to spend the entire day in bed with her, but he had to take his kid into Boise to buy him a bike, an early birthday present.

Trevor would finally become a teenager in a few weeks, and he and his dad had planned this trip to Boise to get a Specialized Vegas bicycle. They hardly ever spent time alone these days, and it was supposed to be a big deal. Now Ballard had totally ruined it.

I'm just a frickin' chore he has to do, Trevor thought as he entered the kitchen. *I'm like taking out the garbage—do it quickly and hold your nose.*

Chapter Two

Up in the master suite, Charlie Smith also was jarred awake by the screechy sound of the intercom coming on. It took her a few seconds to process Ballard's salacious murmurings. Once she realized what was happening, her eyes snapped open and she looked at the clock. A little after six a.m.

Holy crap! That man is an idiot!

She hoped that Trevor wasn't up yet. Safely tucked away in his room, he'd have no way to hear any of his father's conversation. She turned over and pulled the covers up past her ears. No use. She couldn't block out his words. Or that smarmy tone in his voice.

Charlie suddenly heard through the intercom the sound of intense banging on the door to the guesthouse, followed by her son screaming at his dad.

Oh my God! What more can happen in this house? A shot of panic coursed through her. She quickly got out of bed, frantic about what this latest event was going to do to her son psychologically.

Charlie threw on her robe and hurried downstairs to find Trevor stomping into the kitchen.

He stopped when he saw her and pressed his hands against his temples. "Jeez, this pain. Why do I get all these headaches?"

"Hey, Trev. Considering what you've just been through this morning..."

"I wish you and everyone else would please stop saying the stress of the divorce is too hard for me to handle."

In fact, Charlie was very worried about her son. He began to be plagued by these bad headaches soon after she and Ballard separated, and while they were sporadic at first, they seemed to sweep over him more frequently these days. He had a history of stubborn sinus infections. She hoped he wasn't developing another one.

"Why don't you lie down?" she suggested.

"I'm okay."

He didn't look okay. Charlie led him into the great room. She saw the sofa and the tangle of his blankets half on the floor, a clue to where he spent the night and a testament to the haste with which he fled the house to confront his dad.

Hunched together now, they both cried.

Behind them the two-story picture window afforded a panoramic view of a vast expanse of Payette Lake. A stunning glacial body of water that was a catch basin for the region's countless high lakes, rivers, and melting snow, its beauty still had the capacity to stop her in her tracks.

Outside it appeared to be a crystalline morning just like the day before, with a hint of fall in the air. The leaves on the Aspens, silver birch, and some of the pines surrounding their property, and many among the forest of tamaracks and larches on the other side of the lake, were starting to change to their vibrant autumn hues. With the tourists gone, and their boats that had churned the lake for months now safely stored until next summer, the lake was a serene mirror. *The calm before the storm*, she had mused absently a few days earlier, while sitting outside on the deck to collect her thoughts and gaze at the silent lake for a few minutes. *Is this morning that storm?*

Normally in September Charlie loved being in these mountains that made up part of the Payette National Forest located about two hours by car northwest of Boise. This morning she wished that she and Trevor had stayed put in Boise where they had relocated last year. Ballard wanted Trevor to go to middle school in a bigger and more challenging school system in preparation for high school and then college. Getting into a top-tier university was especially important to Ballard, who once was the district attorney in a tiny Pennsylvania town but gave up the law to live in California where he joined his in-laws' business and sports empire.

Charlie just wanted out of McCall for any reason. The winters were increasingly hard to take. When Ballard suggested it, she readily agreed to relocate to Boise but to continue to spend weekends and summers at their lake house, providing the best of both worlds for Trevor.

However, soon after settling into the new home and giving Charlie *carte blanche* to remodel at will, Ballard increasingly seemed to be drawn back to McCall for what he claimed were store matters, until he almost never stayed with her and their son at all.

He even turned down a request from Trevor's middle school basketball coach to help with his team. "Why won't he do this, Mom?" Trevor had asked her. "He always wanted to be a coach in McCall."

"You know I can't answer for your dad. He says he's busy at the store."

"I miss my dad," Trevor lamented again and again. "I thought we were going to live here like a family."

"I did, too, Trev."

Then 9/11 happened. Charlie decided that their family needed to be together. Right away. Besides, the idea of being sequestered in a tiny village in the mountains made her feel safer. She arranged for Trevor to re-enter middle school in McCall. They hastily returned to their home on the lake where Charlie quickly discovered her husband's infidelity with the clerk from their store. The marriage-ending revelation led to him living in the guesthouse.

And now this morning Trevor was being forced to become involved in yet another unsavory slice of his father's personal life with yet another store clerk!

"Did you hear all of your dad's conversation?" Charlie asked softly.

"Yeah," he admitted, reddening and unable to meet her eyes. "He makes me sick. Why do I have a father like him? I hate him!"

"No, Trevor. You don't hate *him*. You just hate the *things* he does."

Trevor sighed and looked away, dismissing her inept attempt to mitigate the emotional repercussion of Ballard's behavior.

Suddenly the intercom once more emitted its hair-raising noise. *Now what?*

Ballard's unrepentant voice echoed through the house. "If you still want to go to Boise with me, Trevor, I can be ready in five minutes."

"You don't have to put yourself through this, Trev," Charlie said sympathetically. "I'll take you."

"No. I need to do this."

"How do you feel? What about your headache?"

"I'll take two Advil," he told his mother. "And I'll be okay."

CHAPTER THREE

The headaches did not go away. Just before Trevor's birthday in mid-October, the pressure in his head increased. He began to see the world as if he were on a dingy in rocky seas. Intermittently dizzy, his gait became unsteady for a few minutes at a time, and the nausea that accompanied both of these sensations felt like the one and only time he got seasick.

One night, his mom noticed him veering off course as he walked through the great room toward the stairs leading up to his bedroom.

"You okay?" she asked. "You look like a drunken sailor. You didn't get hit in the head at football practice, did you?"

"Everyone gets hit in the head at practice, Mom. That's why we wear helmets! I'm fine," he insisted. "Just got up from the couch too fast, that's all. Made me dizzy for a second."

He waited for her to quiz him further, but she turned back to some long legal document she was reading. He quickly went up to his room and lay down. That didn't help. He got dizzy again and had to sit up. Very still.

The truth was, he was scared. But he wanted to keep playing football and knew his mom would get him off the team if he weren't careful. He just couldn't admit to himself that he might be really sick. *Like really, really sick!* So far, he managed to keep some other new symptoms from his parents, like the fact that he began to throw up just about every day.

~

By November fifth, however, he was feeling wasted before the day was half over, and he had to put his head down on his desk in class just before lunch. Luckily they were doing individual reading assignments, and none of his classmates noticed. Mrs. Bingaman, his teacher, did, though.

She was his teacher once before when he was in fifth grade. In Trevor's estimation, Mrs. Bingaman, a tall, slender woman with dark hair, dressed and acted like a borderline hippie. And she had a reputation of being really hard. He'd gone into her fifth grade class with some trepidation but had learned so much from her and found her very caring. He learned another lesson: appearances can be deceiving. She knew he was a hard worker and wouldn't slack off in class without a good reason. Out of the corner of his eye, he saw her walking toward him now. He wasn't surprised.

"Hey, Trevor. What's up?" she asked.

He sat up. His head felt really heavy. He saw her face through flashes of light. "I have a pretty bad headache, Mrs. Bingaman."

In fact, it was one of the worst he'd experienced so far. It had started in the early morning as a dull pain, and he thought he might be able to control it with a few Advil. But an hour into the school day he was in the boys' bathroom barfing. That only gave him temporary relief.

Now just a few minutes until lunchtime, the pain bore into him full-force. He had hoped he could hold out, but it became impossible to focus on his class assignment. It was as if someone were pounding on his head with a hammer—from the *inside*.

"Trevor, you look pretty pale," his teacher said. "Maybe you should rest in the nurse's office until you feel better."

He nodded and gathered his books and papers. On the way to the nurse's office his vision became fuzzy for a few seconds. The flashes of light returned. He leaned against one of the metal lockers lining the wall and closed his eyes, grateful that the classrooms hadn't yet spilled out into the halls for the lunch recess.

Although finally able to continue on, he concluded that he couldn't deal with all these new symptoms alone any longer. He would have to come clean with his mom and dad and tell them what was happening to him.

"I have a bad headache," he told the nurse. "My teacher said for me to come here."

The nurse was sympathetic and took his book-bag from him while he settled onto a cot. He lay back, his head resting comfortably for a few seconds as the coolness of the fresh pillowcase pressed into his neck.

While she was feeling his forehead for fever, then deciding to take his temperature, Trevor heard the lunch recess bell ring. Doors banged open, kids' voices rang out, and a thunder of footsteps moved by the nurse's office toward the cafeteria. He would have given anything to be in that herd of students like before—talking, joking, and laughing among his friends.

The nurse removed the thermometer. "Normal," she announced.

"I have to sit up," he said suddenly.

"Are you feeling better?" she asked hopefully.

"Worse. I'm dizzy with my head back, and the pain is ..." He bent over and rested his head on his knees. "I'm kind of sick to my stomach." He straightened up and took a few deep breaths to try to overcome the feeling.

"If you have to vomit, let me know right away." She put a little curved plastic dish by his side.

The pounding in his head got worse. "I really think you should call my mom," he said suddenly. "I have to go home. I don't feel right."

CHAPTER FOUR

D espite persistent insomnia, Charlie zipped around on nervous
energy these days. She spent the early morning exercising in
their gym on the lower level of the game house, a two-and-a-
half story open-beamed structure with spectacular lake views. Forty-five
minutes on the Stairmaster at Matterhorn level. Thirty minutes of free-
weights. Thirty-five minutes of Tae Bo to Billy Blanks' DVD. When she
finished her grueling routines, she barely had broken a sweat or made a
dent in the morning and wondered if she should start over again.

Instead, she scurried the thirty yards through the frosty morning air
back to the main house. After showering, she threw on some sweats and
her Uggs, pulled her hair into a ponytail, then phoned her best friend,
Else Fuller, to see if she wanted to meet downtown at Mountain Java,
their favorite coffee shop, for another episode of the Smiths' personal
soap-opera: "As Your Stomach Turns."

Charlie couldn't wait to tell Else that she had enjoyed a moment of
complete clarity earlier in the morning in the middle of her last Tae Bo
high kick: *I'm gonna be okay.* It was Trevor who worried her now. He
seemed to have become more lackluster with each passing day. Hardly
any appetite. Even less energy. Fewer and fewer friends coming over to
play. Headaches. Bursts of anger at his father. Sometimes even at her.
Clearly he was depressed and refusing to admit it or talk about it with

her, or anyone else for that matter. Else had tried to draw him out, but that hadn't worked.

"Hell, this divorce has shaken him up. He doesn't know who to trust. Plus, he's a teenager now. Even if I am his godmother, why would he want to confide in an old bag like me?" she told Charlie as they sat across from one another sipping steaming mugs of mocha cappuccinos.

"Always fishing for compliments," Charlie deadpanned. In fact, Else was still beautiful and youthful well into her late sixties, with her red hair and fiery Irish temper and humor.

"Everything you say may be true," Charlie said. "But it's more than the divorce. I just can't put my finger on it. I'm worried sick."

"This too will pass," Else promised. She finished her coffee and told Charlie she had to run. She was off to show some prime lakefront property to clients from San Diego, their old stomping grounds.

Charlie thought longingly back to her youthful, southern California days. Sure, she had struggled to make ends meet for quite a few years and to get her tiny business on a successful footing. But she never once felt unhappy doing any of it. There's no shame in hard labor, her dad always told her. He'd been a construction worker, even once owned his own business, and after that went belly-up he dusted himself off and started again. The thought quickly crossed her mind that she could always return to San Diego if she wanted to. Live year-round in 72-degree weather.

Else and Charlie decided to meet up again in a few days for dinner, maybe splurge at The Epicurean at the Hotel McCall, have steaks and a nice bottle of wine.

⌒

Charlie drove west on Lake Street past her store, Out-A-Idaho. Ballard's car wasn't there. Neither was the clerk/girlfriend's. It was almost eleven o'clock. The doors were open for business. *Who's minding the store?* Charlie drove another fifty feet and pulled into the parking lot for Paul's Market, found a space in front, and went inside to meander and try to drum up some enthusiasm for a dinner menu. *That's all my life is these days. Exercise, taking care of Trevor who doesn't want me to take care of him, and buying food for dinners that neither of us will eat.*

Picturing how thin Trevor was getting, she decided to make him one of his favorite meals: chicken Parmesan and Caesar salad. She opted also to throw in her special home-baked cheesecake that he loved. Even after putting the ingredients for the feast into her cart, she continued to go up and down every aisle as if she might have forgotten something she would need later. She did manage to wile away some significant time, which of course would cost her at the checkout stand. Always purchasing way too much of everything. Not that anything at Paul's was all that inviting. Charlie tried not to shop there that often. But it was the best McCall had to offer, and she had no choice.

When she needed to seriously restock her provisions, she usually made the two-hour trip down the mountain to Costco in Boise. That could be a tricky drive in the winter when a snow or ice storm could make navigating the winding roads treacherous. In the summer, Paul's Market held one extra lure for Charlie besides convenience of location. It was the place where she got to chat with her summer friends. They were long gone now. A new wave of loneliness washed over her as she turned and walked up another aisle.

~

While Charlie stashed her purchases into the back of her SUV, she noticed that the temperature outside was dropping, and she felt frozen through and through. Lately it didn't matter how many layers of clothes she put on.

In more recent years, winters had seemed to wall her off and erode her ability to cope. She had mentioned that to the court-appointed psychologist who had interviewed her at the start of the custody part of the divorce. He rewarded her honesty by reporting to the judge that she suffered from "light deprivation" and perhaps a little depression, and suggested that she should invest in one of those special lamps that mimicked sunshine. She and Else had a good laugh over that one.

Else had added, "Maybe you should have told the shrink that joke going around about McCall: 'the town of four Ds—Divorce, Depression, Death, and Disease.' That would have made him give you a prescription for Prozac!"

Charlie smiled at the memory as she turned on the ignition, turned up the heat, and tried to turn off her negative thoughts. Slipping off her Isotoner gloves, she flexed her fingers and sat waiting for them to thaw.

At last, she turned out of the parking lot and pointed her car east on Lake Street toward home. Once more she had to pass the strip mall she and Ballard still owned together, where Out-A-Idaho was located. She missed those days when she could pop in at will to see what the Idaho artisans had sent to her for approval, stay for hours talking and working and stretch out the intervals between loneliness. She missed the days when a store clerk was just a store clerk and not some potential new soul-mate for her husband.

You've got to snap out of this mood, girl, she admonished herself. *It is what it is.* Even so, she seemed unable to stop her mind from flitting from pillar to post of good and bad memories of her life here.

Charlie slowed down to let a rusty pickup truck pass her on Lake Street, and the old coot driving the wreck made her think of her friend, J.R. Simplot. He was responsible for her and Ballard's first visit to McCall at the end of the 1980s soon after they got married.

Most of the time, J.R. and his wife, Esther, resided in Boise. But they loved McCall and summered at their massive, but rather rustic, compound across Payette Lake from McCall's town center. In its heyday, their estate doubled as the location for the famous 1940 Academy Award–winning film, *Northwest Passage.*

Simplot, who began his career hoeing rows of potatoes, became a billionaire who boasted a reputation far and wide as "the potato baron" of Idaho. There was more to him than potatoes. He had his hand in just about every business enterprise in the state, including phosphate mining, fertilizer companies, cattle ranching, and founding MICRON Technology, one of the biggest computer chip makers in the world.

Eventually his businesses owned a fleet of planes. It didn't matter. Always the eccentric, J.R. drove from state to state in a rundown car. He bragged that he had worn the same ski outfit for forty years. Charlie could attest to it, since she had skied with him and had seen the tattered, worn, red one-piece suit with her own eyes.

J.R. supplied more than fifty percent of the potatoes to McDonald's for their delicious French fries. It was that business connection that led Ballard to get to know him. When he married Charlie, Ballard encouraged her to become friendly with the Simplots, too.

"You've got to visit us in paradise," he told the Smiths when Ballard said he was interested in buying land in Montana or someplace similar. "Our little corner of northwest Idaho is about to become the next Sun Valley."

"What's he been smoking?" Charlie commented wryly to Ballard after they took J.R. up on his offer and made a trip out to tour the area.

The center of town was decidedly unimpressive, dominated by the burned-out remains of a sprawling lumber mill, with only its mammoth rusty teepee-shaped burner intact. Apparently the mill caught fire under suspicious circumstances in 1984. Now it was the end of the 1980s, and to her way of thinking, it remained an eyesore of immense proportions. She was told that when the mill was operational and the chimney working, a nasty plume of smoke wafted over the town at all times.

She couldn't deny the natural beauty all around: the lake was shimmering, the forests lush, and the land along the lake and inland immensely affordable. And if J.R. did turn out to be prescient about the future plans for the little hamlet, it could one day rival any of those other resorts.

Within a year of that first trip, they returned to find the rusty burner gone, and it did appear that developers were coming out of the woodwork with plans to transform the town into another luxurious destination vacation spot.

Charlie became more enthusiastic. Ballard wasted no time buying an expanse of lakefront acreage on Lick Creek Road east of the town center in desirable Pilgrim's Cove at Shady Beach, planting their roots in a field of trophy estates blooming like wildflowers. Their neighbors would be the scions of the Albertson's Market chain family, the UPS families, and more of their ilk.

"Work your magic, baby," he told Charlie, after they hired architects and builders. With an unlimited budget, a fertile imagination, and the desire to achieve perfection, Charlie indefatigably pursued her and Ballard's dream, eventually turning their little piece of Idaho into a gem worthy of a Hollywood movie set.

While other homes rivaled hers, to be sure, and in some instances far surpassed the Smith's in size and scope, the town itself never did become that luxurious destination those first developers had in mind. McCall exuded neither the glamour of Aspen nor the cosmopolitan allure of Sun Valley. It oozed none of the planned quaintness of Vail. Not even the authentic cowboy feel of Jackson Hole. Their only movie theater closed down. Upscale shopping venues did not exist. No bookstores selling bestsellers thrived, although there was one used-books store on a side street in a quaint clapboard house. Marginal restaurants, at best.

None of this bothered her when their stays in the dream house on the lake were measured in weeks and months. Charlie sighed inwardly as she drove around the Hotel McCall, then continued east. She eyed the patches of snow on the ground that fell the other day and probably never would melt now that the temperatures were descending for the duration. Her mind turned to balmy San Diego again. She smiled at the memory of her "Gidget" days on the beach, learning how to surf and playing hooky from school with her boyfriend.

She thought about her niece, Lori, who still lived there with her husband and two daughters. Charlie suddenly remembered today's date: November fifth. Lori's birthday. She would go home, start her preparations for dinner and then call Lori and have a really long chat.

Only fifteen years older than her niece, Charlie thought of her brother Denny's daughter as the sister she never had. Lori uncannily resembled Charlie in her looks and had the same husky voice and guileless, gregarious personality. Charlie smiled as she thought of all the fun they always had together. Lori's daughters Lexis and Marisa were Trevor's age, and they got along famously.

Charlie felt her spirits rise. *I've got to cowgirl-up and get my game-face on for the rest of the year,* she resolved. Thanksgiving was one of her son's favorite holidays, and it was but a few weeks away. Last Thanksgiving was a horribly depressing time because Trevor had just learned that his parents were separating. She vowed to make up for it this year. In fact, she was going to insist that Lori and her family come to McCall to spend the holiday with her and Trevor. She'd ask Denny to drive down from northern Idaho as well. It would be just what the doctor ordered for her son—and for herself, too. Her older son, Jimmy, already was planning on being there. He doted on his little brother and had told Charlie recently he wanted to be with him as much as possible, because he seemed so lonely.

She slowed her car a bit as she cruised by the local McCall golf course where Trevor first learned to play. He told her a few months back that it was a sport he intended to conquer. She laughed, reminding him how hard a game it was but telling him she admired his determination.

She turned onto Lick Creek Road that led to her house. To her right she spotted the fairway where Trevor outdrove her for the first time last summer. "You're hooked," she had told him then. He smiled proudly and gave her a little punch in the arm. *Yeah, this is something we can do together. Laugh at together. Agonize over. Maybe I'm worrying too much and everything will turn out okay.*

Suddenly her cell phone rang. It was Trevor calling from the nurse's office. He sounded dreadful. Her skin prickled as he cried, "My head is killing me, mom. I'm scared. I wanna go home. Please come pick me up."

Chapter Five

Charlie didn't even take home the groceries. She careened around corners, took back roads and slammed into park in front of the school. She ran inside and found Trevor waiting for her in the main office. His face was blotchy, his eyes red. He looked miserable. He was wobbly when he stood up.

"Do you need help walking, Trev?"

"No. I just want you to please make this pain go away," he whimpered. When they reached the car, he barely could turn to put his seatbelt on.

"I think you need to go to the emergency room. I'm taking you there right now."

On the way, Charlie phoned Ballard to let him know what was going on and to meet her at the hospital. She got his voice mail.

"Can we drive by the store to see if my dad's there? I want him with me, too."

Charlie made a detour into the Out-A-Idaho parking lot. Ballard's car still wasn't there. She called the store—no answer. She called his cell phone again. Still no answer.

Trevor moaned in pain. "Let's go."

Dr. Jennifer Gray, the physician on call, treated Trevor. As she took his temperature and vital signs she suggested that he probably had the flu. After she flashed a light into Trevor's eyes, he got sick to his stomach and bolted to the bathroom across the hall from the examining room to vomit.

"Feeling better?" Charlie asked hopefully when he returned. He shook his head. She implored Dr. Gray to send Trevor for a CT scan.

"I really don't think it's necessary," the doctor told her.

"But I do! Something just doesn't feel right!"

The doctor still refused, discounting the vomiting and sensitivity to light. She offered that if this wasn't the flu, it quite possibly could be a migraine. "I see by his chart that he gets sinus infections, doesn't he?"

"Well, yes," Charlie conceded.

"It could be that." Dr. Gray prescribed some medication and sent them home.

———

The next day, Ballard left town without saying goodbye. He was bound for Colorado to take some furniture from Out-A-Idaho to his eldest daughter, Allison, and to see her newborn daughter for the first time.

Charlie expected him to call to learn about Trevor's trip to the emergency room, but it was Ballard's ex, Linda Smith, who phoned her eventually. Over the years, the two women had developed a semblance of a relationship, especially once Charlie became an integral part in the nurturing of Linda's daughters.

Linda began hysterically crying a minute into the conversation. Apparently Ballard had experienced chest pains while visiting Allison, had rushed to a local hospital where he had some tests. They thought he might have suffered a heart attack. He was headed to Scripps Memorial Hospital in La Jolla, California, for further evaluation.

"This is awful," Charlie said.

"I fear for the kids," Linda lamented. "If something were to happen to Ballard, I just don't know what they would do."

"I know. They all are so attached to their father. He sure controls the girls' lives, even now that they're all adults."

"That's true," Linda admitted. "Oh God! Do you think you should even tell Trevor about this? How's he doing?"

"He's been sick, himself, lately. I'm worried about him. Ballard getting sick could really be tough on him."

They chatted for a few more minutes about Ballard's heart problems. Charlie peppered her with questions about the severity of the attack. Linda didn't really have any of the answers.

Charlie decided to call Joan Kroc. If anyone would know what was going on with Ballard, it would be Joan. In many ways, she was more tuned into Ballard's life now than anyone else in the family. Her granddaughters kept her up on all of the details of his various love affairs and business dealings.

"Do you think it was a serious heart attack?" she asked Joan.

Joan replied sardonically through a loud exhale of smoke, "I always thought you needed to have a *heart* to have a heart attack."

Charlie laughed. "So I guess that mean he's okay?"

"Oh yeah. The girls told me he had a stent put in to open a blocked artery. He's calling it heart *surgery*, but these days it's practically an outpatient procedure. I'm more worried about you." Joan wanted to know how the divorce proceedings were moving along.

"Great. I'm sleeping like a baby—up every two hours crying."

"That's my girl," Joan chortled. "Where there's laughter, there's hope. But promise me this, Charlie. You must keep a strong heart. I want you to land on your feet."

~——~

Later that same day, Charlie finally reached Ballard.

"Ballard, I know you're not feeling all that great. I still need you to listen to me for a minute. I'm worried about Trevor's health. You know I had to take him to the emergency room." Ballard seemed to recall her message. "A doctor he saw there put him on ten days of medication for a sinus infection. I think it's more than that. I have a gut feeling…"

He interrupted her. "Don't worry about it. He's all right."

"Will you just call him tonight, Ballard?" she begged. "He really wants to talk to you."

Ballard said calling Trevor would not be a good idea. "Do not say anything to Trevor about my heart attack."

After a bit of back-and-forth, Charlie agreed with Ballard's decision not to alarm their son.

CHAPTER SIX

Trevor diligently took the medicine Dr. Gray prescribed, but the headaches persisted. It was like having a really mean ogre stomping around in his head morning, noon, and night. Tormenting him.

"I just feel so weird," he told Charlie more than a week later as he picked at his dinner.

"Weird? How?" she replied.

"I don't know. Just *weird*. I can't explain it," he shot back, dropping his fork onto the plate with a clatter that hurt his ears. All of his senses seemed frayed.

The very next morning, a searing pain in his head accompanied by flashing lights jolted him awake, and he vomited profusely. It was overwhelming for Trevor to throw up so abruptly and so forcefully that he couldn't even make it to the bathroom. He felt like he was being turned inside out.

He cried out for his mother.

"Oh, Trev. What happened?" she said upon coming into his room.

"I threw up. I couldn't even get to the bathroom."

"Let's get you cleaned up. We're going back to the clinic."

This time Trevor got to see his regular doctor, Scott Harris. Dr. Harris, a native of McCall, was an easygoing family practitioner. He always made Trevor feel like more than a mere patient. That connection extended to Mrs. Harris, who had been Trevor's third-grade teacher.

Trevor now had to endure another physical exam. Afterwards, Dr. Harris poured over the notes on Dr. Gray's chart and then listened intently as Trevor explained how awful he had felt for the past week even while taking medication: pulsating pain, pressure, flashing lights, dizziness, and nausea.

"I wish Dr. Gray had given him a CT scan," Charlie stated.

"Well, let's get him one today," Dr. Harris agreed.

The next morning, Charlie thought that Trevor should take a day off and rest at home.

"Why?" he asked. "I'm okay, Mom. Really. I can't miss school."

Seeing how important this was to him and proud of how seriously he took his responsibility as a student, she reluctantly agreed to let him go.

She barely was out of the school parking lot after having dropped off Trevor when her cell phone rang. It was Dr. Harris.

He said he found something "disturbing" on the CT scan. He wanted her to come in to see him right away. Dr. Harris' somber tone of voice made her heart race wildly. With Ballard out of town and ailing in San Diego, she called Else.

Else didn't answer.

I can't go alone, she panicked, white-knuckling the steering wheel and beginning to shiver with fear. She pulled over to think. Finally, she turned to another friend, the town's local veterinarian, Dr. John Park.

"I'm just so damned scared," she told him. "I want to make sure I get it all. And you have a medical background."

"I understand," he replied. "Don't worry." He agreed to be her eyes and ears during the session with Dr. Harris.

John was waiting for her in the parking lot outside McCall Memorial Hospital. A short, stocky man, he exuded an aura of kindness about him. He wore typical laid-back work attire—plaid shirt, Levi's, and Sorel boots. The look in his eyes this morning was anything but laid-back; it was one of concern for her and Trevor.

"My gut is telling me this is not going to be good," she said, as they entered the examining room where Dr. Harris had said to meet him.

"Let's just take one step at a time," he gently admonished her.

"Is it bad?" Charlie asked Dr. Harris the minute they settled down for their conference.

"That's hard to say, Charlie. The scan showed a spot on Trevor's brain. At the base of his neck. I can't say for sure what it is."

"A tumor?" Charlie murmured.

Dr. Harris nodded. He glanced worriedly for the briefest instant at John and then looked back at her. That nearly imperceptible exchange between the two men spoke volumes to her: *This is bad.*

"Charlie, we're such a small hospital," Dr. Harris went on. "Trevor needs an MRI. I think you must take him down to Boise to get more definitive tests done. Right away," he added, in what Charlie felt was an even more emphatic and serious tone.

Suddenly Charlie's mind went blank, but her body reacted, and she was unable to stop herself from vomiting. After apologizing profusely to Dr. Harris for her emotional reaction, Charlie and John left.

He helped her into her car. "Please sit with me for a minute," she implored.

He settled into the passenger seat. "Is there anything…"

Erupting in sobs, Charlie didn't hear clearly the rest of what John said. He tried to soothe her and convince her not to jump to hasty conclusions, but she realized he couldn't calm her.

"I have to talk to Joan," she blurted, punching her number into her cell phone. She wiped her tears away. Tried to control herself long enough to talk.

Before getting two words out, though, Charlie became hysterical once again. She thrust the phone at John. "It's Joan Kroc," she mumbled. "Tell her…"

He quickly explained who he was and what Charlie just learned.

He nodded and answered a few questions, then handed the phone back to Charlie. "Just listen to her."

Joan told her, "You have to get control over your emotions. Now is the time for you to be strong. Even though it's frightening, you have to help Trevor get through this. Remember, I will be there for you. Always."

Finally, Charlie felt herself calming down. Joan had that kind of effect on her. Almost from the beginning, she and Joan clicked emotionally. Through the years, Charlie sought out Joan for advice, for pep talks, and for friendship. They became confidants, sharing the ups and downs, the joys and sorrows, of their intertwined families.

"Charlie, you must get Trevor down to Boise immediately," Joan said emphatically. "Waste no time. I'll get doctors lined up for him in San Diego—or any other city, if things don't work out in Boise."

As Charlie put her phone away, she told John, "She'll help us get through this."

"You're lucky to have such a woman in your life."

"Don't I know it! We…Ballard and I…we owe Joan everything. And I mean *everything!* She and Trevor are close. It's so sweet to watch. I could hear it in her voice—she's really broken up about this. You know, she insists he call her Grandma Joan. You have no idea how much that means to me and Trevor. I feel like she's the glue that holds this whole family together."

CHAPTER SEVEN

Trevor was glad he insisted on going to school. For some reason he felt pretty okay today. Manageable nausea. Less pounding inside his head. It was almost easy to forget for a few moments at a time that he was awaiting the results of the CT scan from the day before. Whenever the thought that the scan results could be bad broke through into his conscious mind, he forced it down like a prairie dog coming partway out of its hole and then darting back in.

Trevor definitely harbored suspicions that whatever was wrong with him was more than a sinus infection. Even so, he couldn't grasp any possibility that went too far beyond something very treatable, like a bad strain of the flu or maybe even a food allergy that could be cured with a simple diet change.

Then the school bell rang, and it signified more than just the end of the school day: back to reality, and that meant his scan results.

He found his mother waiting for him in the parking lot. He eyed her for unpleasant facial signs as he settled into the car.

"How was your day, buddy?" she asked, smiling at him.

"It was okay."

"Anything good happen at school today?"

"Mom, have you heard from Dr. Harris?"

"I saw him earlier," she said.

He and his mom had a very strong connection. He could tell immediately just by looking at her, even when her voice seemed nonchalant, that there was something wrong.

"It's not a sinus infection, is it, Mom?"

"No, sweetheart, it isn't," Charlie admitted, tears welling up in her eyes and spilling over. "We're on our way to see Dr. Harris now."

Dr. Harris led them into the big conference room. The fact that they were in this particular room instead of a small patient cubicle actually was the first moment that Trevor couldn't escape the prospect that something momentous might happen in his life. Perhaps his mom's tears weren't exaggerated?

While they arranged themselves in the chairs, the doctor put Trevor's scan on one of those lighted boxes on the wall. Then Dr. Harris' demeanor turned more serious when he began to address him and his mom. None of the usual small talk.

"Trevor, you have a mass at the back of your head," he said, getting right to the point.

Cool! Trevor thought. *This doesn't sound so bad.* The word "mass" did the trick. Some of the building anxiety seeped out of him, and the thought of returning to being a normal thirteen-year-old took its place.

But Dr. Harris wasn't through; he added that in medical terms this mass was known as a brain tumor. At this point, Trevor could tell how hard Dr. Harris was trying to fight back any sound of sympathy and uncertainty in his voice. A sense of doom filled him. That new, awful word, tumor, reverberated through the room. *This is no joke. Oh man. Will I ever see fourteen?*

All at once, Trevor felt tears brim in his eyes. He blinked and swiped at them, barely finding the courage to ask Dr. Harris, "Am I going to be okay?"

Trevor scanned Dr. Harris' reaction: every nuance, every tic. *He knows me so well, he likes me so much, and still he can't smile.*

Hesitating, Dr. Harris said, "I really can't answer that for you, Trevor."

Mom, you better start carving my gravestone.

———————

Everything sped up. His mom spoke really fast to Else on the cell phone in the car. His godmother was going to come with them to Boise. His mom drove like a maniac to their house where they threw a few belongings into a suitcase, then picked up Else and began the twisting trip down the mountain.

Trevor crushed himself into a corner of the backseat. Else and his mother were in the front. He really loved his mom and adored Else, a constant figure in his life from the time he was born. But they weren't making this easier on him with their silence. Usually they chatted and laughed the entire way down the hill. Today, Else's soft crying filled his ears and made him even more scared. *What does she know that she isn't telling me?*

He turned his head to gaze out the window at the rolling grasslands and then at the intermittent rapids out of which rose sharp, towering mountains. Every year this seasonal scenery was the same. He could set his watch by nature's cycles. It comforted him. Trevor suddenly was struck by the unsettling thought: *My life might never be the same. And worse…I might never see any of this scenery I love ever again.* He couldn't bear to look at all this beauty any longer. He shut his eyes.

By six that evening, Trevor and Charlie sat rigidly on the edge of their chairs across the desk from Dr. Bruce Cherny, a chubby pediatric neurosurgeon with big, brown, sympathetic eyes. The Boise doctor had studied Trevor's CT scan and confirmed that he had a mass, which would necessitate an MRI in the morning.

Trevor took to the surgeon right away. He acted confident, and he never once intimated that the tumor lurking in Trevor's brain was something bad like cancer. Trevor nearly breathed an audible sigh of relief and sat back in his chair.

His mother was a bit more composed now, too, and spent a lot of time talking before and after the doctor's appointment with Grandma Joan.

She told Else and him that Joan spent the two hours they were driving down to Boise on the phone working her medical contacts.

"She's done a thorough check of Dr. Cherny," said Charlie. "According to her personal physician in San Diego, Cherny has a great reputation. And she's okay with St. Luke's, too. The Kroc Foundation donated a Ronald McDonald's Room for children with cancer. I guess the hospital went through a lot of checks and things back then. That sealed the deal for her."

"So, I'm staying here?" Trevor asked.

"Grandma Joan thinks we should make a final decision after the MRI in the morning."

On the way to their Boise house, they stopped at a pharmacy to fill a prescription for Decadron. Dr. Cherny said it would eliminate some of the edema, or swelling, in Trevor's brain.

He explained to them in his office, "Trevor's headaches are the result of the brain tumor blocking a major route of fluid drainage. It creates swelling, leading to excruciating pressure. My hope is that the release of that pressure will take away the pain and those flashes of light."

Within hours of taking his first dose, it worked. Trevor slept the night pain free for the first time in weeks.

Rested and with no headache the next morning, Trevor faced the MRI with a bit less trepidation. In some ways, he felt more annoyed than scared. He went back to grousing about the inconvenience of this whole experience, behaving like a normal kid who preferred to be outside playing with his friends.

"Even taking a grammar test would be better than this," he told his mom and Else before being escorted to the inner rooms of the radiation lab. "Besides," he argued, "I've already gone through the CT scan. How different can they be?"

He soon learned from the tech that an MRI was more complicated. It required having dye injected into his body. The unsettling thought of having chemicals circulating inside of him set him on edge and gave him chills. Also, he was going to have to spend forty-five minutes in a tube lying completely still. Stuffed into that cylinder, he tried to keep a happy image of himself going through football practice. However, the machine made so much noise, it nearly shook all those good memories out of his head.

Afterward, they met with Dr. Cherny again. He was amenable to a telephone consultation with Joan and then Ballard, during which they all agreed with Dr. Cherny's conclusion: Trevor must undergo surgery the very next afternoon.

Knowing the inevitable oddly settled Trevor down. *Dr. Cherny's calm. I'll be calm, too*, he decided. Trevor was good at calming himself. He was, after all, a Mighty Mite. It was going to be like taking on a scary black diamond ski run for the first time: standing on the precipice hunched over; staring down the face at the moguls; the fear of failure gripping his stomach for a few seconds; the push-off; the exhilaration of navigating the turns and bumps, making it safely to the bottom; and then looking up and saying with a laugh, *What was so scary about that?*

As they walked to the car, Charlie said, "Guess what?"

"I don't actually have a tumor and we're going back up to McCall?"

"Almost as good. The family's all going to fly in. Starting tonight."

"My dad, too?"

"Sure thing."

CHAPTER EIGHT

News spread fast. Soon their house on Winterwood Lane was bursting at the seams, the kitchen and family room echoing with the lively voices of relatives and friends who came by to lend moral support before the surgery in the morning. Everyone seemed determined to maintain a party atmosphere to keep Trevor's mind off what he was about to face.

Ballard arrived in the early evening from San Diego with his daughter, Amy Smith, and her fiancé Frank Ragen.

Sprawled on the sofa in the family room watching TV with his uncle Denny, Trevor flew off the couch and into his father's arms the minute he spied him. It was as if all of the bad blood between them was forgotten because Ballard was there for his boy. Trevor really wanted to look up to his dad again, to feel safe because he had once more taken his position as the man of the house, the protector.

They both burst into tears. For Trevor, they were tears of relief. Over his dad's shoulder he noticed his mom standing near the kitchen sink watching them. Her eyes were red-rimmed, but at this moment she looked happy and relieved.

Ballard asked to talk to Trevor in private. They settled near each other on the sofa in the library, a secluded, wood-paneled room at the front of the house away from where everyone else had noisily congregated. As happy as he was to have his dad near and to tell him about the things he'd been going through, like CT scans and MRIs, Trevor realized with some alarm that he felt just as alone after their short talk as he did before it. He wasn't sure if his father was too preoccupied to ask the right questions to draw out these scary, innermost feelings, or if he was too afraid to put them into words.

~

Arriving earlier that afternoon from northern Idaho, Uncle Denny had already put his dibs on one of the two guest bedrooms. Else claimed the other. A late arrival, Ballard drew the short straw—the downy couch in the family room. He offered to go to the hotel with the others, but Trevor begged him to stay close.

Trevor shared the old master suite with his mom because her new one was still under construction and walled off with plastic wrapping.

Trevor heard his mother get up and down throughout the night. Toward dawn, he finally fell into a deep sleep. The homey smell of bacon stirred him awake. He was disoriented and couldn't recall at first why he was in Boise. It felt like a typical morning for a few more seconds. Then his mother, standing at the foot of the bed, reminded him to take his Decadron pills. *Oh yeah. Those. Tumor. Surgery.* It took so much effort to pull back those covers. It was as if they weighed fifty pounds. Trevor really didn't want to get out of that warm bed and face his last morning as he knew it. *Cherny's calm. You are calm*, he repeated in his mind.

~

In preparation for the three o'clock surgery that afternoon, the growing entourage of family and friends crammed into several cars and arrived at St. Luke's Hospital surgery wing at one o'clock. The normally innocuous red brick hospital building surrounded by leafless trees now appeared ominous to Charlie. The weather was turning, the afternoon cold and raw. Her nerves were raw, too, and she felt as if she were on the verge of a breakdown.

Their group virtually took over the surgery waiting room. Charlie's son, Jimmy Walls, was there, of course. Her brother, Denny. Lori and her girls, Lexis and Marisa, had jetted into town early in the morning from San Diego on Joan's sleek, luxuriously appointed G-4 along with three of Trevor's four half-sisters and several other family members and boyfriends.

Grandma Joan stayed home in Rancho Santa Fe. Charlie wasn't surprised. At this point in her life, Joan preferred to remain in the background, attached to the goings-on via the telephone. Else became a de facto conduit of information for Joan, who phoned her every few minutes for updates about everything that was going on, demanding all of the details no matter how small. Joan had already spoken with Charlie about how she felt she could serve Trevor best by running the show from the wings. Charlie concurred, so grateful that Joan insisted on being an integral part of her son's treatment that she could have communicated with smoke signals, and it would have been fine with her.

While the others milled about in the waiting room, Charlie and Ballard accompanied their son into the surgery prepping area. They stayed beside him as the nurse wheeled him down the corridor toward the double doors leading to the operating suites.

The effects of the pre-op drugs appeared to have caused Trevor to become almost giddy. He babbled about how hungry he was and how he planned to eat steak and mashed potatoes. And *corn. Lots of corn.*

"Poor thing, he must be starving," the nurse commiserated, "what with no food today or last night, and it's almost four o'clock."

Charlie said, "Actually, I gave him a few bites of a bagel very early today to take with his Decadron pills."

"Good Lord! I can't believe you let him eat!" the nurse exclaimed.

Charlie defended her actions, explaining that the directions said to take the medication with food, and the doctor insisted that Trevor must take it even this morning to relieve his edema. No one told her that she should disregard the explicit instructions on the bottle.

"Well, we might not be able to do the surgery now," the nurse huffed. "I'll have to check with Dr. Cherny." She left them in the hall while she raced off to find the doctor.

"Let's get this show on the road," Trevor moaned over and over. "I'm so ready for this. Steak. Mashed potatoes and corn. *Lots* of corn," he rambled.

Dr. Cherny appeared in no time. He patted Trevor's shoulder sympathetically. Charlie could tell it was dicey because the surgeon stood silently stroking his mustache for quite a while. Then he finally announced his verdict: even though it was several hours after eating, he didn't feel comfortable proceeding with the surgery.

Charlie reminded the surgeon that it was hardly any food, and it was very early in the morning when Trevor injested it. He said he had to think about it some more. He sent the Smiths out to the waiting room while the nurse brought Trevor back to the prepping area.

Within half an hour, Dr. Cherny showed up in the waiting room where he advised the parents, each standing in their separate camps of loyalists, that he would postpone the surgery until Monday morning. Ballard glared at Charlie. Amanda Smith Latimer pitched a fit about her grandma's plane leaving, causing her to have to take a commercial flight back to San Diego days later.

They bundled Trevor up and took him home.

⌒

After the orderly wheeled her son away from her on Monday morning, Charlie felt claustrophobic and had to put some distance between herself and her well-meaning family and friends. She paced alone up and down the corridor leading to the surgery suite. Worrying. Agonizing. Rehashing the events and strain of the weekend when she and Ballard were forced to spend time under the same roof for the sake of their child. Feeling anew the animosity of her stepdaughters, Amy, Holly, and Amanda, who barely said two words to her. Ballard ditching them all for hours on end, acting like a teenager in lust, and leaving his son without a father to dote on him. Charlie experiencing waves of fear, feeling like she might lose it. Staking a separate space outside on the patio. Staring. Shivering. Remembering how different things were thirteen years ago when Ballard and her stepdaughters lovingly surrounded her while she gave birth to Trevor.

"The tension's so thick you could cut it with a knife," she had confessed to Joan during one of their many long-distance conversations over the weekend.

"I know. Amanda told me."

Amanda always told her grandmother everything. As she paced the hospital floors, Charlie thought about one particular phone call from Joan immediately after coming back from St. Luke's on Friday once Cherny aborted the surgery plans. Joan had tried to mitigate Charlie's guilt, imploring her not to beat herself up about the bagel.

"Who can think straight at a time like this?" she said to Charlie. As always, Joan continued to phone with all the right things to say to help her get through several more days of anxiety and fear. "And I'll leave the plane for the girls so they don't have to fly commercial."

Poor dears. Such suffering. Flying commercial! Charlie could show them a thing or two about true suffering by forcing them to look into the rooms of the children with cancer up and down the corridors of this floor, all of them in various stages of painful recovery or dying.

The enormity of these sick kids' tragic plight, and what might be in store for Trevor, left her drained. She sought solace in the cheery Ronald McDonald room by herself but soon was seated with her head in her hands, bent over in sympathetic pain.

While the family awaited updates, Dr. Cherny and his team went to work in a brightly lit, high-tech surgery suite. They placed Trevor under general anesthetic with his head slightly elevated. They shaved the right frontal region, washed the entire area, and draped it in a sterile fashion. After that, a horizontal incision was made and the outer part of his skull was breached. Using a special drill, they made a bur hole. Soon, minute particles of bone like dust became visible under the intense light. Next, a drain was inserted in front of the external auditory canal.

At this point, Trevor entered a period of continual decompression. What followed were more extensive preparations, including the insertion of IV lines that allowed the infusion of antibiotics. When they were certain Trevor's intracranial pressure was stable, he was turned onto his stomach on a special table.

Dr. Cherny methodically worked his way deeper into Trevor's brain, opening him up layer by layer, splitting muscle down to the occipital bone on the way to reaching the tumor in the cerebellum. During this time, Trevor was monitored closely to be sure that his intracranial pressure remained normal.

When the surgeon finally reached the area of the golf-ball-sized tumor, it was near the arachnoid and two projections called tonsils, which he could see pulsating. He split the tonsils, which led into a very soft and suckable tumor that was mildly hemorrhagic. Several sections of the tumor and surrounding area were sent to the pathologist on call. He would freeze these sections in order to rapidly determine if the tumor was malignant or benign, and if all of the tumor had been removed, leaving clear margins. The pathologist's preliminary diagnosis was a "probable astrocytoma" of a low grade. At this point, Dr. Cherny continued to excise the remainder of the tumor, which he now described as both soft and hard in sections.

Once Dr. Cherny was satisfied that he had cleared all the margins, leaving no discernable tumor behind, he began the process of closing Trevor's skull. He sutured and grafted areas, making them airtight to prevent cerebral spinal fluid from leaking. Finally the surgeon reaffixed the bone with plates and screws. Trevor was extubated, awakened, and put on an ICU bed for transfer to the critical care unit.

Eight hours had passed.

CHAPTER NINE

When Dr. Cherny finally appeared in the waiting area looking exhausted, he told the family that Trevor came through surgery quite well. He then offered the caveat: He came through as well as could be expected "under the circumstances." The circumstances were that his head was swollen and his face misshapen, but that was normal.

No, thought Charlie. *Normal is Trevor on the couch watching a football game with family and friends, laughing and horsing around. Normal is Trevor on his motorbike or riding his horse out at the ranch. Normal is my son on his snowboard racing the wind down a hill. Normal is Trevor on our boat dock in McCall, cannon-balling into the water.* Normal was when Charlie walked through town in summer, and locals stopped her to say with a smile that her cheerful son seemed to live in the water, either on his wake-board or swimming, and some referred to him "that cute boy on the lake."

Dr. Cherny further alarmed Charlie with the warning that the next twenty-four hours were critical, still touch and go. He tempered that unwelcome news with a promising update: The frozen-section pathology report indicated the tumor might be an astro...something, a name Charlie never quite got, only that whatever it was might not be malignant.

Family members streamed in to see Trevor for snippets of time in the ICU. Their descriptions were disheartening. Charlie was the last to go in, so afraid of what Trevor might look like that her legs nearly gave out before she got to his bedside.

It was worse than the doctor described. Trevor lay nearly inert in the bed, small and frail, pale as his pillow with tubes and IVs and drains coming out of his body and brain. Dr. Cherny referred to all these medical accoutrements as "life-saving methods post-surgery."

Trevor tried to speak. It came out in gurgles and groans.

"Sssh," Charlie said. "You're going to be just fine, honey. Rest."

A moment later, Charlie fled to the Ronald McDonald room where Denny was holding together their side of the family. She fell onto him and began to sob. "He can't talk anymore," she cried.

A laconic, no-nonsense sort, Denny now offered his sister the insight he gleaned from years of caring for a wife who suffered through a debilitating stroke while still a young woman and who still was incapacitated. He suggested that Trevor's garbled speech most likely was a result of having had a tube down his throat. This made sense. Charlie regained her resolve and went back in to be with her son.

~

She remained a constant presence at Trevor's bedside, tearing herself away only after Ballard insisted she go to dinner. She sat disconsolately at the table with her eldest son, Jimmy, pushing her food around the plate.

"You have to eat, Mom," he begged. "I can't stand to see you like this."

"I'll just throw up."

He went on exhorting her to pull herself together. "Look in the mirror. You're fading away."

Jimmy was right, of course. She had caught a glance of herself in the mirror of the fourth-floor ladies' room this afternoon. It was a startling moment of reality. Before the problems with Ballard escalated and Trevor's illness sprang up, she was a lithe, athletic woman with energy and enthusiasm to spare. This afternoon she saw herself as Jimmy did now: too thin and sad with a careworn expression etched deeply into her face. Her once dancing, sky-blue eyes were cloudy with conflict and fear. Even her hair seemed to have lost some of its luster.

"Please pull yourself together! For Trevor, if for no one else," he urged.

"I shouldn't have left him lying there like that. You know I only came to dinner so Ballard could have some time alone with his son. Trevor will need him more than ever now."

Ballard's alone time with Trevor didn't last long. He phoned Charlie, demanding that she get back to the hospital because he wanted to leave. She didn't need any prodding to do just that. Dr. Cherny said that nurses would be monitoring the drops of fluid coming out of the drains in her son's body. *She* felt compelled to count every drip herself, because the more there was in the next twenty-four hours the better chance Trevor had to survive.

Jimmy drove her to the hospital and stood watch outside the ICU, in case his mother and brother needed him. Late into the night, Charlie finally insisted he go home.

The hospital arranged for Charlie and Ballard to each have a room for the night down the hall from their son's. She accepted; he did not. They got into a semi-heated discussion about him going off to a hotel when Trevor's life still hung in the balance.

"Look, I need a real bed to sleep in," he argued. "Don't forget I've been in a hospital lately, too."

Charlie thought, *So what? This is your son.* She was about to say this when Trevor started to babble. He appeared to be focusing on them with something on his mind. But the noises he made were still nonsensical.

"See. He's out of it and won't even know if I'm here." Ballard left soon after.

Trevor felt his mother in the chair next to him. Nurses hovered throughout the night, or what he guessed was the night. They gently moved him around the bed, checking on the tubes, especially the one in his brain. Oddly, he felt no pain. He had trouble breathing, though, and several times thought he didn't have the strength to draw another breath. His new mantra, *Dr. Cherny's calm,* repeated in his head like a newsreel loop.

Just before dawn, Denny showed up in Trevor's room. "I'm all packed up and ready to head out," he whispered to Charlie. "Hate to leave you, but I have a long drive home. The wife needs me up there."

"I know," she said softly. "Can you stay a few minutes longer?"

"Sure."

"Do I look like a hairball the cat just threw up?" she asked.

"That'd be a yes!"

She smiled briefly as she sat back in the chair that had become her roost last night. Denny leaned against the window ledge. They both stared at Trevor, who sounded stressed with each intake of breath.

"I didn't think he'd make it through the night once or twice," she told her brother.

"He's a trouper. He'll pull through."

A few more silent minutes passed. Denny walked over to give Trevor a kiss on the forehead. Charlie stood up, stretching and cracking her stiff neck.

Denny hugged her tightly. "Hang in there," he said. "And call if you need anything…anything at all."

"I will."

At the door, he asked directions to Ballard's room. He wanted to go say goodbye to him, too.

"Don't bother," Charlie said. "He stayed at the hotel last night. Said he needed a real bed. A hospital bed wouldn't do."

"God forbid he should be inconvenienced. Selfish bastard. You'd think he'd sleep right here on the floor if he had to."

"You'd think," she replied.

Denny left. She could tell her brother was livid with Ballard for not being there for Trevor. She realized she was completely alone now: no brother, no Ballard. She was overwrought by the distressed sounds Trevor had made throughout the night, increasingly petrified that he would die. What if he took a sudden turn for the worse? Could she handle it by herself?

CHAPTER TEN

Joan phoned Charlie a little while later. "How's our boy doing?"
she asked.

"I'm right next to him," Charlie replied. "Been in a chair by
his bed all night." She glanced over at her son. His face was massively
swollen, and he was barely able to open his eyes. "You should see him,"
Charlie whispered. "I'm so damned scared."

"I know you are, sweetheart. Be strong. And give Trevor a big kiss
from Grandma Joan."

"I will."

"Is Ballard with you?"

"He checked into a hotel last night. Said he needed a comfortable
bed to sleep in."

"I guess we know what that means. I warned you about that predator
years ago. The girls around?"

"They should be here soon."

It seemed that Joan did not keep Ballard's latest AWOL behavior a
secret. When Ballard showed up at St. Luke's later in the morning, his
youngest daughter confronted him. "Why didn't you stay at the hospital
last night?" Holly demanded. "Trevor needed you."

"I needed my comfort," Ballard replied defensively.

"If you needed comfort, Dad, you could have gotten it from your family!"

Charlie overheard this emotional exchange on her way to the bathroom. *You go, girl!* she thought, proud of Holly for doing what was right and risking her father's wrath.

Holly was the only one of Ballard's daughters who had lived with them for extended periods of time. During those years, Charlie developed a close relationship with the girl. When Holly suffered through some severe conflicts, inflicting pain on her family and harming herself, it was Charlie to whom she turned. She had always trusted her step-mom. Joan often said she was indebted to Charlie for helping her beautiful and youngest granddaughter to survive. Since the divorce proceedings, however, Holly barely spoke to Charlie. Even now in the middle of castigating her father for his inappropriate behavior, she refused to cast so much as a glance Charlie's way.

Ballard avoided eye contact as well as he edged past Charlie into Trevor's room. When she returned from the bathroom, she was surprised to find Ballard already gone. Instead, she discovered Trevor clearly distressed and sobbing about his dad's health. He still had trouble talking, but he kept trying to ask questions about Ballard's heart attack.

Charlie could feel her insides churning as she vividly recalled Ballard's exact words and stern admonition not to tell their son about his health problems so he wouldn't be scared. What could possibly make it okay now to sandbag him so soon after surgery? Nothing! Intense rage rose up in her. It took all of her self-control to keep from charging from the room to find Ballard and treat him to one of her best Tae Bo high kicks to the jaw.

Instead, Charlie sought to minimize the emotional toll of Ballard's horrid revelation by explaining that the heart attack was not serious. She emphasized that his father was totally fine now.

"I don't believe you," he said haltingly in a raspy voice. "I heard my dad. He's scared. He was crying really hard."

Charlie climbed onto the bed and put her arms around her son. She told him that she had good news—preliminary reports said that his tumor wasn't cancer.

Even that couldn't stop Trevor from crying over Ballard's bad news. Over the next few hours, Charlie settled into her chair next to the bed, watching Trevor drift in and out of sleep, waking each time to ask more questions about his father's health.

"I know Dr. Cherny has made me better," he said one time. "He's amazing."

"He sure is, Trev," Charlie agreed.

"But now I have to worry that my dad might die."

CHAPTER ELEVEN

The only thing that kept Charlie going in those first two days of Trevor's recovery in the ICU was the possibility that his tumor was not malignant. On the third day, that last glimmer of hope was dashed when she and Ballard met with Dr. Cherny in a cramped conference room on the pediatric ICU floor. He introduced them to Dr. Eugenia Chang who was a pediatric oncologist. When another stranger, a man wearing one of those identifiable clergy collars, also entered and joined them, Charlie's whole body felt like it was closing in on itself.

The doctors spoke in the scariest of tones: soft and serious. Their faces, too, were implacable as they explained that the final pathology report showed that Trevor had an aggressively malignant cancer requiring extensive chemotherapy and radiation.

Charlie erupted into gut-wrenching sobs, then leaned across the small table and grabbed Dr. Cherny's arm, squeezing it hard. "You can't let my son die!" she cried. "Don't you let him die!"

Both doctors remained stoic, waiting patiently for her to stop weeping. At last, they explained that the family and Trevor must do everything asked of them, which they said would be harder than anything they had ever undertaken, and they would do everything humanly possible to keep him alive.

Ballard had his head on his arms on the table but looked up when Charlie addressed Dr. Cherny. "Can we wait to tell him a few more days until he's stronger?" she begged.

Drs. Cherny and Chang readily agreed, saying it was a very good idea.

"Ballard?" Charlie said.

He promised not to say anything, either.

———

Escaping from the conference room, Charlie went for a walk on the hospital campus grounds, needing some time alone to stop crying and to clear her head before facing her son. The piercing chill of the November winds matched the iciness that spread throughout her body.

As she meandered in a fog of misery, she couldn't stop her thoughts from going back in time to when *she* was a defenseless child, tormented and molested for two years by a friend of the family, then raped by him in a barn near her house in Encino, California. Only her family's relocation to San Diego saved her from further assaults. It was a terrifying pastiche of images she never consciously allowed to surface.

Lately, however, the repressed, unwanted memories bubbled up. They populated her dreams in weird combinations and, at odd times, overwhelmed her during her waking hours. She aimlessly meandered, lost in thought. *Why did this awful secret have to reappear now? I need to be strong for Trevor. Strong for whatever lies ahead.*

What she really needed was for the damaged little girl still inside her, still holding the secret of her molester's deeds, to be locked away somewhere—for good. "Don't tell your parents, or I'll hurt them," he had warned her a few days before the Schaefer family closed up their house and moved away. "I'll know if you do." Charlie believed him. David Diffenderfer was big and burly. Powerful. Scary. Some truths are better hidden away. Safer for everyone concerned. She did it, too. Kept the secret. Survived.

No one who crossed paths with the gregarious, bubbly teenaged beauty and homecoming princess would have guessed that under that intoxicating exterior was a damaged child. No one who ever watched her pull herself up again and again, laughing at her failings and striking out bravely once more, would ever guess that sometimes a fear washed over her that felt like the beginning of paralysis. What she let others see was the fearless Charlie...the one who could beat back death, if need be.

But could she do it? *Cancer. My beautiful son has cancer.* This was a new species of horror. She could feel the weight of it pushing her lower than any place she had ever been before, worse even than being defiled in that barn, with no *deus ex machina* this time to swoop down and save them. *How am I going to find the strength to will both Trevor and myself to survive?*

CHAPTER TWELVE

The next day, the doctor removed the catheter in Trevor's bladder. It was a milestone on his road to recovery, or so he thought. Even though he was unsteady and had so many tubes still attached to him that both a nurse and Charlie had to assist him to the bathroom, his belief in Dr. Cherny's ability to have cured him completely remained unshaken.

He didn't mind that his sisters went home to their lives. He found it harder to accept that his father also left town a few days after the surgery. He was puzzled that his father chose to be up in McCall instead of staying in Boise near him. When he did come to see Trevor, it was maybe for an hour or two. Even then his attention was divided; Trevor spent most of their time together watching Ballard talk on his cell phone. His dad developed a pattern of calling to tell Trevor a specific time when he was arriving and then not show up until hours later. The drain of unfulfilled anticipation left him emotionally depleted.

Charlie literally camped out at the hospital, determined to be upbeat and hide reality from Trevor for a few more hours, a few more days. She made friends with all the nurses, aides, and social workers on Trevor's case. She began to take an interest in the other young patients on the fourth floor, many of whom had been in the hospital for weeks at a time fighting their cancers.

Charlie was now officially a member of "the fourth floor moms." It wasn't a club to which she had any desire to belong. She couldn't believe how many other mothers there were. The social worker assigned to assist her and Trevor told her pediatric cancer was on the rise in every state of the country.

"How can that be?" Charlie asked.

"How many hours do you have for me to tell you?"

She wanted to know more, but for now Charlie's hours would be consumed with caring for her son, who finally seemed ready to be moved to a real room.

———————

Before he could be transferred, Trevor needed the drainage tube removed from his brain. Dr. Cherny gave him two shots, one on each of the stitch lines he was about to make. The shots were to numb the top of Trevor's head. With each shot, he felt more of a burn rather than a sting.

He still was too weak to open his eyes for more than a few seconds at a time. He heard a scratching sound, which was the only way he knew the doctor was doing something to his numb head. The sound and sensation made him think of a car in winter having its windshield ice removed by a scraper. When he was done, Trevor's head was shaven in two places with stitches everywhere.

Trevor managed to find a silver lining in all of this: the swelling in his face was going down, and he knew he could live with all of the discomfort at this point, because once he left the hospital, this ordeal would be behind him for good.

The rest of Trevor's hospital stay became a revolving door of well-wishers. The San Diego contingent left, but Charlie's local friends visited in droves. Jimmy Walls was a trouper. Trevor called his older half-brother Bro, and he practically lived there as much as Charlie, trading nights with his mom in the room St. Luke's had given her to use.

Then one day toward the end of his time in the hospital, Tina Gould showed up with her son, Chris, who had been Trevor's best pal. She also brought Paden, her older son. Tina and her husband Bo had worked as caretakers of the Smiths' McCall estate from 1997 to 2000. The family had lived in a modest two-story gatehouse at the entry to the Smiths' long driveway. It was during these formative years of Trevor's life that he developed his friendship with Chris. The Goulds lived in Boise now, and he rarely saw him.

The idea was to leave the boys alone with Trevor. Charlie told him it would help his recovery to have a couple of so-called normal hours. She and Tina went out for a cup of coffee and a long talk.

But the plan didn't work out that well. Trevor's eyes still fluttered closed all the time even though he wasn't tired, and that worried Chris and Paden. Conversation between the boys was stilted, too. Paden and Chris said something to Trevor, and he tried to answer, but he couldn't speak that well and with his eyes moving of their own volition the whole experience was beyond awkward. He couldn't help but notice that they seemed almost panicked by his behavior. For the first time, Trevor thought that if he didn't get his body and brain back to normal soon, he might lose all his friends.

To make matters worse, later that same night Trevor rang for the nurse on duty to take him to the bathroom. He was still too weak and uncoordinated to walk by himself. He felt her grasp him tightly as he passed out.

"Trevor, I can't hold you," she blurted as he came to and felt himself dropping out of her arms to the ground.

She ran to get help, and Trevor peed in his pajamas. Lying there all wet, he felt like a fish out of water, like he didn't belong anywhere anymore.

⌐⌐⌐

Trevor was scheduled for a MRI the morning of his release from the hospital. It was the day before Thanksgiving. They would be spending it down in Boise. He wished he could be up in McCall going snowboarding. He felt considerably stronger by this time, however, and was certain he would be back up on Brundage Mountain by Christmas. If he shut his eyes, he could almost feel the cold wind on his face and hear the slick sound of his edges carving through the powder.

Ballard promised to be at the hospital in time for this final MRI. Trevor stayed up worrying the night before. *Please be clear. Please let me go home.* Although Dr. Cherny had told him a day or so ago that the tumor was all gone, Trevor still felt panic each and every time. The fear only subsided once the doctor told him everything still looked cancer-free.

After the MRI, they wheeled Trevor back to his room to wait for the doctor to come up and say he could finally go home. Ballard had been a no-show. Trevor couldn't contain his disappointment and said something to Charlie about being sad that his father didn't care enough to come and support him. She evaded his comment by telling him instead that Dr. Cherny was bringing another doctor with him.

"What kind of doctor?"

"An oncologist," she answered.

"What's that?" Trevor asked, just as his father finally arrived.

Ballard barely said a word. He hardly looked at Trevor.

"Why didn't you show up for the MRI, Dad?"

Just as Ballard opened his mouth to say something, Dr. Cherny and a woman doctor walked into the room. He said hello to them instead.

"Trevor, I want you to meet Dr. Chang," said Dr. Cherny.

Trevor smiled at the pretty Asian woman who appeared to be in her late thirties. She was the one who spoke, taking over. Her voice was soft and soothing to Trevor's ears. At this point, he still didn't know what an oncologist was, so at first what she said didn't register in his mind.

Dr. Chang said, "We have the final pathology report now, Trevor. Unfortunately, it shows that your tumor is malignant."

Trevor looked at her blankly, his eyes still fluttering open and shut of their own free will. Sensing his hesitation, the oncologist quickly added that this meant he had cancer. He glanced at his mother, whom he now recognized was trying to keep herself under control as the doctor went on to describe the treatment for a large medulloblastoma.

Just the word, **MEDULLOBLASTOMA**, sounded ominous. It seemed like something in a scary science-fiction movie. Then, Dr. Chang mentioned radiation and chemotherapy to make certain that the cancer cells did not spread anywhere else. At this point he still couldn't process much of what she said. He just kept thinking that he had cancer, and that meant he was going to die.

Once, he saw a movie, whose name escaped him, where the hero learned how and when he was going to die. The way it was played out fascinated him. Now this kind-looking woman was standing at his bedside scaring him beyond belief by telling him between the lines that his death would be from cancer, and from the look in everyone's eyes, probably very soon. It wasn't at all like the movie. Knowing was awful. It made him feel as if he were being pulled under water, and he was having trouble holding his breath. It was like he had a thousand pounds of pressure on his chest, every muscle in his body was tensing up, and all he wanted to do was scream for someone to let him surface.

The atmosphere in the room deteriorated rapidly. Tears ran unchecked down Ballard's face. Charlie verged on hysteria. The doctors murmured that they would leave the family alone for a few minutes of privacy and disappeared.

Trevor turned over onto his stomach, burying his face into his pillow. "I'm going to die! I'm going to die!" he kept choking out between sobs.

Ballard's crying grew louder. Charlie's sobs escalated into a keening, heart-rending wail.

Trevor felt as if they all might cry themselves to death right then and there. Ballard approached the bed, and Trevor felt him rub his leg briefly. He heard his dad's footsteps cross the room, the door open and close, and then he was gone. A fleeting, panicky thought crossed Trevor's mind: *I hope he doesn't have another heart attack because of me.*

Charlie and Trevor waited for him to come back to help them gather up Trevor's few belongings and leave the hospital. He never did return. Charlie finally called Bro. He drove them home to their house on Winterwood Lane.

Chapter Thirteen

A few days before Trevor began his radiation treatments in early December, he was allowed to make a final visit with his McCall classmates and enjoy a weekend visitation with his father.

The day at school turned out to be traumatic for Trevor, tense and unbearable at times. Even though his closest friends greeted him enthusiastically, they were almost too solicitous and deferential. Everything felt scripted to Trevor, as if they were playing parts in a "How We Greet Trevor Smith" play.

At lunchtime, Trevor stood amidst his old group nearly mute and unable to take part in the conversation. It was demoralizing. He used to dominate recess chatter on any subject important to his friends. He wasn't surprised that no one broached his surgery and what it was like, or how he felt now that he had cancer. Not that he would have known where to begin if they had asked. He stood out like a sore thumb in the cap he wore to cover up the scars and stitch lines. His eyes still bothered him, doing that fluttering thing.

He already had begun to miss his coveted place in the center of the popular crowd and with the athletes, two areas he dominated a few months ago. It amazed him to see how fast a person could become a nonentity, a subject of curiosity rather than friendship. The idea of being with kids in some other town who didn't know him before the surgery, and who wouldn't know how much he'd changed, began to seep into his consciousness.

The entire weekend in the guesthouse with his dad was depressing. Little talk. Less laughter. Trevor felt powerless to keep his already dark mood from plummeting. He became increasingly quiet and withdrawn.

———

Down in the main house, Charlie had Else Fuller for company.

"I know you don't want to be alone," Else said before Charlie could open her mouth. "So, I'm staying here with you."

"I don't know what I did to deserve such a good friend."

"Hey, you guys are the best show in town, and I have a front-row seat. Without you and Ballard locking horns, I'd have no drama in my life. I'd just be at home playing video poker on my computer!"

Charlie smiled at her. "I hope Trevor's having a good time with Ballard up there." She cast a glance toward the guesthouse location.

"Trevor'll be okay no matter where he is. I just hope Ballard doesn't come apart."

"It's hard on him, I know. Sick kids. He's not that good in situations like this."

Else added, "We'll see what he's made of, that's for sure. How about some wine?"

"I don't want any."

"Come on," Else insisted. "It'll relax you."

"Maybe you're right."

Charlie opened a bottle of Chardonnay. She poured two glasses, and they sat reminiscing about the past.

"God, remember that first time I saw Ballard with Joan?" Charlie asked Else as she got up to stoke the fire.

"You mean at the Hotel Del Coronado in nineteen-eighty... when was it?"

"1987. That big fundraiser. We were at that front table when you said..."

Else chimed in, "...get a look at that hunk coming in with Joan Kroc."

"And I said, 'He seemed taller in photos.' And you told me something I'll never forget: 'You don't have to be tall when you have a powerful mother-in-law like Joan Kroc behind you every inch of the way.'"

Else laughed and reminded Charlie how she'd cajoled her into going on a date with Ballard because they'd make such a great-looking couple: a real Ken and Barbie.

"I do remember. I was going through my divorce and didn't want to get involved. But you talked me into giving it a try."

"Sorry. It seemed like a good idea at the time."

Charlie sighed. "It was great for awhile, Else. It really was. And I have Trevor. So how much can I complain?"

"Remember at the beginning, Ballard kept sending you those cards and letters saying you were his soul-mate?"

"Soul-mate." She laughed. "What a bunch of bullshit! I had no idea that was his MO for getting women," Charlie said. "I didn't even know what one was until he started talking about it. But I fell for his romantic line. Hard. He made me believe he was a compassionate man. He said and did all the right things. You remember the way he just swooped in and took over the care for my mother when she was dying? Like he knew I was falling apart at the thought of losing her, and he would be there to take her place."

"I have to admit he outdid himself there. Setting her up in his La Jolla house and making a hospital suite out of the living room for her. Round-the-clock care."

"The whole nine yards. Then chartering that private plane to take her to the Bahamas to live near that clinic so they could perform miracle cures on her."

"But there were no miracles there," Else commented.

"No. And there were no miracles that could keep the real Ballard from showing up right after she died and our honeymoon was over. I couldn't believe someone could change that much so fast. I keep thinking about what Linda warned right before my wedding: 'Ballard's not what he seems. He gas-lighted me for sixteen years and made me think I was going crazy.'"

They both sat quietly, lost in their own thoughts.

"Look outside, Else," Charlie said. "It's going to snow. I better put more wood on the fire."

"Look how easy that is for you. Piling on those logs like 'Paula' Bunyan!"

"Yeah. Who needs a man?" Charlie said with a laugh.

"You know what they say: a dog will never leave you, but a man won't pee on the carpet."

"Are you sure?" Charlie asked with a grin.

"That's food for thought," Else replied, getting up to pour herself some more wine.

"Speaking of food—what should I make for dinner?"

"Hey, let me take you out," Else suggested.

"I don't know if I should leave."

"Trevor'll be okay for a couple of hours. Anyway, we're just a cell phone call away."

"You're right."

"We never did get to the Epicurean," Else reminded her.

"Sounds good to me."

Located in the center of town on the land that once was the McCall train depot, the Hotel McCall's Epicurean Restaurant dominated a prime spot with a wonderful view of the lake.

Their waitress, a sylphlike Scandinavian named Lolo, was typical of many of the McCall locals—she worked more than one job and knew everybody in town. Thus, it was not odd for Lolo to offer her best wishes for Trevor's speedy and full recovery while seating them at their table.

"You know, Charlie," Lolo went on. "Trevor's not the only sick kid up here. My stepson is only sixteen, and he's fighting testicular cancer. Charlie, everyone's saying that if a kid like Trevor is getting sick, too, there's a real problem. I don't know what the hell is going on up here!"

When Lolo left to fill their drink order, Else said, "You know what Lolo meant, don't you? That Trevor's the golden boy of McCall, from a wealthy family with every advantage."

"If that's true, it goes to show you: money can't buy health."

"Exactly. If he's getting cancer, too, then there has to be something more to all of these illnesses."

"I don't know if I ever told you this," Charlie said, "but once we became full-timers, we'd go to parties and would hear gossip… rumors…about all the sick people here in McCall. Honestly, I never gave it much thought."

"We've all heard stuff like that. Remember Doris Gardiner*?" Charlie nodded and smiled. "She was raised here and told everyone not to swim in the lake because it would make you go crazy! We all laughed and said that she was just a bit of a sweet old loon herself. But what if she was right? Oh God." Tears welled up in Else's eyes. She began to weep quietly, dabbing at her eyes with a tissue.

Charlie felt her eyes water, too. As she reached for Else's pack of tissues, a woman sitting at a nearby table piped up. "You know," the woman said. "I couldn't help overhearing your conversation. I don't live here, but I'm thinking of taking a job as a nurse at the McCall Hospital. I'm from Sun Valley. We have problems there, too. Everybody says it's because of all the mining that went on for years."

"You're kidding!" Charlie replied, turning in her seat to get a better look at the woman. "I thought it was just up in northern Idaho. Coeur d'Alene area. Where there are Superfund sites."

"Nah," she replied, "it's everywhere. No regulations for years. It all comes home to roost eventually."

Else was sufficiently recovered to speak again. She offered, "I bought my home over by the Shore Lodge on the west side of town. The young woman who sold it to me was dying of cancer. I got it for a steal."

Lolo had walked up by this time to bring them their salads. "I knew her. Nice gal. I've heard of other people living over there who also got cancer."

"What the hell is going on here?" Charlie murmured.

"Toxic exposure's a funny thing," the nurse told them. "It could sit there for years and just come up and bite you much later. I know a woman at my church in Sun Valley. When she heard I was thinking of moving here, she just about had a fit. Said that she grew up in McCall. Her daddy was a lumberjack. She said he wasn't all that educated, but he did know a thing or two about this town. He wouldn't let his family drink the water. Said they dumped every goddamned thing they could think of in the lake back in the day."

"That's comforting," Charlie said. "We get our water from the lake." She warily eyed the water goblet in front of her then said, "Pour me another glass of wine, Else!"

Charlie and Else sat up half the night talking about the possibilities of something environmental being the cause of Trevor's brain cancer. But what?

As the hours passed, Charlie's memory of days gone by improved. Little things that never bothered her before now stood out in *bas relief*. The lake water was getting warmer. But it was a glacial lake over three-hundred feet deep. Some kids she knew didn't even wear wet suits anymore to swim. Should that have been a red flag?

She remembered Kyle, a sixteen-year-old boy who died of brain cancer just two years ago. The son of a local land surveyor, he had lived his entire life in McCall.

"Oh, my God!" Charlie exclaimed. "There's another boy, too. The son of Trevor's soccer coach. He came down with cancer in 1998. I can picture it so well, because his dad shaved his head at the same time his son lost his hair from chemotherapy."

"What if there are even more young people in McCall sick with cancer like these boys?"

"This is pretty scary stuff. I have to find out," Charlie said emphatically.

Charlie had graduated with honors from the 'School of Hard Knocks.' A high-school dropout, married at seventeen with a baby on the way, she had to become resourceful once she got divorced and became a single mom living on welfare for many months before starting her own business. As she often described her rise: "I pulled myself up by my bootstraps even before I could afford the boots."

She transformed herself from being a part-time model and effervescent hostess at golf tournaments in San Diego to co-owning with her former sister-in-law a business coordinating a bevy of attractive women to drive golf carts around the course during corporate and charity golfing events. Charlie garbed her gregarious gals in white short shorts, pink tee shirts, and jaunty caddy caps, and they served food and drinks to the tournament participants.

After finally going out on her own, Charlie's Caddies became so popular in San Diego that the president of a fledgling golf-club company, Cobra Golf, approached her to do promotional events for his tournaments. They became known as The Cobra Charmers. She achieved success by tackling a task head-on and plunging into the fray without worrying if she could actually succeed.

Else agreed that they should look into it as soon as possible.

———————

Charlie was up and dressed early the next morning, making breakfast and still thinking about how to figure out what may have caused Trevor's cancer.

The phone rang. It was Trevor.

"I'm not feeling good, Mom. I'm real weak. Can I come be with you in the main house for a while?"

"Of course you can," she replied.

"I'll be right down."

She thought, *What am I doing? I have no extra time for sleuthing.*

Chapter Fourteen

A few days before Christmas, Charlie was outside putting the finishing touches on the fragrant cinnamon spice and pine wreath on her front door when Ballard phoned.

"How about spending the holiday up here?" he suggested.

"We've already made plans to be in Boise," Charlie told him.

"I know it's your holiday with him. But Trevor loves McCall at this time of the year. And I'd really like to be with my son."

Ballard was right. Trevor did love the McCall holiday atmosphere. He did want to see his father more. He was terribly insecure because of Ballard's inconsistency even before the cancer diagnosis.

"Okay," she said. "I'll make the changes. We'll be there."

On Christmas Eve day, Charlie and Trevor piled into their SUV, while Bro trailed in a second car. Secreted in his backseat was Charlie's Christmas present to Trevor, a twelve-week-old pug she christened Elliot, after the boy in the movie *ET*.

Slowly caravanning up to the mountain resort on treacherous roads in a snowstorm, they arrived in McCall in the late afternoon. Driving through town on the way to the lake house, Charlie felt a poignant twinge for the loss of her idyllic past as she drank in the familiar bustle of pre-Christmas activity of a small town.

Trevor was rail-thin by this time, vomiting regularly from extensive radiation treatments and a first round of chemo. In fact, Trevor got sick en route at the side of the road at the clearing just before Cascade. Their last-minute lark was turning into an ordeal. Even so, it was right to have changed plans. Trevor was heartened by the notion that his father wanted to spend the holiday with him. From what Trevor also had hinted at, Charlie suspected that he hoped that by getting his parents together in the holiday spirit, they might decide to reconcile. That would never happen, but she also believed that staying in Boise for the holidays and giving in to the illness at this point might take all the fight out of her son.

While Charlie unpacked the car and put away the provisions in the kitchen, Trevor went up to see his dad. Bro waited until he was out of sight to take the puppy out of his car and hide him in the furthest of the three downstairs guest bedrooms.

———

Trevor climbed the stairs slowly and with great effort to see his dad in the guesthouse, remembering with a pang of fear how he was able to take them two at a time just a few months ago.

"So, what are you doing?" Trevor asked him.

"My new hobby. Beads. Beaded bracelets. Necklaces. I'm getting pretty good at making them."

Trevor thought his dad's new hobby was creating more of a mess than his place usually was. His beads and tools were everywhere. It was a challenge finding a place to sit.

Trevor barely made it through an hour. He found it hard to talk to his dad about anything. And Ballard didn't seem to be making any effort to ease the tension between them.

"You're back so soon!" Charlie exclaimed when Trevor came in through the mudroom door.

"It's a mess up there. And he seems too busy to talk to me."

Charlie said, "Too busy? With what?"

"He has a new hobby. He's into beading. I think he's becoming a hippie!"

Charlie burst out laughing. That got Trevor laughing, too.

"I have an idea," Charlie said. "Why don't we ask your dad to eat with us?"

She paged Ballard on the intercom. "You're welcome to have dinner with me and the boys," she suggested. "Trevor would love that."

"Can't," he said. "I have other plans."

"I hope I didn't make him mad," Trevor worried.

After awhile, Trevor became too queasy to care who was having dinner with him.

⌒

On Christmas morning, Charlie and Bro finally handed Trevor the pug puppy they had been hiding for three days.

Charlie could see that this gift was the best medicine he could have gotten. From the moment Elliot nestled in his arms, Trevor seemed like a new person. The mood in the house lifted for them all.

Charlie planned Christmas dinner for four in the afternoon. Ballard was their guest of honor.

She had phoned him earlier to see if he wanted to come down and spend the entire day with her and the boys. "You should see Trevor with that puppy."

Ballard demurred. Said he had to have some time for himself in the middle of the afternoon. He promised he'd be back well in time for dinner.

Having stayed primarily in the back guestroom playing with Elliot, Trevor first realized that his father was nowhere to be found around one in the afternoon. He called him on his cell phone, but it was turned off.

At first Trevor didn't think much of it, even though Ballard told him after the surgery that he'd always have it on in case his son needed him. Trevor understood that he shouldn't have been so scared about the cell being turned off. But it was Christmas. It was getting late. He called again. No luck. By this time, he began to really worry.

"Where's my dad?" he asked his mother.

"He promised to be back before dinner."

"Well, why did he have to go off at all?"

Charlie shrugged.

While Trevor was working himself up into a state, his mother worked busily in the kitchen basting the turkey and getting all the other side dishes prepared. From two until four o'clock Trevor kept phoning his father, leaving messages that became increasingly urgent.

"What if he had an accident in the snow, Bro?"

"Don't worry," Bro said. "He's fine."

"But what if he had a heart attack and no one is around to save him?" he said to Charlie.

"He knows dinner's at four. He'll be here."

Nothing either of them said placated him. He made himself sick with worry by dinnertime, and Ballard still was not answering his phone or making an appearance.

They waited and waited. Just before 5:30 p.m. they decided Ballard really was a no-show and sat down at the beautifully decorated table filled with everyone's favorite dishes. By this time Bro was as glum as Trevor and Charlie. They didn't have to say what they all felt: Christmas dinner was ruined, reduced to a desultory exercise. Trevor barely ate two bites of his food.

Ballard showed up after six in the evening without any explanation or apology. Charlie turned to the sink and didn't say a word to him as he sauntered past her through the open kitchen toward the great room.

Trevor lay resting on one of the couches, his earlier anxiety having been replaced with a deep and growing anger at having been treated like a second-class citizen.

A fire blazed in the river rock fireplace. The fragrance of pines filled the air. Bro was sprawled across the easy-chair, having tried without success to lighten the somber mood. Like Charlie, he gave Ballard the silent treatment.

Trevor, on the other hand, would not be silenced. "Where were you?" he demanded.

"I was visiting some friends," Ballard replied lamely.

"Friends, or your girlfriend and her kids?" Trevor shot back more loudly. "And don't bother to lie. 'Cause I know that's where you were."

Ballard said nothing.

Trevor went on, his angry tone tinged with childlike exasperation. "We came all the way up here to be with you, Dad! You asked us! So why would you want to spend Christmas with them rather than me?"

Instead of answering, Ballard turned and walked back through the dining area and kitchen, slamming the mudroom door on his way out. No one heard another thing from him for the rest of the night.

———

The next morning, clumps of Trevor's blond hair began falling out. It was a real shock. He looked into the sink in his bathroom and saw strands of hair. *Hey, what's this?* He glanced up at the mirror and saw empty spots on his head where his blond hair used to be!

Later, while resting on the couch, he pulled out more tufts of hair. "Mom," he called out. "Come look at this."

"My God!" she said, as she barely pulled and more hair came away in a clump.

By this time, Trevor was panicked. "I have to call my dad."

"Okay," Charlie replied. "But do you think you should after what happened yesterday?"

"I have to." He got on the intercom. "Dad," he said fearfully. "My hair's falling out!"

Ballard responded with alacrity, contacting a woman who cut his hair at a local shop called Rumors. She said she'd come in right away and see what she could do for the frightened boy.

Trevor was thankful his dad let him bring Elliot, whom he cradled in his lap as they made their way in silence in his father's Suburban to the shop across from the McCall airport. In what was becoming a series of disasters in his life, Trevor couldn't imagine how they were going to resolve this latest.

After a quick consultation, Trevor climbed into the stylist's chair and had his entire head shaved. Afterwards he tried to avoid the mirror, but he couldn't help catching a glimpse of himself before they left. *Who is this pathetic boy? I'm thinner than a concentration camp survivor. Whiter than a ghost, with black shiners for eyes. Bald as an egg, with ragged scars like cracks scattered all over.*

He noticed his father could barely look at him as they drove home. Elliot didn't seem to mind as he licked his face. "Hey, boy," Trevor whispered into his little ear, "Guess I'm officially a cancer kid."

*The Smiths' Pilgrim's
Cove Compound:
Payette Lake,
McCall, Idaho*

*The Lake House:
Ballard and Charlie
with Trevor and
his sisters*

*Fourth of July:
Charlie and Trevor
on the deck of the
lake house*

Golden Moment: Trevor and his dad, Ballard, at a McDonald's convention

On the Field: Trevor in seventh grade at Payette Lakes Middle School, in September 2002, just two months before he was diagnosed with brain cancer.

Trevor the Mighty Mite: Trevor accepting his award for the J-7 slalom race at Brundage Mountain, McCall, Idaho. The Payette Lakes Ski Club sponsors the Mighty Mite program.

Joan's Jet: Family members land in Boise after flying in Joan's G-4 from San Diego for Trevor's surgery on November 15, 2002. From left to right: Troy Latimer, Amanda Latimer, Lori Schaefer, Amy Smith, Frank Ragen, Mildred Smith, Lexis and Marisa Milisic, and Scott Walther

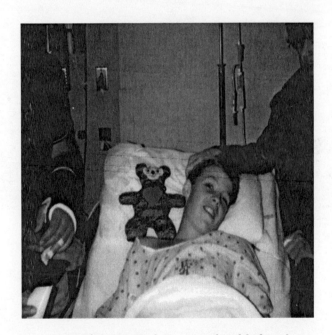

St. Luke's Hospital. Trevor sedated before the first scheduled surgery on November 15, 2002. Trevor is comforted by Charlie on right.

Charlie and Else in the 1980s.

Early Days: Charlie, age six, in front of her Encino, California, home with her brother Denny in 1956.

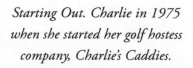

Starting Out. Charlie in 1975 when she started her golf hostess company, Charlie's Caddies.

Cobra Charmer: Charlie (second from right) at work hosting a golf tournament in San Diego in her new role with Cobra Golf Company.

Hotel del Coronado: Joan Kroc with Senator Gary Hart and Ballard Smith at the Hotel del Coronado in San Diego, California, 1987. It was at this fundraiser where Ballard first met Charlie.

Ballard and Charlie's Wedding: La Jolla, California, January 23, 1988. Special guest Steve Garvey (left) once played for the San Diego Padres and the Los Angeles Dodgers.

Socializing: Chub Feeney (former president of the National Baseball League and then-president of the San Diego Padres), Joan, Ballard, and Charlie at a party at Joan's home in Rancho Santa Fe, California, 1988.

Trevor's Radiation Helmet: This is the protective gear that Trevor wore during his radiation treatments, five days a week.

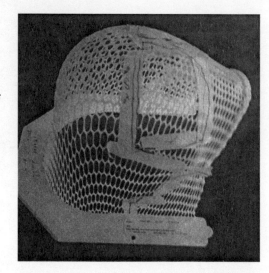

Get well letters from Grandma Joan

Dear Trevor & Charlie,

Thank you for the special gift you sent for Christmas - I loved the love bird candle and everything else!

Trevor, you are a very strong, courageous young man. I am so positive about your recovery and if love from everyone who knows you will heal, you will make astounding progress in your recovery. I love you all so much

Hugs & More! Grandma Joan

Dec. 13- 2002

Dear Trevor,

I hope you will like the books & the game -

Grandma Joan thinks of you many many times during the day. I know you are having a lot to deal with right now but I believe 100% that you will recover fully.

I love you & am so proud of your strength & courage -

Grandma Joan

From the right to know and the duty
to inquire flows the obligation to act.

Dr. Sandra Steingraber

Part Two:

FIGHTING BACK

CHAPTER FIFTEEN

Boise, Idaho
Spring 2003

Trevor sat in his yellow flannel pj's at the kitchen table, struggling to eat his breakfast. Elliot lay splayed at his feet, occasionally tickling his ankles with his velvety tongue. Trevor reached down and scratched a favorite spot behind his ear. "How's it going, my little chemo dog?"

"You have to try and eat, Trev," Charlie urged. His body was so frail and shrunken. Poked and prodded. Sallow complexion. *How many more months of this can he take?*

"I will," he promised earnestly. It almost made her cry. It was a wonder she had any tears left. These days crying felt like her job. She ministered to Trevor all day, then spent half the night in her room sobbing.

He dutifully took a spoonful of cereal. Slowly worked it around his mouth. Half-gagged. "There," he announced after he managed to swallow it.

"Mouth sores still bothering you a lot, huh?"

He nodded. "I wish they would go away, already."

"Dr. Chang said they will. It just takes time."

Charlie sat down next to him with a cup of steaming tea. Her breakfast. Lately, she almost ate less than her son. Her brother joked recently that she was so pale and skinny her legs looked like out-of-bounds stakes on a golf course.

Trevor suddenly eyed her with unexpected intensity. "Mom," he said, "I'm so angry that this happened to me."

"You have every right to be." He'd been talking to her like this for a couple of weeks now. Just a few words here and there, hinting at the depths of his despair.

"But maybe all this happened for a reason."

"Oh?"

"You know how you've been hearing about problems up in McCall? Environmental ones?"

"Right."

"Remember how you said that because I got sick a lot of the town's people are sitting up and taking notice of all the people who got sick, too? Maybe something positive will come out of what happened to me so other kids don't have to suffer."

"Trevor, you are amazing!" She got up and hugged him.

Charlie was about to encourage him to open up more about his feelings and his hopes when the phone rang. It was from the outer gate to their complex. Their landscaper was there to plant flowers into the recently thawed ground around her woodsy property. *Spring's officially here*, she thought, and felt her spirits flutter upward as she buzzed the gate open.

"I have to talk to Vicki outside for awhile," Charlie told Trevor. "She's brought dozens of flats, and I need to talk with her about where to put them."

"Go ahead. I'm fine."

"Try to finish that bowl of cereal."

Half an hour later, Charlie and the landscaper strode into the family room from the patio. Vicki removed her soil-encrusted gardening gloves and slipped out of her lace-up rubber boots before entering the house barefoot.

"Wow, what a great place. I see now why you chose all those blues and yellows. The flowers go great with the color scheme inside. What style is this decor, anyway?"

"Country French," Charlie replied, glancing toward the kitchen and noting that Trevor was still sitting at the table, staring into his bowl of cereal.

"Hey, bud. This is Vicki."

"Hey," he said, barely lifting his head or managing a smile.

Vicki started to say hello but stopped, a shocked, wide-eyed look spreading across her face instead at the sight of an emaciated Trevor.

"I…uh…" he started to say, then gagged and covered his mouth. He made a dash for the sink and vomited. He looked up at his mother and shrugged helplessly, then rushed from the room.

"I'm so sorry," Charlie said to Vicki. "Trevor's going through chemo for brain cancer. Sometimes the nausea sweeps over him without warning."

"Poor kid. Don't worry about me. I just feel so bad for him," said Vicki.

"This has been the year from hell. Mouth sores are the latest. So tired he can hardly get out of his pj's anymore. Sometimes he can't even lift his head off his pillow. More pain and suffering than any child deserves in ten lifetimes."

"Seems like there's a lot of childhood cancer going around these days."

"Yeah. I've gotten to know so many parents on the fourth floor of St. Luke's Hospital. That's the pediatric cancer floor. We're all scared.

Bewildered. Feeling like we belong to a club none of us wanted to ever join."

"It's got to be hard on families," Vicki commented.

"Oh, it is. Parents break up. Lose their jobs. Their homes. Siblings getting emotional problems. I saw one mother last time we were at MSTI...that's the Mountain States Tumor Institute at St. Luke's. Anyway, she was tending to her six-year-old with cancer while trying to hold and contain her younger child who was autistic. She told me that her husband left her two months before. She lost her job because she couldn't afford childcare for the little one and had to stay home."

"You're divorced, too, right?"

"Yeah. His dad has visitation rights every afternoon here. One to five p.m. Court ordered it. He lives up in McCall. Sometimes he comes. Sometimes he doesn't. Trevor and I are pretty much going through this alone."

"My friend, Sue O'Dell, lives in McCall. I remember her telling me about all the brain cancers in that area."

"She sure is right about that! Trevor is just one of *five* brain cancers in the past year. There's lots more cancers of all kinds and other diseases, too."

"She knows a lot of people with big mouths up there. If you know what I mean."

"Hmm. I'd like to talk to her."

"Consider it done."

A few days later Vicki phoned Charlie to say that her friend, Sue, would like to get together. "If you're going to be home this afternoon, can I bring her over to your house?"

"Absolutely."

Within the hour, the three women were seated in the family room talking a mile a minute. Sue was a warm, intelligent woman who cared deeply about Valley County. She also firmly believed that there was something off about all the illness and wanted to help in any way she could.

Charlie told them about her encounter at the Hotel McCall with the waitress Lolo and the job-hunting nurse from Sun Valley. "What both of those gals said got me thinking. But at this stage that's all it is: a jumble of thoughts."

Sue explained, "I began to suspect that there was something really wrong all the way back in 1995. My friend, Mike Stewart, got involved researching a possible breast-cancer-cluster case. Bunch of nurses from the local hospital."

"I know who Mike Stewart is," Charlie told Sue. "The man who owns and publishes *The Long Valley Advocate*?"

"Yep. That's the one."

"I've seen him around town. But honestly, I just don't know when I can break away to get up there any time soon. Trevor needs me..."

"I understand," said Sue. "What if I arrange for Mike to come down here to talk to you? No one knows more than that man. He's your guy. But I can't bother him if you're not really committed."

"Trevor and I have been talking about this. The other morning he told me he feels that maybe he got sick for a reason. Maybe to help others. It's something he wants me to do. I'm willing to take a shot at it!"

Sue smiled. "I was hoping you'd say that."

———

Mike Stewart drove down to Boise on a day in mid-April when Trevor was in the hospital getting his four days of chemo infusion, and Charlie was able to break away for a couple of hours.

They met for lunch at a local eatery, where they could sit outside and enjoy the lovely, crisp spring afternoon. Charlie and Mike hit if off immediately. In his mid-forties, the newsman sported a close-cropped beard, was casually dressed, and had a spirited look in his eyes and a ready smile. He was easy to talk to, unselfconscious, and willing to help her.

He talked more than he ate, diving right into the topic at hand. He shared with Charlie some of what he knew about the illness patterns in Valley County, informing her that he first became alarmed back in 1995.

"That's when we moved to McCall full-time," she remarked. "Although we had our house long before that."

"Well, as a seasonal resident, you probably would never have heard about the problems."

"I heard things, but never really thought much about it."

"It came to my attention, however, that some local women could be part of a breast-cancer cluster. I started researching what the causes might be with a friend, Dieuwke (Duka) Spencer, who's with the Central District Health in McCall."

"And what happened?" Charlie asked.

"We had amassed some damaging data, when we were told that it wouldn't be a good idea to pursue it."

"Wow. And you listened?"

"Yeah. I was a lot younger back then. A hungry new publisher-owner. I had a newspaper to put out and copies to sell. Duka didn't want to get fired."

"I understand," Charlie told him.

They spoke about what Charlie had learned so far. Not much. Mostly what Lolo had told her, plus all that innuendo interspersed with very few facts she had gleaned since moving to McCall full-time. She admitted that she was an absolute neophyte and really didn't know where to turn next. "I may not be a scholarly type, but I know how to get things done," she promised him.

"Let me think about this for a few days," Mike told her. "I'll come up with a plan. Figure out who you need to contact."

"Bring 'em on," she said.

"I like your spunk," he replied. "Most mothers in your shoes would wilt at the thought of ruffling all those official feathers. I don't think Valley County will know what hit them."

Later, as she ruminated on the meeting with Mike, Charlie rehashed their conversation. He had told her that he loved nothing more than shutting the doors to his weekly newspaper housed in a storefront on the main street of Cascade and going biking or river rafting for days at a time. He admitted rather shamelessly that he possessed an encyclopedic knowledge about and loved every inch of northwest Idaho. Where to fish. Where to hike. And even more important, where all the businesses had come and gone for decades. She hoped he also knew where all the bodies were buried.

Chapter Sixteen

"D-Day," Charlie crowed to Mike as they walked into the government building on Hilton Street in Boise, which housed the Idaho Department of Environmental Quality (IDEQ) offices. A few weeks back, Mike gave her an assignment: call this list of people and get us appointments. Now it was May twelfth, and she successfully had arranged their very first one-on-one session with Jeff Fromm, the head toxicologist at the IDEQ.

"The first of many D-Days, I hope," Mike said.

Fromm was waiting for them in the main foyer. Slight of build and wearing glasses, he had a stale, professorial air about him. He warmly greeted Mike, whom he knew fairly well, and shook Charlie's hand graciously. He then led the way back to his first-floor office. There was another man already seated there.

"Meet Monty Marchus," Fromm said. Marchus stood to shake their hands. "He's the head of Water Quality Control here. But he worked on the water issues in McCall for several years."

"I'm so happy you could be here, too," Charlie said. She sat down, waiting for them to begin the conversation. Silence. As they stared at her and Mike, she wondered, *Are we having a quiet contest? So this is how you want to play it? Here goes.* She dived right in, telling them in a rush who she was and why she was there this afternoon. She became more emotional than she wanted to be as she concluded, "I think you can understand why I have to ask you outright how you plan to address so many cancers in McCall?"

"And how that squares with the documented problems with the water quality over the years," Mike challenged.

It seemed neither of the officials wanted to reply to either question. They took turns equivocating, conceding only that the McCall's water filtration system was still "a work-in-progress." They both refused to accept the idea that this glacial lake from which most of the residents got their home water was problematic enough to warrant a closer look than the normal tests done every two years by the DEQ.

"Wait a minute. I thought you were doing the testing every year since 1995," Mike offered.

"Budget cutbacks. You know how it is," Marchus said.

Mike quickly eyed Charlie as if to say: we sure do know how it is. "So, every two years is sufficient? Do you have any documents to that effect?" Mike asked.

"Documents proving your assertions. Because I'd like to see them, too," Charlie added.

"We'll have to get back to you on that," Monty responded immediately.

"Right," Jeff added. "I'm sure we can allay your concerns."

They continued to talk in circles about water-testing schedules and the "work-in-progress" filtration system for another few minutes. Charlie finally couldn't take their stonewalling any longer.

Time to get personal. She removed an eight-by-ten photo from her satchel. "This is my son, Trevor," Charlie told the two men, showing them a recent image of a very ill Trevor.

Jeff nodded and mumbled something that sounded like, "I'm sorry he's been so sick."

Monty didn't even want to look at the photo. In fact, within a few seconds of Charlie having produced it, Monty abruptly announced that he had to leave for another appointment.

"I want to help you out," Jeff said in a confidential tone once Monty fled the room. "We have a newly formed group called the Cluster Analysis Work Group (CAWG), and I will get you in touch with them. They do good work, I'm told."

He took her phone number and then announced that he enjoyed meeting with her and Mike but had to cut the session off at this point. He offered to walk them out to their cars. On the way, he divulged conspiratorially that he was working on a potential brain-cancer cluster in eastern Idaho.

"Where?" Charlie inquired.

"I can't disclose any specific information about it," he replied.

Once he left them, Mike and Charlie stood in the parking lot talking for a few more minutes.

"Mike, it's like the CIA around here: If I tell you, I'll have to kill you!"

"Look, I'll see what I can find out about this super-secret eastern Idaho cancer cluster. Fromm is a nice-enough guy. Comes across open and empathetic, but he won't help you, you know," he told Charlie.

"And Marchus seemed even more gun-shy," she replied dejectedly.

"Yeah. They construct smokescreens shrouding the truth. Taunt us with half-revelations leading nowhere. Or, just up and leave the room like Monty did today. Maybe you can do better than I have."

"I have to," she said emphatically.

Charlie stewed for a week over the memory of that ineffective meeting with Jeff Fromm and Monty Marchus. She had phoned Fromm a few times to see if he would give her a contact name for the CAWG. It was an ongoing game of telephone tag.

She reached Mike at his office in Cascade. "I'm getting nowhere with Fromm. I have to get my hands on those McCall water documents," she said.

"Easier said than done," he reminded her. "No one wants you to see them. At least not the most incriminating ones. I've reported for years about the ongoing problems, and the reports I've been forced to use reveal just the tip of the iceberg."

"There has to be a way. I just haven't thought of it yet."

A few days later, Charlie left Trevor at home with his tutor and his father and drove to the DEQ office. She knew from her constant phoning that Fromm was safely tucked away in eastern Idaho and wouldn't be anywhere near the office for several days. She strode purposefully into the building and stopped at the front desk. The receptionist looked up expectantly.

"Hi," Charlie said like she was greeting an old friend. "I'm here to go over some documents on McCall water. Jeff Fromm assured me they'd be ready for me to review."

"Jeff's not here today, hon."

"Oh gosh. Now what?"

"Oh, don't worry. I'm sure Mr. Fromm just forgot to tell me. You'll need to sign in and get a badge to allow you into the documents section, though," the woman explained.

She walked Charlie down the hall, got her the badge then led her into a little cubicle with a table and a chair.

"You can sit here," she said, "while I get what you need. What years specifically do you want?"

"Everything you got," Charlie responded brightly.

In about fifteen minutes, the woman returned with a stack of documents a foot high. After dumping them on the table, she added, "I have more if you need them."

Though Charlie was licking her chops at the sight of all these files, feeling like she was at a moonlight sale at Nordstrom, she expected it would take someone knowledgeable at least a week to go through them carefully. For her it would take a millennium. *What was I thinking? Be careful what you wish for!*

The woman left her alone, and Charlie phoned Mike. She told him how she wrangled her way into the documents room. "I got my hands on a shitload of files. I don't know where to start."

"You're turning into a regular Erin Brockovich!"

"Hardly. *She* knew what she was doing."

"Take a deep breath."

He explained how she might scan quickly to find some of the more important documents. Which she did. Then she went down the hall to the receptionist's desk and asked if she could make copies. The woman took them from her and disappeared.

She called Mike again. "I think I have some really exciting stuff here," she said. "From what I can see, it's no wonder Monty walked out on that meeting last week."

"I think it was the photo of Trevor that did it. But you're right: they don't want us little people to know the truth."

When Charlie left the building, she was weighed down with two satchels stuffed to the brim with documents dating back more than a decade. Mounds of potentially incriminating information. Memos galore. As she sped away, she thought, *You guys all just screwed with the wrong mother.*

Charlie spent several hours every evening going over the purloined documents, learning the vocabulary, the charts, and the symbols. It was like being a first-grader all over again. Mike was the recipient of many late-night phone calls where he had to explain the data to her.

The going got easier. Then Charlie came upon a memo about a letter Monty Marchus had written concerning the water filtration system back in 1991. The sender of the memo, Robert Braun, stated:

> *I am not convinced McCall has much of a leg to stand on. They have been sitting on their hands, knowing their compliance deadline is just around the corner. They have made no effort either to monitor and document that they can meet the filtration exemption criteria, or to protect their water source by controlling runoff, watershed activities, or sewage overflows, all which make the lake vulnerable. Maybe CT is an option, but we need to corporately agree on a policy as soon as possible. Being an informed citizen, I might prefer to drink filtered water rather than water that has been chlorinated to death.*

She phoned Mike and read it to him. "What do you think?"

"What I think is that you should make copies of everything. Then drive up here with the duplicates as fast as you can. We have a Big Payette Lake Water Quality Meeting tomorrow in McCall. It's at the library. You need to be there."

She arrived at the library and went downstairs to the meeting room just as the session started. Nearly all of the seventy-five chairs were taken.

Everyone turned to eye her. For the first time, she felt like an interloper. She took her seat next to Mike Stewart and handed him two mammoth envelopes containing the copied documents. A woman near them in the audience watched the hand-off taking place. Mike nodded at her. She nodded back.

Partway though the meeting, Charlie raised her hand to speak. "My name is Charlie Smith," she said. "I lived in McCall full-time for eight years starting in 1995. My thirteen-year-old son has brain cancer. I think he got it because of some environmental lapses allowed in this town. I want to find out what they are, not only for my son's sake, but for all of the other children who have suffered and will suffer in the future if nothing is done."

Murmurs went around the room. A few frowns. Even more nods of sympathy.

Then she stated, "From what I've been hearing at this meeting, the problems with the water aren't so very different today than they were back in the 1990s, when the filtration system was suspect." She paraphrased some of what she learned so far, including her worries that not enough attention was being placed on various contaminants, like mercury. "Wouldn't it be possible to make a connection between these toxins and the growing number of cancer cases among our youth and the adults, too?"

The head of the Water Quality committee, Peter Johnson, a thin, gray-haired man in his sixties, replied that as far as he was concerned, there was no correlation between the water in the lake and any illnesses. However, they would be happy to see any recent data that she could produce to show them otherwise. "This is why we organized this committee. To keep our water safe," he added.

"I will get the documents for you," she said to him. "In due time."

She retook her seat. Almost immediately, the woman who had watched with interest as Charlie gave Mike the folders, scooted over and sat down next to Charlie.

"I'm Tonya," she whispered, handing Charlie her business card.

Charlie scanned the card: *Tonya Dombrowski* was the head of the DEQ office in Valley County. She eyed her more closely now. The woman was reed-thin with medium-length brown hair. No makeup. Had that granola look.

"Mike's told me about you," Tonya whispered. "Give me a call. I'd like to talk to you further."

"Will do," Charlie replied.

She suddenly noticed the time on the wall clock. She turned to Mike. "This is going longer than I expected. I really have to get back to Boise."

"That's cool. I'll stay and let you know if anything else comes up. Thanks for these," he said, patting the envelopes on the chair next to him.

As she walked to her car, Charlie heard someone call her name. She turned and saw a husky, older man waving her down.

"I'm Paul Woods," he announced. "Head of the USGS here in Idaho." He must have seen her confused look, for he added, "United States Geological Survey. I am so very sorry to hear about your son's brain cancer. What a shame."

"Yes, it is. Especially if it could have been prevented," she added.

"Well, yes. *If* is the operative word here."

"You're a scientist. Can you help me get to the bottom of all these cancer cases?" she implored.

"I believe I could help you. However," he paused, "I, uh, have a conflict of interest. You know how it is—a job to protect for a few more years. As you will find with most of us, our hands are tied, but we are entirely sympathetic to your cause."

"If you can't help, then why did you follow me out?" she asked.

"I just wanted you to know that some of us think you shouldn't back off."

Chapter Seventeen

Since 1934 when it was founded, the Arid Club was a private dining establishment in downtown Boise. In more recent years, the venerable institution moved to a shady grove of cottonwood trees next to the Boise River. The rustic two-story building remained a good-old boy's retreat, still accepted as *the* place to conduct business in a low-key, social setting. Captains of industry, politicians, and other well-heeled members of the Boise aristocracy rubbed elbows with one another without looking like they were trying too hard to get what they wanted. It wasn't until the early 1990s that the Arid Club admitted women as members for the first time. Despite this, it remained a favorite haunt of nonagenarian J.R. Simplot, who played gin rummy there every day in the upstairs card room. Word had it the billionaire rarely ate there because he thought the food was too expensive. He preferred McDonald's.

Today Charlie spied J.R.'s little handicap scooter, with its watch-out-for-me flag, parked in a spot reserved for him a few steps from the front entrance. A couple of years back, she almost turned her old pal into her hood ornament when she entered the club's parking lot and he pulled right in front of her without looking.

"Women," he had muttered, when she rushed over to see if he was okay.

This afternoon, Charlie was en route to a lunch meeting with Cecil Andrus, the former governor of Idaho and U.S. Secretary of the Interior. A mutual friend suggested that she must talk to Andrus, probably the last Idaho politician in the past two decades outwardly sympathetic to the plight of the environment when overused and overrun by business.

A receptionist told Charlie she would find the governor at his favorite table on the entry level overlooking the picture windows. Two men fawning over Andrus at his seat turned out to be a state senator and the CEO of a major land-development company. Charlie shook hands with them, and they left. Always known as an impeccable dresser, Andrus appeared nattily attired in a hounds-tooth sports jacket and a federal-blue tie. Ever the gentleman as well, he rose from his chair upon her arrival and now helped her take her seat.

He jumped right in, interrogating her in a compassionate way about Trevor and his illness. Within a few minutes, Charlie filled him in about the harrowing surgery and its aftermath, and the grueling treatments.

"I wish he could have been here today, too," he said.

"I wish he could, too, Governor. It was bad timing. I dropped Trevor off at Camp Rainbow Gold yesterday. He'll be there a week."

Rainbow Gold was a camp for childhood cancer patients, open for one week every August in Ketchum, Idaho. When Charlie broached the idea of Trevor going at the end of his summer stay with Ballard up in McCall, he told her it didn't sound like much fun. She reminded Trevor of all the times he had called her during the summer to lament the disappearance of his old, carefree life on the lake; how he had avoided all of his old friends; how he could not do any water sports he loved; how lonely he was. She finally had talked him into giving this camp a try.

"It's a special place," Andrus agreed. "We Idahoans are lucky to have it."

"When I got there, I saw kids with no legs, and kids with IV bottles dragging their chemo carts around. They all had smiles on their faces, though. They were having fun in spite of the awful cards they've been dealt. I could see why they call it Rainbow Gold. I sure hope Trevor will get something positive out of this experience. He's had so much sadness, pain, and upheaval in his life these past few months."

"Cancer is a devastating disease for the entire family," Andrus commiserated, revealing that his daughter had suffered a bout with it in her twenties. He told Charlie she was fine now, living near Boise.

"This disease is like an epidemic for families in Valley County. I'm sure we're in the middle of a cancer cluster," Charlie said.

As they discussed this awful possibility, it came out that in addition to their main home in Boise, for many years the Andrus family had owned a vacation home in Valley County.

"Our place is on the banks of Cascade Reservoir," he explained. "So, what's happening up that way is important to me."

"I read a frightening report recently," Charlie told him, "that in 1993, a herd of cattle wandered down to the reservoir in Cascade to drink from it. A few hours later, they *all* keeled over and died."

"Oh, yes. I know about that. What a disaster!"

"This report I read links the deaths to contaminated water coming out of McCall and settling into the shallower Cascade reservoir. As you know, the Payette River runs through Payette Lake and empties down into the reservoir. The city of McCall puts treated water back into the lake, and of course, it ends up in the reservoir, too. According to every report I've read, the McCall filtration system has never worked correctly. So, the treated water is suspect. I'm still researching more definitive answers about that."

At that moment, J.R. Simplot made his way through the dining area. He waved at the governor as he passed into the foyer, obviously on his way toward the elevator that would take him up to the card room.

"He's amazing," Charlie said.

"Even though we've locked horns on some issues, he's been a good friend."

"In preparation for our meeting, I read your memoir, *Politics Western Style*, and found it inspirational."

"I'm happy to hear that. Anything in particular?"

"That section about trying to get a stream-protection law to stop the use of the Snake River as an open sewer."

"Yep, in the '70s we had at least twenty-three industrial plants and two municipalities dumping untreated wastes directly into the river."

"And you had to get J.R. to stop dumping his potato peelings and everything else into the river. I thought it was eye-opening when you said he told you that was why he built his plant right where he did: so he could conveniently dump the waste products."

"But he was always reasonable. Once I promised him I'd treat him no differently than any other businessman, he agreed to cooperate. Hell, he figured out a way to take those peelings, divert it all, and feed his livestock with it. Made even more money as a result!"

"I laughed out loud when I read that excerpt," Charlie said. "I could just picture the exchanges between the two of you. Another section spoke volumes to me as well. When you wrote about how there was this idea that recreation, wildlife, and timber harvesting and mining could all exist side by side. And then you said that it didn't quite work out that way: You'd never seen people enjoying a picnic in an open-pit mine."

"And I still feel that way, Charlie. That's why I admire what you're trying to do, especially with a sick son to care for as well. If there is something going on up at Cascade, or in McCall, I want to know about it."

Over dessert and coffee, Charlie questioned the governor about which local agencies in Boise might assist her in her quest for answers.

"I suggest you get in touch with Chris Johnson. He's the head of the Cancer Tumor Registry. He'll be able to help you with your cancer-cluster study."

Within the week, Charlie found herself sitting across from Chris Johnson of the Idaho Cancer Tumor Registry. Using Cecil Andrus' name certainly opened that door quickly. And the wiry man with the pale complexion and short dark hair was nice enough—until she handed him the list of brain cancers in McCall alone for the past year and launched into her impassioned plea for help.

"You have to understand how these things work," he intoned. "You have only seventeen hundred or so full-time residents in your town. Hardly significant enough to even warrant a study of a possible cancer cluster."

"How can that be?" she asked.

"We refer to that as 'statistically insignificant.' We would never be able to get a proper scientific result to know if these cancers represent a cluster or not."

"I don't get it," Charlie exclaimed. "Five brain cancers in young people are statistically insignificant?"

"In a word—yes. You're wasting your time pursuing this."

"That man has no compassion," Charlie moaned to Mike on the phone later in the day.

"It comes with the territory. It's as if these employees are programmed to find reasons not to look into problems. For years we've been told that our towns are too small to be useful in any study."

"*Every* town in this state is small," she reminded her friend. "Well, he won't stop me."

Mike chuckled. "No. I don't suppose he will."

"I'm coming up to Cascade tomorrow," she said. "Big conference over custody. I'll be down the street from you at the courthouse. I could stop by."

"Better yet, why don't we go out to see Stibnite, if it's not too late? Ever since you read me Andrus' quote about no one enjoying a picnic in an open-pit mine, I've been thinking that you should see the area. And I haven't been out there in a very long time."

"I'll be too wiped out after sparring with Ballard." She told him about Trevor's fervent wish to move down to Boise to live with her, and her ex-husband's increasingly adamant fight to prevent it. "I'll stay over in McCall. Let's drive out the next morning."

CHAPTER EIGHTEEN

T*he Long Valley Advocate* newspaper office occupied a small space among a block of retail stores on Main Street in Cascade. Charlie knew the area well, since it was down the road from the Valley County Courthouse where Ballard had thrown a whale of a tantrum the day before.

Charlie parked and went inside. Before she could announce herself, Mike Stewart stuck his head out from a doorway leading to another section of the no-frills building and said he'd be just a minute. She took the opportunity to look around. Posters and other tacked-up headlines from times past crowded the brick walls. Machines and past editions of newspapers piled several feet high cluttered just about every inch of the interior space. Somewhere among it all was a desk and a counter.

"You'd win the grand prize for a paper drive at grammar school," she joked, when he appeared.

He chuckled, claiming he was in the process of cleaning it all up.

"Somehow I doubt that," she kidded, picking up a front page from four years before.

"Yeah. You're right. Ready for a wild adventure?" he asked.

"You bet."

Before they left, Mike called out to his assistant, who strode out from the back room. Mike introduced him as his second-in-command and someone who might want to buy the newspaper in the near future.

"So you're thinking of selling?" she asked, as she followed Mike out of the store.

"Always," he replied, stopping to tie an errant lace on his scuffed hiker's boots. They went right along with his semi-wrinkled khaki cargo shorts and a well-worn Batman tee shirt.

"The call of the wild, huh?"

"Something like that."

"I think you should drive," Charlie said, as she handed Mike the keys to her SUV.

"Good idea. Lots of dicey back roads."

They headed out on Route 55, which doubled as Main Street for the few hundred yards it took to traverse the dusty town of Cascade.

"So, how did it go yesterday?" he asked Charlie.

"With my ex?"

He nodded, then turned off Route 55 and headed north on Warm Lake Road.

"Picture this scene," Charlie said. "Me, Ballard, my attorney, and Ballard's attorney in one small conference room down in the courthouse basement. The atmosphere was explosive. A few minutes into the meeting, my attorney brought up Trevor wanting to move down to Boise. Ballard's face turned a bright red, and he ranted, 'You don't know what my son wants. And even if he did want to go live with his mother, he shouldn't be allowed to decide what he wants. He's only thirteen.'

"My attorney was shocked. He said, '*Only* thirteen? At that age, Trevor should have a say.' There was legal precedent, he started to argue. Ballard interrupted him, then screamed that he was a 'f-----g liar.' With that, he got up and slammed out of the conference room."

"I found out about that last night," Mike admitted. "The court clerk, Dana Davis*, gives me a heads up about pretty much everything going on down there. Said she and the bailiff heard Ballard shouting like a crazed maniac all the way upstairs in her office. The bailiff almost went down to see if you were all right."

"We were fine. Physically. Just stunned. Ballard's poor lawyer sat there with his jaw down to his chest. My lawyer said that he'd never in all his years of practice had anybody act like that. Ballard never came back. End of session. Nothing accomplished."

Mike glanced her way. "I think Ballard should consider anger-management counseling."

"Been there, done that. Hoffman Institute several times. Didn't help. I think he failed at it more times than he flunked the California Bar exam."

"I'm sorry for your suffering."

"Fool me once, shame on you; fool me twice, shame on me. The fact is, Mike, I did a disservice to my son by not leaving Ballard sooner, and poor Trevor's paying for it."

When they reached the South Fork Road turnoff, Mike began a nonstop narrative about the business history of the county, emphasizing the vast extent of the mining and milling that went on for more than a century.

"Cecil Andrus addressed the ramifications of all that in his book," Charlie recalled. "Raw sewage dumped into the rivers and lakes. Mining companies going bankrupt and pulling up stakes without remediating the land. Then there's all the milling. It makes my head swim to think of what might have been going on while Brown Tie and Lumber was up and running in McCall for all those years."

"I've been trying to get to the bottom of that mill operation since I moved here. Boise-Cascade bought the company from Brown. Closed it abruptly in the early 1970s. I heard it was because they were about to get some big fines for pollution. They owned another big mill down in Cascade, too.

"The Cascade mill had an ongoing problem with contamination," Mike went on. "The latest is that they're in discussions with the EPA about cleaning up about twenty acres of petroleum contamination at the mill, so the land can be sold. From my reporting, I've learned that the ground was saturated with hydraulic oil, lubricating oil, grease, and diesel fuel from vehicles and mill operations from as far back as 1928, when the mill first opened."

"Could it have been the same up in McCall when they owned it?"

"Absolutely," he agreed. "Down here in Cascade we found something else: wood preservative in the soil. Most likely, creosote. A carcinogen. I've talked to a guy who owns a company out of Boise who was hired to clean up the contaminated ground."

"Jeez! What are they planning on doing with the land?"

"Turning it into a park."

"Like the park on the old mill property in McCall?"

"Yep."

"I read Warren Brown's memoir, *It's Fun to Remember*. In it, he talked about how his family's mill operation was the only thing going in McCall for decades. The town was there so the lumberjacks and other mill workers had a place to live. They used the entire lake as a log pond. Brown never imagined the town would change from its original purpose: a support base for logging and milling. Certainly not become a destination resort and recreation area with people and boats filling the lake instead of logs. No wonder they didn't care about the quality of the water back then," Charlie said.

"The question is what exactly did they dispose of?"

"Right," Charlie said. "It's so amazing to me that I used to look at the natural wonders that are all around us at this moment and take them for granted. I used to think that such vast beauty could never be diminished. Or compromised. Not anymore. Now I'm coming to understand that ignorance and greed could very well jeopardize it, as well as the health of the people."

"Astute observation," Mike concurred. "Wait until you see Stibnite."

~

Eventually South Fork Road narrowed and became a country lane. Their pace slowed as they drove along the South Fork of the Salmon River.

"What's going on down there?" Charlie asked, when they came upon a Fish and Game officer who had created a blockade in the water.

"I don't know. Let's find out."

They pulled the SUV off the road and scampered down the embankment. The friendly official seemed happy for the interruption. He explained to them that the Service was attempting to study the effects of contamination on the migration, spawning, and survival of salmon, which he was capturing to tag for further study.

"I guess it's not only humans who suffer in these parts," Charlie observed.

"You got that right. Fish and wildlife are as fragile as children," the game warden said.

All at once, the man walked away from her further into the water, which rose almost to the top of his hip waders. He pushed against the stream, dipped his hands under the clear surface and trapped one of the tagged fish.

"Here," he said, unexpectedly thrusting it into Charlie's arms where she stood on the bank of the river.

"Oh my God!" she exclaimed. "This sucker's heavy!"

She was told that the twisting, muscular salmon weighed more than twenty pounds. Although enjoying the moment, it was difficult not to remember the underlying reason for this outing, and she wondered if salmon like the one wriggling in her hands would last as a species in the years to come.

———~———

"What did he mean about children and fish being similar?" Charlie asked Mike once they were back in the SUV.

"Glad you asked! I read something about that in an interview with Dr. Sandra Steingraber. Have you heard of her?"

"Isn't she that biologist and cancer survivor?"

"Yes. She writes extensively about cancer and toxins. I'll give you her famous book, *Living Downstream*. She is adamant in her belief that many cancers in children are environmentally caused."

"I heard about her at St. Luke's from one of the nurses who has been telling me about the huge number of new pediatric cancer patients coming in to the clinic every day."

"In the particular journal interview I read, Steingraber discussed the kinds of cancers in children that are not family related. Not genetic, in other words. She indicated that research shows that these cancers are rising rapidly. She also said that since children don't smoke, drink, or have stressful jobs, you really can't argue that they live badly and cause their own disease. She also talked about how the latest information indicates that not only small children but adolescents are especially prone to being adversely affected by toxins in their environment because their bodies are changing rapidly, too."

"Children and fish? Shit, Mike. What did Trevor do all day, every summer of his life? Swim like a *fish* in the lake!"

———~———

By car it took them another forty-plus, very bumpy minutes to reach Stibnite along the unpaved Johnson Road, a rutted and potholed expanse of compacted dirt. Crows, gliding on the air currents over the summit from Charlie's front door in McCall, could have gotten there a lot faster.

Mike pulled over to the far side of the road so Charlie could get out and take a closer look. Looking down a steep embankment was a site that left her without words to describe. The once-thriving mining town was littered with crumbling structures that cascaded like jumbo pick-up sticks down fire-ravaged and denuded hillsides. What charred and leafless trees remained loomed out of ashy mulch, looking forlorn and without any hope of revival.

"Was there a fire here recently?" Charlie asked.

"No. This is from the 1994 fire. Do you remember that one?" Mike said.

"Yeah. We were in McCall. I saw the hills burst into flames from the main restaurant at Shore Lodge. Are you saying our fire burned this far?"

He nodded.

"Interesting. And what are those silly-looking hills and those inky pools down at the bottom over there?" she asked, pointing toward manmade earthen pyramids and several huge pools filled with standing black liquid.

"The mini-mountains are the left-over mine tailings from World War II and afterward, when tungsten and antimony were mined. This area supplied most of the ore needed for the war. The black pools were the above-ground, cyanide leaching pits. Those came much later. Back in World War II, this entire mining district was called 'the Glory Hole.'"

"Nice," Charlie chuckled.

"Pyrite, arsenopyrite, and gold were the most prodigious minerals in this area, known as the Yellow Pine District. Geologists surmise that as the earth layers formed, these three minerals were deposited first," Mike explained. "Later came strata of fine-grained tungsten minerals, followed by antimony-silver minerals. Finally, there's stibnite, which is tungsten crystallization."

"Now don't faint, but I actually knew that antimony and tungsten were mined up here for the war effort, making Idaho the largest producer of these minerals in the country at that time. Turned those ores into munitions. I did some homework, too," she said with a smile.

"Oh, I forgot. You never sleep."

Charlie laughed. "And I let my fingers do the walking these days. You can't believe what you can discover on the Internet if you just keep pushing the keys."

"Okay. Then you probably know that this entire area has been mined for over a century."

She nodded. "I read that in the early days most of it was carted down to Boise and other Idaho towns for processing. After making this bumpy drive, I would guess that it couldn't have been all that safe."

Once they got their fill of the view from the road, they moved the SUV to an off-road area and parked there.

"You up for a hike?" he asked.

"Sure. Let me get my camera."

They set off on a climb that took them into the hills above the ravine. Walking carefully around and between scarred and rotting tree trunks, Charlie snapped photos along the way.

It was slow going, so they stopped frequently to regroup, and Mike took these pauses as a time to fill her in on more of the history of the area.

"The mining companies thrived during the war," he told her. "It was a boom town up in these hills. More than two thousand people lived here then. But two things happened: the war ended, and the lodes of antimony and tungsten were depleted," he explained. "No one needed that much of it now, anyway. The post-war years were all about mining gold and silver."

"I heard all of it came to a screeching halt."

Mike nodded. "When prices dropped. They pulled out and left behind mountains of fine-grained tailings as you just saw. You know,

Charlie, some people argue today that these millions of tons of tailings are even more harmful than coarse spent-ore, since it has the potential for rapid migration."

"Rapid migration," she muttered, thinking she'd have to look into that further.

By now they were high above the mining area and could look through the slender tree limbs down at the abandoned site. It looked just as desolate from this vantage point. "Why hasn't anything grown back up here?" Charlie asked, her gaze sweeping the expanse of pathetic forest.

"Every year I hear there's going to be a reclamation project started. But I'm not sure it would make any difference. Perhaps nothing grows because the land itself may be irreparably damaged from heavy-metal soil contamination."

"That's horrible," Charlie commented.

"It's what happened to the forest region up in northern Idaho after the Great Fire of 1910."

"Tell me more," she said, as they turned and began to make their way back.

"As the price of gold went up in the 1970s, exploration in the Yellow Pine District resumed with a vengeance. From 1979 to 1991, the Canadian Superior Mining Company constructed and operated a successful state-of-the-art extraction process.

"What made all this new gold mining possible was that extraction methods became more sophisticated, and smaller veins of gold could be removed from the rocks. However, to get at it, they had to use a dangerous method known as heap-leaching, which required above-ground, open cyanide pits like the ones you just saw. Sodium cyanide was sprayed twenty-four hours a day over the piles of ore, leaching out the gold. According to descriptions by those in charge, the pads were a foolproof, impervious material that would prevent pollutants from entering the groundwater."

"Okay—you can't possibly buy that B.S.?" Charlie exclaimed.

"I agree with you. From my snooping, I've learned that people who worked here knew that they couldn't prevent seepage and spills. They knew about horrendous truck accidents on the way up to the site with cyanide and even worse ones going away from the site with poisonous residue. In other words: a nightmare."

"Yesterday at the courthouse, I was talking to Dana Davis and that other clerk about coming up here with you. They both told me that their husbands worked this mine, and they both got arsenic poisoning."

"I can see why," Mike said. "The spray certainly had to get into the wind up here. But if you discount that, and all went according to plan in the spraying, the gold attached to the cyanide. When the leaching was finished, the pad was sprayed for a day with fresh water drawn from the river. Finally, the pads were sprayed with vast amounts of chlorine designed to neutralize any remaining cyanide."

"Who are they kidding?" Charlie nearly shouted. "Chemicals like cyanide and chlorine can be extremely toxic to humans, sometimes even fatal."

Mike nodded.

There was little more to say as they gingerly maneuvered the last few yards of these blighted hills and murky streams, stopping to shoot more photos to document the padlocked door to the only intact structure still standing—a tin-sided warehouse with an enormous skull-and-crossbones symbol of poison and the words: Do Not Enter. Cyanide.

When they reached the car, Mike piped up, "Oh, I forgot to tell you this—I got hold of the National Priorities List (NPL). They report that there are continuing mining-related disturbances all around Stibnite. They've detected heavy metals and cyanide in area soil, groundwater, seeps, and sediments."

"You mean, we're being exposed right now?" she asked.

He smiled sheepishly. "I suppose."

Now, there were more vehicles parked in the dirt near Charlie's car. One boasted an official government seal.

"I think this is Bruce Schuld's pick-up," Mike said. "Let me see if I can find him."

"Isn't he that Mine Waste Projects Coordinator from DEQ? One of the guys on the list you gave me?"

"Yeah."

"I never got around to calling him."

"There he is." Mike pointed toward another expanse of ground on the other side of the cyanide shed. "Let me see if he'll talk to us."

Mike wandered off and returned with Bruce. Charlie found him to be outgoing and pleasant. He explained to them that Stibnite was about to go through a process of reclamation.

"And that means?" Charlie asked, noticing that Mike was trying not to roll his eyes.

"We're going to try to improve the land in various ways, including planting and some more cleanup."

"Well, I think we should be heading back," Charlie said, after another few minutes of chit-chat. "Nice to meet you, Bruce."

He gave Charlie his card. Said she could call him whenever she needed information.

As they drove away, Mike opined to Charlie, "I feel sorry for him. He has to say that stuff about a reclamation project. Every year. Just like I explained to you. Guys like Bruce have their nuts in a vise. They get into this work because they love the outdoors, they have scientific minds, and they want to do good. Then they have to dissemble just to keep their jobs. It's hard on them. My problem is that I can always see things through their eyes, too."

"I used to, Mike. Not anymore. My sympathies lie with those who have no voice. Who speaks up for them? Who goes to the mat for them?"

CHAPTER NINETEEN

The drive back to Cascade took them through a town called Yellow Pine. About fourteen miles south of Stibnite, Yellow Pine sat in the northwestern part of the Yellow Pine Mining District. For more than a century, Yellow Pine possessed the area's only general post office and a landing strip, making it the default epicenter of the mining activities in this ore-rich mountainous region of Valley County.

Structurally the town still vaguely resembled the way it was in its halcyon days, with one main street and a saloon on every corner. Upon closer inspection, Charlie could see how the paint was peeling off of the buildings, roofs needed repair, and Mike told her the post office was now tucked away in the sheriff's home and administered by his wife.

"The Yellow Pine Saloon is good," Mike said, when Charlie suggested they make a pit stop and have lunch.

"Sounds great," Charlie agreed. "I've been here before. Rode in on my horse with Ballard and a guide a few years ago."

They pushed through the louvered swinging doors and entered the old-fashioned restaurant and bar. Its darkly wooded interior included exposed, rough-hewn log beams and walls, wagon-wheel chandeliers, and rusty rifles mounted on the walls along with black-and-white photos of the early Yellow Pine days. Charlie admired the pool table and the impressively long, gleaming, waxed-wood bar.

The bartender, a heavyset man in a chef's apron, started gleaming, too, apparently happy to have some customers mosey in. The town had looked absolutely deserted as they drove through it.

"Sit anywhere," he said.

Before too long, a waitress* appeared from a back room and ambled slowly toward Charlie and Mike.

Charlie muttered sardonically under her breath, "She looks like she's been rode hard and put away wet."

Mike stifled a laugh.

She handed them their menus. "What can I get you?" the scrawny woman asked in a husky cigarette voice.

Charlie and Mike both ordered beers, burgers, and fries.

"Glasses or…?"

"Bottle will be fine for me," Charlie replied. Mike concurred.

She stuck her pencil behind her ear and sauntered away.

"How'd you like to live up here full time?" Mike whispered to Charlie.

"Sounds good…count me out! Seriously, how many people do you think live here now?"

"Pretend you're a reporter, Charlie. Ask her."

"I don't want to pry."

"But then you'll never know what you want to know."

"Okay. You're right."

When the waitress had given the bartender the order and returned with their ice-cold beers, Charlie asked her if she minded answering a few questions about Yellow Pine.

The woman tucked a mop of frizzy, dyed yellow hair behind her ears and smiled broadly, revealing a gap of a couple of missing teeth on one side. Charlie noticed her pretty blue eyes nearly hidden under drooping lids. "Not at all, hon. Shoot."

"What's the year-round population here?" Charlie posed.

"I'd say near to seventy-five in the summer. Down to about twenty of us in the winter. Why you want to know? You writing a story about us mountain folk?" she asked.

"No."

The woman shrugged her head toward Mike. "I kinda recall you had came up here before for that newspaper of yours."

"Good memory. But that was to report on the Harmonica Festival," Mike said.

"Yeah. One good thing going on. Mostly, though, reporters cart theirselves up here from time to time to write about what to do with all them other problems."

"What kind of problems?" Charlie asked.

"We're on every environmental shit list the government has."

"So I heard. From Mike. But I'm just a mother," Charlie told her. "I have no ax to grind. I've never been against mining, per se. Mike's a friend of mine, and I asked him to help me find answers about why my son came down with brain cancer in McCall. I kind of think it may all be related to the mining up this way. And those lists that you're on."

"Well, I'm sorry to hear about your son. Cancer's like the common cold up here. At one time or other, my whole family lived up in these parts. A lot of 'em had came down with cancer."

"So, you grew up in Yellow Pine?" Charlie asked.

"No. Stibnite."

"Really," Charlie exclaimed. "Can..."

Just then the bartender called out.

"Hold that thought, hon," she said. "I might could help you, but first I got to get your food."

She came back balancing the plates of wonderful smelling fries and burgers, put it all down in a perfunctory manner, and left them before Charlie could pursue any further questions.

"You'll be lucky to get her talking," Mike told Charlie, between huge bites of his burger. "Friendly and wary, forward and elusive at the same time. The history of this area makes them that way. They knew there were serious problems, but they needed their jobs and learned to look the other way. Their approach to life almost gets stamped into their genes."

"That's what I meant earlier at Stibnite. Those without voices," Charlie reminded him, watching the woman walk outside, barely waiting to light her cigarette before the swinging doors closed behind her. "Who steps up for them?"

"I have a feeling it's going to be you."

"I need to know a lot more if I'm going to be an effective advocate. Like, what the hell is the difference between being a Superfund site and that thing you mentioned... the National Priorities List?"

"The Comprehensive Environmental Response, Compensation, and Liability Act (CERCLA). Quite a mouthful. Maybe that's why it's also called Superfund. It was created around 1980 to respond to communities that had suffered excessive health and safety problems from toxic contamination. Superfund operates in three ways. One, the agency can come in at the snap of the fingers when there's an immediate threat to health or life from toxic contamination. Two, they can create a longer-term assessment on how best to clean the spills or releases. Say, a six-month window. Still critical, but not an outright emergency. And three, they have the option of a non-time-critical response, in which they make more far-reaching plans.

"The National Priorities List is a list of sites that have a long-term planning window and reclamation costs that exceed two million dollars. Stibnite and Cinnabar and Yellow Pine are all on the List and have been for years. Some people have argued that Stibnite should already be a Superfund site because it is so polluted and still poses an extreme health hazard. But somehow the politics of the whole thing have kept this area out of that final designation."

"It always comes down to politics," Charlie groused. "I think the people up here have suffered enough. It's time for them to get really angry."

"Oh, they're angry. At everybody. Jerked around by big mining companies. Heads spinning from double talk of big government."

"Yet they don't rise up and demand change."

"Maybe that's where you come in," Mike said. "Give these folks a direction."

"I can't spiral off in too many directions, Mike."

"Why not? If they're related."

"My life's hard enough right now."

"Nowhere near as hard as their lives have been. I read somewhere that in the early days, the houses the company built for the miners and their families in Yellow Pine had no foundations and were made of green lumber. Every winter the damned things would slide off their plot of land right onto the landing strip. They'd have to reset them every spring."

"Was it the same in Stibnite, too?"

"I think they had foundations under the houses there, because I read that the shacks were literally lifted off their foundations in the late '50s and early '60s and hauled out to towns all over Idaho. Even McCall."

"I know those tiny cottages," Charlie said. "The ones right next to the old mill site. Often wondered about them. Who lived in them up here? Now I know. People like our waitress."

"Most likely her parents or grandparents."

The waitress strode back inside and over to them. She asked if they wanted another beer. More fries?

Mike patted his belly and said no.

She smiled at him and cast a glance at Charlie's nearly full plate. "That one eats like a damn bird."

"But everything was delicious," Charlie insisted. "Hey, would you mind answering another question for me?"

"Shoot."

"You said you lived up in Stibnite."

"Yep. Like I said, growed up there. Daddy worked the mine."

"Any idea why the area still looks like it does?"

"Hell if I know. Nobody ain't never told us a damn thing. It makes me so sick, I like to throwed up! Not sure I'd of believed their bull, anyway. Excuses and lies. That's all they give us."

Charlie eyed the waitress sympathetically. "Us, too," she murmured.

CHAPTER TWENTY

After dropping off Mike in Cascade, Charlie continued on to McCall. She planned to pick up a few things from her storage unit but had a burst of renewed energy and decided to head out to Warren. Once a booming gold mining site and the oldest town in Idaho, it was an easy drive northeast from McCall on East Lake Street, then along Warren Wagon Road. The route wound through some breathtaking scenery.

During the winter, she and Ballard often had ridden snowmobiles from their home to Warren with Trevor and the girls. It was always a bumpy ride because that time of year the road was like a washboard. It was so hard on their kidneys and backs that Charlie always offered kidney belts to their guests to wear, along with helmets, for the trek up there. A couple of times the Smiths had made a trip to the village around Labor Day to attend the Arts, Crafts, and Back Country Treasure Fair, a much smoother ride at that time of year. She and Else almost went morel mushroom hunting in Warren. It became an excellent place to seek out these fungi as a result of the many fires in the area in recent years. Somehow they never got around to it. This afternoon would be a new experience: She seemed to recall that Warren also had hills of abandoned mine tailings.

A virtual ghost town with no more than twenty full-time residents, Warren consisted of basically one dirt road with a tiny motel, a restaurant

127

called Warren Tavern, a gas station, and a makeshift market. A few other cabins were scattered about. It was a far cry from its boomtown days at the end of the nineteenth century and into the first half of the last century when the town bustled with as many as five thousand people, many of them Chinese.

She found what she was searching for at the airstrip. Off to the side were mounds of mine tailings left behind decades ago. As the closest mining area to McCall with direct water drainage into Payette Lake from the north end, these toxic, abandoned piles might have impacted the health of the water in their lake and the lives of those who lived around it.

If it were earlier, she might have headed farther out to Cinnabar, another ghost town between Warren and Yellow Pine. Once a major mercury producer, Mike told her that like Stibnite, it was on the National Priorities List (NPL). Instead of risking back roads late in the day, she settled on a quick visit to the McCall Public Library before heading back to Boise. She recently had learned that there was a virtual data mine tucked away in a separate small room devoted to periodicals and historical books about all of Idaho, with an emphasis on McCall and Valley County. She headed right for the musty, closed-in space at the back of the library.

In the course of rifling through every book, treatise, and magazine, Charlie unearthed promising articles and tracts about Warren and Cinnabar. She found material about the history of the old mill in town and its closure, too. By this time, it was quite late, so she made copies of as much as she could about both the mill and the mining districts to review as soon as she returned home.

———

Charlie's cleaning crew found her the next morning asleep at the kitchen table, papers spread all around her.

It embarrassed her for them to see her like this. In fact, Charlie normally kept all of her research locked in her bedroom walk-in closet. Who knew what trouble prying eyes could cause?

"I'm sorry, ladies. I'll just clear the table and get out of your way," she said, hastily getting up and trying to pull all of the documents into a pile before anyone could see them.

Julie, the head housekeeper who had worked for Charlie for several years, piped up, "Finally, something for us to actually do. You usually clean the house before we get here."

"The new me. Knock yourself out!" Charlie joked.

One of the other cleaning ladies offered, "Here, let me help." She began scooping up a few documents at the opposite side of the table.

A look of panic came over Charlie's face.

The woman quickly set them down. "Sorry."

"That's okay. I'm just weird about people looking at my research."

"I couldn't help but notice...are you doing something about Stibnite?"

"Oh, kind of. You know that area?"

"I used to live there."

"Really? What's your name?" Charlie asked.

"Angie*. I guess we were never formally introduced."

"I guess not. Nice to meet you, Angie." Charlie scooped up the rest of the documents and left the breakfast room with them in her arms.

As soon as she got into her bedroom, she stashed them all in her crowded closet and locked the door. She was certain she was on the road to discoveries that would upset a lot of people. No need to explain what she suspected before it was time. Some of that blowback already had hit her. During his summer with his father, Trevor had spilled the beans about her research. Ballard became incensed. Her attorney informed her that she was going to be deposed about her so-called "work." He was certain they would attempt to paint her as some wacko trying to poison her son toward his father and the town where he lived. "Bring it on," she told her attorney.

As she washed her face and brushed her teeth, she realized that it might have been a fortuitous accident that this new girl, Angie, saw the documents. Perhaps she could give Charlie some more firsthand information about Stibnite that might prove useful. Despite Mike's urging, Charlie found it difficult to probe into people's lives, as she had yesterday with the waitress. Perhaps Angie would become another notch on her brand-new interview belt.

Charlie found the woman scrubbing Trevor's bathtub. "Can I talk to you for a minute?" she asked.

Angie stood up, holding her rubber-gloved hands out in front of her and pushing a few strands of gray hair out of her face with her arm. She stood smiling at Charlie but not speaking.

"Angie, I was wondering if maybe you could help me out? I'd really like to know a bit more about Stibnite."

"I don't know how much I can help. But I'll try."

"How about when you finish with Trevor's room, meet me outside on the patio?"

———

Charlie phoned Mike to tell him that she'd gotten some great background data from her library treasure hunt, but his cell went right to voicemail. She made herself a cup of strong tea and found a comfortable spot on the patio. She thought about Mike's admonition to check the river flow patterns, because he thought that the Salmon River tributaries might not flow toward Payette Lake. She had looked through everything she copied until her eyes had grown bleary, but she had found no answers. She decided to contact someone with DEQ in Boise, or perhaps even drive over to Boise State later in the day to see if any geology professors there could help her out. She was in the middle of making notes about her next steps when Angie came outside.

"Have a seat," Charlie said.

"Thanks." Angie settled next to Charlie at a wrought-iron table sheltered from the sun by a covered patio. "It's nice out here. The sound of the water in the stream seems so peaceful. And you have a really nice pond."

"Pretty different than Stibnite. Water up there wasn't so clean and clear. Ponds and streams were murky. Ominous. Like nothing could really live in it and look normal! Is that how it was when you lived there?"

"Yeah. Pretty much. Everything was polluted. Went fishing once and reeled in something with three eyes. I'm not kidding!"

"I've heard about that around Warren, too. Did your family work the Stibnite mines? Or do something else up there?"

"Yeah. They were miners. Are you thinking about buying property up there?"

"Hell, no!" They both laughed. "I'm trying to learn if the contamination from the mines has any relationship to all of the illness in Valley County. Primarily McCall. I don't know if you heard that my son is recovering from brain cancer."

"Yeah. I heard. So it's for him?"

"Yes. And the other kids who have suffered, too. So this is really important. I'm reading as much as I can. What you can remember and tell me could make a difference."

"Gee." She exhaled loudly. "Let's see. We lived up there to mine gold."

"When was that?"

"Eighties. Our house was down in Yellow Pine. My dad drove up to Stibnite and worked the mines. My mom worked in the lab there, too."

"What lab?" Charlie asked.

"The one with the chemicals and such. Arsenic. Cyanide. Chloride. You name it. I tried to get a job in the lab, too. When they did my physical, they found out I had a bum heart and refused to let me work there. It was dangerous—health-wise. Made you wear special clothes. Kind of like a hazmat suit. Had to remove everything at the end of the day. Sometimes you had to take a shower before leaving the lab."

"Because of the arsenic and cyanide?" Charlie suggested.

"I guess. They claimed all the bases was covered as far as the health thing was concerned. But that ain't so. People got hurt. Got sick. Accidents happened. And then there was all them piles of crap left out like little mountains. It's really windy up there. Swirling in every direction. Fine stuff blowing all around off them hills. Mom had constant headaches."

"Can you recall anything else?" Charlie probed.

"Not really. Things definitely went downhill with each new company that took over. I mean, like I said, it was pretty hairy up there most of the time. Then I got married to a miner. That was even worse."

Charlie said, "I get it."

"Yeah, I heard you ain't married no more. So, my memories are all pretty jumbled up with my personal stuff. Well, I best get back to work."

"Me, too," said Charlie, standing up with Angie and going into the house. "Look, if you remember anything else, just call me anytime."

"Mostly I try to forget about my life up there. But if something comes to me, I'll let you know."

***

Charlie spent several more hours going over the documents about Stibnite she had collected at the McCall library. All of the data seemed to confirm what Angie mentioned about the deterioration of the mining sites with each successive owner from 1945 to the end of the 1990s. In fact, the history of the area seemed even worse than what Mike and Angie had told her. Charlie felt certain that the disregard for the health and welfare of those who lived at or around Stibnite radiated out to districts and towns farther afield. Hell, McCall was only thirty-eight miles over the ridge from Stibnite. There had to be some relationship between the two places. She just had to establish that the water flow patterns were consistent with her findings.

To that end, she phoned the geology department at Boise State. No one was there to help her. She left her name, phone number, and a brief explanation of what she wanted with a secretary. Next, she decided to phone Bruce Schuld, who had given her his card up at Stibnite. Certainly he would know about water flow patterns. He was out of the office and in the field.

She found the cards for Tonya Dombrowski and Paul Woods and stared at them for a full five minutes before deciding to phone them, too. Neither was in the office. She left messages and then sat at the kitchen table writing down lists of what she now knew and what she still needed to learn about the mining area. Between these brainstorming sessions, Charlie wandered the house, making sure every nook and cranny was spic and span for Trevor's homecoming the next afternoon.

She had talked to the director of Camp Rainbow Gold on the way home in her car yesterday. Apparently, Trevor was having a ball. Feeling well. His balance was improving. *Thank God*, she thought. *He'll need that to latch onto, since he's not going to be happy when he hears that nothing came of the meeting at the courthouse about his living arrangement and custody requests.*

———

The phone rang a few minutes before eight p.m. It was Angie, the housekeeper. She told Charlie she thought of something else: there was a lawsuit between the federal government and one of the owners of the mine up in Stibnite. She didn't know what company, only that everyone who lived and worked up there hoped it would lead to a massive cleanup. Then it all got hushed up. Nothing came of it.

"Were you still there?"

"No. It was right after I left. Maybe the end of the '90s," Angie said, though she wasn't even sure about that.

"Well, thanks, Angie. I'll look into it."

Charlie pulled out her reams of papers and went back over every inch of the copied library data. She went through her notes about the Canadian Superior Company, which had mined the area in the 1980s. They leached about 200,000 tons of ore and produced more than one thousand ounces of gold from their five heap-leach pads, which they completed in 1982. They also had to reclaim previous tailings left behind. Charlie was amazed to learn that this particular 77-acre site contained about 4.2 million tons of finely ground waste left from the earliest days of the Bradley Mine ownership back in the '40s. She was certain these tailings were still there, making up part of the "hills" that she viewed from the road upon arriving at Stibnite with Mike.

She dug further and learned that between 1984 and 1990, several companies bought and sold the Stibnite claims. By 1987, the area was the leading gold producer in Idaho. From this point forward, the DEQ continually found reasons to cite Stibnite's various owners for increasingly shoddy practices. In addition, the Idaho Department of Health and Welfare cited the companies for low levels of cyanide in Meadow Creek. Supposedly it was coming from leached ore that had not been fully neutralized. They also were cited for diesel fuel leaks. Even more citations followed, citing problems with transporting waste products on Johnson Road, poor water quality, and hazardous wastes violations.

According to the United States Forest Service (USFS), in 1994, the residual tailings pile still was approximately 1,200–1,500 feet wide, 2,200 feet long, and 50 feet thick. It was highly susceptible to liquefaction. Worse still, Meadow Creek meandered through the tailings, and the fine-grained material was easily eroded. Superior rerouted Meadow Creek around the tailings and built a retention berm to try to prevent tailings from being carried downstream. The data all led Charlie to conclude that they were not entirely successful.

This was all good stuff, but she still found nothing about a lawsuit between the federal government and any of the companies that had left those living in Yellow Pine and Stibnite angry and confused.

She phoned Mike Stewart. This time he picked up.

"Got anything good?" he asked.

She told him about her sleuthing at the McCall Library, her growing cache of data, and how she had interviewed a woman who worked on her cleaning crew whose family and husband once lived in Yellow Pine and worked in Stibnite.

"I'm so certain we are on the right road here," she said excitedly, adding that Angie had just phoned her with news about an important lawsuit, albeit without any information to go on. "Do you know about that?" she inquired. "Federal government and one of the later mining companies?"

Mike said he didn't know what Angie was referring to. "But I have news for you, too." He'd done some preliminary research on the flow of the South Fork and the East Fork of the Salmon River. "Bad news, Charlie," he said. "Everything seems to veer away from Payette Lake. The water theory is not going to cut it, I'm afraid."

"But McCall is downstream from Stibnite. What if there are even smaller tributaries meandering west into Payette Lake? These waterways are known as juvenal fluids."

"Hey, could be. You should check that out."

"I plan to."

"But I wouldn't bet my house on it," Mike insisted. "It's a bitter pill to have to swallow, since we both wanted Stibnite to be the smoking gun here. I mean, it's so polluted up there still. Latest reports show it still has the highest arsenic levels in the entire country. It would have been like shooting fish in a barrel to have that be the answer we wanted. But you're going to have to take a different tack. Maybe something closer to home."

"Like Warren?" she asked. "I have data on what went on there, too."

"Absolutely. And don't forget about the mill," Mike suggested. "You said it was a priority. And it should be. I know there is a lot of information on the mill's past that has been hidden from the public. I've been trying for years to get a look at it."

Charlie pictured the plume of noxious smoke that had wafted over the town for decades before she moved there. "I got a lot of data on the mill at the library, too. I haven't forgotten about it."

"Then hop to it."

"As soon as I get Trevor settled. I heard this afternoon that he won't be granted the right to start school here in Boise. He has to stay in McCall after all."

"He comes first. But promise me you won't lose hope and give up."

"Mike, *that's* not even an option."

CHAPTER TWENTY-ONE

Charlie pulled into a parking space across the street from the DEQ office in Cascade. It was in the same block as *The Long Valley Advocate*. "Do you want to come in with me?" she asked Trevor.

"Nah. I'll wait here with Elliot. Take as long as you want," he added with emphasis.

Charlie knew what he meant: He was on his way to be handed over to his father in McCall for the coming school year, a prospect he desperately had hoped to avoid. At her house this morning, he'd looked so forlorn. Moping at the breakfast table. Lamenting his flippant decision in early 2002 to continue to live in McCall even after Charlie told him she was planning to relocate full-time to Boise. Wondering how a year later, with everything in his life changed, only this court order seemed to have been carved in legal stone.

Trevor had remained sullen for most of the ride up the mountain, staring out the window, absently petting Elliot and listening to music with his earphones.

"I feel like a FedEx package being delivered to a business," he had said to her as they crossed Rainbow Bridge. "Why is my dad doing this to me?"

"I don't know, Trev," she had replied.

"And why won't the judge listen to me now?"

"I think he has blinders on."

"Well, it's not fair."

Now they were in Cascade, and Trevor clearly was becoming even more frustrated.

"I won't be long," Charlie told him as she got out of the car. "I have to see if Tonya Dombrowski has some information for me about Stibnite."

"What's Stibnite?" he asked.

"A pretty awful mining area not far from McCall."

She crossed the street and entered the building. Tonya's office was at the end of a long, narrow hallway. There were two desks. No one was there. Charlie noticed boxes on the floor labeled "Stibnite" and "Cinnabar." And "Mining." She was considering taking a peek, when a woman came down the hall and asked if she could help.

"I'm looking for Tonya Dombrowski," Charlie said.

"She's out of the office on appointments and won't be back until later this afternoon."

Because of the designated drop-off time for Trevor to Ballard, Charlie did not have the leisure to wait for her return. "Please tell her Charlie Smith was here."

She walked outside and saw that Mike Stewart was leaning in the window and talking to Trevor. "Hey," she called out.

He stood up. "Trevor's telling me he's on the way to his dad."

"Yep. I thought I'd take a chance to see if Tonya was here. I noticed a ton of boxes, some labeled Mining and Stibnite," she told him. "We can't wait around, though."

"Yes, we can, Mom!" Trevor piped up.

"Your dad is expecting you at a specific time. Court Order," she told Mike.

"Whatever," Trevor mumbled, under his breath.

"There was a box in Tonya's office labeled Cinnabar, too," Charlie said to Mike.

"Not surprised. Cinnabar ranks right up there with Stibnite. Maybe not quite as horrible. But in its own way, a horror story, too. In 1992, the Forest Service found the site so dangerous that they did a 'time-critical' removal of tailings located adjacent to Cinnabar Creek. The surface runoff bled into the creek endangering Chinook salmon, bull trout, and steelhead. The Service also demolished large fuel tanks and removed the smelter roaster that was located in Cinnabar Creek."

"Actually right in the water?" Trevor asked.

"Yep. In the 1950s, that smelter had been used to roast the ore— mercuric sulfide, otherwise known as cinnabar— to produce free mercury vapor and sulfur dioxide gas. In 1998, the Forest Service had to go back in and address the continuing erosion of a waste pile into Cinnabar Creek. Earlier this year, the Forest Service was back again, removing more toxic tailings that had eroded into the Creek."

"Wow, Mike. You sure know a lot about this stuff!" Trevor exclaimed.

"And your mom will know even more by the time she gets done doing her research," he replied.

Charlie said, "Hate to break up this love-fest, but we can't be late."

"Good luck, Trevor," Mike called out as they drove away.

"Where is Cinnabar?" Trevor asked, in a more animated voice than before.

"It's between Yellow Pine and Warren."

"Warren? We used to go out there."

"Snowmobiling in winter. Remember that?"

"Yeah. I remember when Else's grandson, Royce, came to visit, and we tried to jump those piles of snow out on the runway."

"Oh, my God! I do remember that. This guy came running after you and screaming to get away. I can't believe it. Those snow mounds were the abandoned mine tailings that I saw a few weeks ago. They're still there."

"I wish I could stay in Boise with you and learn more about all this stuff."

"I'll try to keep you up on whatever I'm doing, Trev."

"It's not the same. And you know it."

Trevor fell silent, staring out the side window again, and petting Elliot.

———

"This is so cruel, Mom," he blurted as they turned into the parking lot of Out-A-Idaho, the prearranged meeting place. "I don't want to live here with him. I should be in Boise near my doctors. Why won't he understand?"

"I don't know, bud," she replied, feeling like a broken record.

"My dad doesn't go along with court orders when he doesn't feel like it. How many contempts does he have against him now? *A million?* And nothing happens to my dad when *he* breaks the law. I tell you what. I'm not getting out of the car."

Just then, Ballard appeared and flung open the back door to Charlie's SUV. "Come on, Trevor. Let's go."

Trevor cowered away from him. Ballard started to yell at Trevor—then at Charlie, too. He reached in and grabbed Trevor roughly by the arm, yanking him partway out of the car.

"Dad, stop it," Trevor cried, pulling back. "I'm not staying here with you. I want to go back to Boise!"

"You're living with me." He physically dragged Trevor out of the car. Trevor was having a hard time keeping his balance, which was already compromised from his chemo treatments. He was half-standing, half on his knees. His father stood over him screaming, "There is a court order, and you are going to follow it."

The first day of school was hard for Trevor. He was depressed and embarrassed. He had told the kids who had asked during the summer that he was really excited to be going back to Boise to live with his mother and to go to school there.

"What happened?" they all wanted to know.

"I don't know. Stupid courts…but I'll be leaving soon." Trevor could not fathom what was going to happen, but he felt if he told everyone what he wanted, it would come true. It had to. He was miserable.

He knew he was a total drag on Ballard's lifestyle. His father was rarely home to attend to Trevor's needs. Instead of keeping a clean house and making wholesome meals, he preferred fast-food restaurants or taking his son to places like Beside the Mill, a decidedly smoky bar/ restaurant in town and Ballard's favorite hangout.

"Why do we always have to go here?" he asked his dad. "I thought you didn't drink anymore."

"I don't. But I like hanging out with my friends."

His dad said things in a way that shut off any further discussion. So Trevor kept quiet and went along. One night while waiting for dinner there, Trevor began to feel dizzy. "I feel sick to my stomach, Dad. The smoke is giving me a headache. Can we please go?"

"I'm not ready to leave. You can wait for me in the car if you want," Ballard said, tossing him the keys.

Trevor sat in the car for over an hour. His hunger grew as much as his anger and unhappiness. He never did get dinner that night.

Finally, Trevor opted out most nights and stayed home alone, fending for himself. Soon it became crystal clear to Trevor that his father really didn't want the burden of caring for a hobbled son.

Trevor retreated from the few friends who still sought him out. He had nothing in common with them anymore. He spent all his time alone. Thinking. Remembering. He came to see his dad as someone who liked to be there at the finish line, greeting the winner. It was clear in every way that Trevor would never be that winner in his life.

———◦———

A few weeks before his fourteenth birthday in October, Trevor phoned Charlie. He was distraught.

Her heart broke at the sound of his cries of unhappiness. She hated the snail-paced court system, the uncomprehending judge, litigious Ballard: everyone who was keeping her boy in such a state.

"Mom, I hate my life. My dad has all my sisters ganging up on me now. They're telling me I'm gonna give him another heart attack if I'm not loyal and do what he wants. I wish I could go to sleep and not wake up."

"Trevor, don't ever say that! If I could get away with it, I'd jump in my car and come get you right now," she told him. "We will get this taken care of. Please hang in there a little while longer."

"I will. I just…" He sat sobbing, then mumbled goodbye. He hung up before she could say another word of comfort or support.

She called her attorney and made an appointment to see him the next day. It was a dispiriting conference in his office. He informed her that their change of custody petition was moving through the crowded justice system as quickly as possible, but obviously not quickly enough.

"Can't anyone see what this is doing to my son?" she cried. "He's fighting cancer and a father who is indifferent one minute, emotionally abusive the next. And Ballard's anger is escalating out of control. He threw a cell phone at Trevor in one of his rages and hit him in the stomach. Doesn't all of this count for anything? What the hell kind of system do we have in this country, anyway?"

Her attorney tried to explain that old adage: in criminal court, the defendant is an awful person presenting his best self; and in family court, the defendants are good people presenting their worst selves. "That's why the judge has to give the benefit of the doubt to Ballard."

"The judge *knows* this doesn't apply in our case!" Charlie exclaimed. "Ballard only wants Trevor because he doesn't want me to have him more. And what's worse, he's willing to sacrifice our son's well-being to get that accomplished."

Frustrated, scared, and distraught, Charlie cancelled a meeting scheduled for that afternoon with Tonya Dombroski, who was in town on other business. The woman was proving to be a valuable source of information. Now, however, Charlie could not possibly focus on anything other than her son's situation.

While at home later that day contemplating what to do next, her niece Lori phoned to tell her she was planning a trip with her daughters to Hawaii in October.

They reminisced about their last trip to the same island, Maui. It was Spring Break of April 2002. Trevor had been healthy then: boogie boarding, surfing, and golfing.

Lori suggested, "Why don't you and Trevor come with us? We could celebrate Trevor's fourteenth birthday together."

"I don't know...there's so much crap going on right now."

"Stop that," Lori interrupted. "It would be so good for him...good for *both* of you. You guys need a break."

"You're right. I'll see what Trevor's doctors think."

Charlie phoned Trevor's oncologist. Dr. Chang agreed that Trevor would benefit from this trip. "I think he's strong enough to fly that distance now. I think the change of scenery will be good for him."

Enthusiastic about this great news, Charlie phoned her son. "Hey, Trev. How are things going today?"

"How do you think?" he mumbled. "It's like every day up here. It sucks."

Hearing the sound of defeat in his voice, Charlie countered with, "I have a deal for you. How would you like to spend a week in Maui with your cousins for your birthday?"

"Really? Dr. Chang will let me go?"

"All clear."

"That's awesome."

On Sunday morning, October twelfth, two days before they were to fly to Hawaii, Charlie and Trevor lingered at the breakfast table in the kitchen of the Boise house. She noticed that his speech was more animated, and his blue eyes sparkled. *If only it could stay this way*, she thought.

She nibbled a muffin, feeling energized while listening to Trevor's high hopes for his return from the islands. He recently had met alone with the judge in his chambers where he had made a fervent plea to be allowed to move down to Boise before the end of the school term.

Trevor's optimism extended to his excitement about seeing his two cousins from San Diego. He was going to try to keep up with them at the beach and the pool. But he also admitted that his greatest fear was that he might not have the strength to play an entire round of golf.

"You do what you can," Charlie told him as she got up to start clearing away the breakfast dishes. "Just remember what your pro at Whitetail told you this summer."

"I know: anything can be tackled and accomplished with the right attitude. I just really want to finish a whole round of golf at Kapalua Bay."

Charlie rinsed off their dishes, smiling every time Trevor jumped up from the table to touch and inspect his new set of clubs, a wish granted to him on October third by the Make-A-Wish Foundation of Idaho. This organization was a godsend. The day the wish-granters took him to the golf store in Boise, the look on Trevor's face when he was handed his new clubs reminded Charlie of the charged joy she had always seen in Trevor when the snows of winter became a raging river once more. *Could these clubs be the instruments to find that path to becoming normal again?*

The phone rang. Charlie turned from the sink. She hoped it was Mike Stewart calling to give her an update on the reporting he was doing on the old federal lawsuit in Stibnite.

"I'll get it," Trevor said gaily. His smile changed to a scowl. Charlie gleaned from the curt way he was responding that it was his father. Ballard had fought this birthday trip, arguing that his son wasn't healthy enough to go to Hawaii. He refused to back down even after Dr. Chang signed off on it in a written memo to the judge. Ballard approached the principal of the middle school and all of Trevor's teachers, asking them to write affidavits swearing that Trevor should not be allowed to miss five days of school. They refused. Every one of these acts was taking a further toll on the faltering relationship between father and son.

All of a sudden, an anguished expression spread over Trevor's face. He yelled out, "No, no! When?"

"Trevor, what's wrong? What's going on?" Charlie demanded, the panicked look on his face causing her blood pressure to surge.

"Mom, it's Grandma Joan," Trevor cried. "She's *dead!*"

Charlie felt her limbs go slack, and she grabbed onto the sink ledge to steady herself. Her mind quickly raced back through all of the times during the past few months when she had waited for the almost daily calls from Joan that had abruptly stopped coming. And those times she phoned, only to be intercepted by a housekeeper and told that Joan was unavailable. She had begun to wonder if what seemed like a sudden brush-off was due to something she had said or done.

She flashed on an image of Joan at Holly's wedding this past May, when she didn't seem like herself. *My God! Did she already know she was dying?*

Charlie took the phone from Trevor. "Ballard, what happened?" she demanded.

"Joan died about twenty minutes ago at home in her bedroom," he replied somberly. He told her his daughters just phoned him with the awful news.

"Oh my God, Ballard. What happened? Was it a heart attack? A stroke?"

"Charlie, you have to keep this from Trevor. Don't let him read the newspapers or watch the news. It'll just be a matter of time before the media gets wind of it. Joan died of brain cancer."

CHAPTER TWENTY-TWO

The latest *USA Today* lay open on the glass table on the veranda of Charlie's ocean view room. She soaked in the detailed article about the death and spectacular life of billionaire philanthropist Joan Kroc. Even now on the fourth morning of her vacation, Charlie remained unable to distance herself from her real life while here in balmy, fragrant Kaanapali, Maui. She could not put the news of Joan's passing so easily aside. *USA Today's* photo spread of Joan was an additional, poignant reminder that Charlie would never again enjoy the special crooked grin and little wink Joan gave to very few, showing her seal of approval. Slowly, the words and pictures on the page faded as personal memories took over.

How vividly she still pictured Joan popping over to chat all those years ago. In her champagne-gold golf cart, she'd putter up the Smiths' driveway from her neighboring Rancho Santa Fe estate early in the day with her hair still in curlers and covered with a scarf. Barge right into the kitchen. Start to light up a cigarette.

"You know you can't smoke in the house," Charlie always reminded her.

"Of course I can."

"Of course you *can't*," Charlie replied every time.

"I'm leaving then." She'd hesitate, eye Charlie, waiting for her to back down.

Charlie would say with a jaunty smile, "Here's your hat. What's your hurry?"

Joan would huff out. Take a few puffs in her cart. Come back inside for a cup of coffee and to chew the fat for a while.

Those were the days. Charlie shook her head, remembering some of those *really* early morning, spur-of-the-moment outings to get a breakfast burrito, pulling up at the drive-through at McDonald's on Del Mar Heights Road in one of Joan's fancy cars. *Impromptu should have been her middle name*, thought Charlie. It was exactly what Joan christened both her yacht and her jet.

Charlie picked up her cup of tea and nestled in the wicker chair, hearing Joan's voice lapping incessantly in her mind instead of the sound of distant waves. She possessed such a distinctive musical lilt in her speaking voice. Undoubtedly, her smoking habit had left a trace of huskiness as well. *When was the last time I actually heard Joan's voice? Gosh, it had to be back in mid-June. June fourteenth...*

"What's cooking?" Joan had asked, phoning as usual to go over in minute detail every aspect of Trevor's recovery. When she was satisfied with Charlie's report, Joan quizzed her about the divorce. She knew it wasn't going well for her or for Trevor. She voiced her worries about her granddaughters being exposed to the parade of women flitting through Ballard's life, and she felt bad that the girls were pretty much out of Charlie's life.

"You did so much for them," she reminded Charlie. "Don't ever forget that." As she had many times in the past year, Joan said again, "It's so important to me that you land on your feet when this is all over."

"Well, Joan—I'm doing my damnedest," Charlie replied triumphantly. "I think you're going to like this. I'm getting into environmental research." She explained to Joan how she had come to think about Trevor's cancer in conjunction with so many others over the past few years, most of them in younger people in Valley County.

"What you're doing is wonderful!" Joan rejoiced. "It's a relief to know that you're embarking on such a worthy journey. Haven't I always told you how important it is to give back? And this is the best way for you to do it. You keep up the good work and don't let anyone stop you."

"Ballard's not too pleased."

Joan huffed and segued into a short reminiscence of her own work on the anti-nuclear weapons project in the 1980s, as well as Linda's deep involvement, and what a stir it had caused in the family. "It reminds me of you now," she said. "Keep a strong heart. It's our connection, Charlie."

Charlie recalled now having been moved to tears by this heartfelt outpouring. She assured Joan that she was in this fight for the long haul. Joan became increasingly effusive as their conversation progressed. She could be wry and acerbic, with a pretty raunchy sense of humor. But on that day, none of that attitude showed up.

With the same emotion, Joan divulged that her niece, Janie, in Minnesota was looking into contaminants like nitrates in their drinking water from nearby feed lots. Joan reiterated that she was so proud to know that some parts of her family and extended family were undertaking societal challenges that she thought were so essential.

Charlie could still hear the regret in Joan's voice as she confessed at the end of that long talk in June that somewhere along the line she might have failed to instill the values of giving back and compassion in her own granddaughters.

If only I had known about her failing health back then, Charlie thought. There were so many "if onlys" in both of their lives...

Joan, however, had no "if onlys" when it came to her pets. She gave her all to them. She often rescued abandoned mutts. Charlie recalled how Joan saved a three-legged dog from the side of the highway. When it died, she interred it in a special tropical grotto on her expansive grounds where all of her deceased pets were laid to rest with appropriate headstones.

Feeling the need to capture her torrent of thoughts in case she decided to speak at Joan's funeral, Charlie retrieved a few loose sheets of paper and a pen from her bedside table and returned to the wicker chair on the veranda. She sat for a few moments letting the humid, aromatic breeze rifling the nearby palm fronds waft over her.

At last, she began to write: *I feel extremely honored to have had Joan Kroc in my life for sixteen years. She was more than the wealthy, philanthropic widow of Ray. She was a benevolent, compassionate, and humble woman that did things on her own terms...*

Charlie stopped, pen poised above the paper, thinking about the constant requests for money with which Joan had been bombarded. Money for this cause, that charity. It sometimes was overwhelming, and Joan had to tune it all out. But there were times when the philanthropist heard or read about a tragedy, and unbidden she sent a million-dollar check to the person or group without anyone asking for it. More times than people knew, Joan gave millions anonymously.

Charlie began to scribble down more thoughts: *I cherish the extraordinary times I spent with her. I recall the day I was at home on our tennis court, Joan phoned, and an hour later she and I were jetting to Vegas. Or another time when we flew to New York just for dinner with Bart Giamatti, the Commissioner of Baseball. Or I'd get a call to come over and dine at her house on Big Macs, washing it down with pink Dom while watching CNN.*

Oh, how Joan loved watching CNN. I can still picture her settled into her favorite recliner with that channel on as background during a conversation. You'd think she was listening to you—then all of a sudden, she'd interrupt and say, 'Hey, did you hear what they just said?' and you'd have to listen along with her. She was the consummate news junkie. She made you want to know what was going on in the world. She was a great role model for me and my son. Joan was a constant presence in Trevor's and my life for so long. She was like a fixture in my world. I never thought her life could be cut short. That she wouldn't be here any longer...

Charlie felt old emotions become new again as she thought back to that time when she first met Joan in the spring of 1987. It was such a strange day. Charlie was at the house in La Jolla visiting Ballard, when Joan popped in unannounced. Joan and Ray owned the home first and then gave it to Ballard and Linda. Linda had moved on. Now this Charlie-with-the-man's-name was filling up the space with her bigger-than-life persona. Charlie sensed from the initial words she exchanged with the stunning woman that the girls had piqued their grandma's curiosity about the very important new lady in Ballard's life.

She and Joan grew increasingly close over the next few months. Despite their age difference, they discovered they had a lot in common: neither went to college—Joan, like Charlie, was a teenage bride and mother at seventeen—and they both did what they had to do to survive during hard times. Joan wasn't the only one who knew how to put a ten-dollar pair of heels with an expensive dress and fool the world.

Building on our relationship, in May of 1987, Joan, Ballard, and I flew back to Chicago on her plane for an annual McDonald's board meeting. The three of us stayed in her usual Ritz-Carlton suite in downtown Chicago. One night while I was getting dressed, I heard piano music and a beautiful woman's voice singing an old Tony Bennett song. I walked into the living room and was surprised to see Joan sitting at this magnificent grand piano playing and singing. What a fabulous voice she had. I could see that she was lost in the music. I learned that night that Joan once was a singer/ piano player in a bar in Minnesota, making ends meet for her daughter and husband, Rollie Smith, who worked on the railroad. That's where she first got to know Ray Kroc, who walked into that bar one night, saw her, and said she was the most beautiful woman he had ever met...

What a great love story, thought Charlie. Ray pursued Joan for years, setting up her husband, Rollie, with lucrative McDonald's franchises. Ray only had so much patience, though, and after waiting and wanting for so long, he convinced Joan to divorce Rollie and marry him.

Joan turned out to be a true romantic, and this side of her came out in full force when she learned that Ballard had proposed to Charlie. Ballard told her of their plans to marry while en route to that annual Chicago board meeting. From the plane, she phoned her personal jeweler in an exclusive store on Michigan Avenue in downtown Chicago and ordered them to prepare a tray of diamond rings for Charlie to see. She especially wanted Charlie to inspect the one exactly like hers. Two weeks later, Ballard surprised Charlie with that ring. To this day, whenever she looked at the *rock*, she thought of Joan and the aura of romance that she helped to build up around that exciting beginning of her life with Ballard.

Joan stayed close to Charlie through the years as a sounding board, a confidant, and a mentor. A surrogate mother and grandmother. In the early '90s in San Diego, when Ballard became embroiled in a game-changing lawsuit against his catering business partners, Premier Food Services, over a joint ownership position in the San Diego Sports Arena, Joan agreed that Charlie must remain publicly loyal, must sit proudly behind her husband in court each and every day. Joan helped bolster Charlie's spirits even after Ballard's humiliating loss when he was found guilty of lying and committing business fraud in breaching his fiduciary duty. Millions of their dollars down the drain. "He'll lose everything I gave him eventually," she had told Charlie back then. "He can't help it. But for the girls' sake and Trevor's, hang in there." And so Charlie bore the brunt of Ballard's continuing humiliation after the caterers' union, angered by his nefarious deeds, plastered his photo on the sides of San Diego Transit buses with the words: "Would You Want to Do Business with This Man?"

And Charlie stayed with Ballard even after Joan could no longer pretend that he was an asset on the Board of Directors of McDonald's

Corporation. Through the years, Joan had painted clearly for Charlie all the drawbacks and constrictions of living in the public arena and having personal and family images to uphold. She understood Charlie's struggle now; she had struggled with that, too...

Joan's life changed dramatically with her marriage to Ray: she suddenly owned a public persona along with status and access to jets and yachts and everything else a woman could want materially. Yet she kept her old friends and added very few new ones. You know, Joan possessed something rare: an ACD—Automatic Crap Detector. It was so astonishing it should have been on display in the Smithsonian. She could size up a person in a nanosecond. If you passed her ACD test, life by her side could be pretty exhilarating. I felt honored to be one of those people she took under her wing. She always told me how much I reminded her of herself at the same age. She said she liked that I was a fighter...

I can still recall how in August of 1987, Joan flew the whole family to the East Coast, where we boarded a yacht moored at the dock on Martha's Vineyard. She chartered the cruiser from her dear friend, Allen Paulsen. After vacationing on his yacht for a week, she decided to buy one of her own. The yacht she christened Impromptu.

I'm not sure she ever used it much. Over time, she seemed to enjoy things less and less, becoming more reclusive, preferring to be home. I think the peace she fought for in the world never quite reached her doorstep. I know that one of the most courageous acts she did at the end was to keep her brain cancer a secret from Trevor and me. Once she knew for certain that she was not going to make it, she didn't want anyone to scare my son with the news that his much-loved 'Grandma Joan' was terminal with the same illness he was fighting to overcome. It explains her sudden silence over the past few months. The almost daily phone calls from her that stopped coming. The calls I made to her unreturned without explanation. The condolence card and flowers I sent when her still-beloved Rollie died two weeks before she did, unacknowledged....the...

The phone in the bedroom of her suite startled her with its jarring ring. Charlie stopped writing, gathered up her scraps of note-filled paper and the newspaper and hurried inside. It was Lori.

"What's up?" Charlie asked.

"Hey, what're you doing?"

"Thinking."

"Stop that! Get your butt down here. We're at the restaurant by the pool having breakfast."

"I'll throw on something and call Trevor in his room."

"He's already down here with us."

"See you in five…"

CHAPTER TWENTY-THREE

Charlie exited the elevator and strolled through the bustling, open-air lobby past the hotel's front desk. She continued down a walkway into bright sunlight, pausing for a few seconds at a pond to admire the pink flamingos and koi. She turned and saw Lori waving at her from the outside dining area. Their table was located in a section of the restaurant close enough to hear the waterfall and the splashing of children in the nearby pool.

Charlie flicked some dried bird droppings off of an empty chair at their table. "Good morning, guys. Anybody want a little bird shit with their omelet?"

"Compliments of our fine feathered friends," Lori laughed.

Charlie slipped into the cleaned seat. "Where's Trevor?"

"Charlie, look over there. He's at the buffet," her ten-year-old niece, Marisa, piped up. Always outgoing and a budding spitfire, the blonde, brown-eyed Marisa, was the one with all the answers.

"Buffet? Well, he must have an appetite today," Charlie replied. "Good for him."

She looked toward the lavish table arrangements: every exotic fresh fruit imaginable, breakfast meats, eggs and waffles to order, and breads and mouth-watering pastries. Trevor was walking back toward them, his limp very noticeable. Charlie could tell that he was concentrating on not dropping two plates, which were piled high for once.

As if reading her mind, Lori commented, "His balance seems improved."

Charlie shrugged. He looked the same to her. But she wanted to believe Lori had some extra power to see miniscule changes for the better.

"Morning, Mom," he said, settling between his two cousins.

Charlie noticed his full plates. Mostly fruit with some toast and jams. "Sleep well?"

"Like a baby," he replied with a grin.

"I know…up every two hours crying," she shot back.

Marisa and Lexis both giggled at the family joke.

"What's on the agenda for today, kids?" Charlie asked, after a few minutes of playful bantering.

Marisa answered as though ticking off a list in her mind: "Pool first. We're going to the waterslide as soon as we finish eating."

"Sounds like fun," Lori said.

"Want to come, Trev?" Lexis asked. Lexis was barely a year younger than Trevor but eons ahead of him socially. Having been a bankable model since the age of five, the tawny-skinned, green-eyed beauty was picked to be the Kodak Girl for the 2002 Winter Olympics in Park City, Utah. That had entailed public appearances, print ads, and TV commercials. Even with all this hoopla in her life, the self-effacing teen remained refreshingly down-to-earth and clearly loved Trevor. She kept trying to include him in every activity since arriving in Maui.

He looked up from his plate of fruit and said, "No, thanks—you girls have fun."

"Are you sure?" Marisa asked. "Come on."

"Do it, Trev. It'll be okay," Charlie urged.

"Nah. I have to go back to the room and do homework anyway."

"You can do it later, honey," Charlie said. "We're on vacation."

"You really want me to try this, don't you?" he said.

"Only if you want to," she equivocated. Charlie felt her heart sink, since this was a replay of the past three days of outdoor activities. One particularly painful time was when Trevor was invited to go into the ocean with his cousins and lasted less than five minutes. At that time, Charlie suggested he could wear a shirt to protect his skin from the harsh sun and just stay in the shallow water. He shot her a look that could kill. It said: *Shirt? Shallow water? Do you remember who I used to be?*

Trevor sighed. "Okay. I'll try."

"You ready?" Lexis asked.

He pushed his plates away and stood up. He took a few pieces of toast with him.

Charlie thought he must still be hungry, but then she saw him throw the pieces to the birds, which swooped in to get them.

Both women watched him trail farther behind his cousins.

"Look how skinny he still is," Charlie commented. "Skeletal."

"What do the docs say about that?"

"That he'll put the weight back on. Eventually. MRIs are clear. Thank God."

"He told us before you got down here that his dad thinks he's dying. Said he overheard him talking about it when he was with him in McCall this past summer. It broke my heart."

"I've gotten calls from friends and workmen up there asking me how much longer Trevor has. I've set them straight. It's pathetic what Ballard is doing to him."

"Trevor said that he's afraid that his limp is something more than anyone is telling him, too."

"Well, I can see it would be hard to know what to believe, with me insisting he's going to be fine, and his dad telling everyone else the opposite."

"Well, what caused that limp, anyway?" Lori asked.

"It's a complication of the chemo. It'll go away. So the doctors tell me." She sat staring off in the distance. A pesky bird made a perfect landing on their table, zeroing in on Trevor's leftovers. She shooed it away. "I wish he could just remember what I told him last New Year's when Ballard left him alone in my house puking his guts out, and he thought he was going to die."

"What was that?"

"He should think of cancer like a bully you have to confront. If he fought back as hard as he could, it would retreat. We sat in his room talking a lot about that. About having courage. Then he asked me, 'But Mom, how can I fight *two* bullies at the same time?'"

"This is just so sad," Lori commented with tears in her eyes.

"It is. I wish Ballard understood what he's done."

"Well, that's Ballard. The only person he cares about is himself."

"Funny you should say that. Trevor told me on the airplane over here that he heard his father tell his girlfriend that *she's* the most important thing in his life."

"That must make Trevor feel loved! Are wedding bells in the future?"

"Not as far as Joan was concerned. She mentioned to me back in June that the girls said he told them he'd never marry her." Charlie exhaled loudly. "So, what's on your agenda today, Lori?"

"I was thinking of doing a spa day. Do one with me… how about a Swedish massage, or one where little Asian women walk all over your back?"

Charlie smiled. "Oh, I don't know."

"Don't tell me you're going to spend the day again under an umbrella reading those reports you brought with you. Remember what you just told Trevor—you're on vacation."

"I like doing it. There's a lot to figure out."

"Give it a rest! How important can it be that you can't pull yourself away from this stuff for one week?"

"I'm learning so much, Lori. Especially about the water problems in McCall. I just went through a water quality report dated back to 1991.

It confirmed what I've thought for a few months now. For years, the people and businesses of McCall just dumped whatever into the lake. And I mean everything—even toilet paper."

"No pun intended—but you're *shitting* me!"

"Really. I'm serious. Then when they tried to reverse the contamination problems by building a new water filtration system, they did a half-assed job. Ran out of money. Couldn't finish. Thought they could fix it with a huge sand dump. That never worked. More testing showed high amounts of chloroform in both the lake and drinking water. Chloroform is a probable carcinogen. And you know how they combated it? They infused the water with chlorine in huge doses. Well, chlorine at that level can cause cancer, too!"

"I *am* impressed by what you're learning. Who's feeding you this info? That newspaper guy, Mike?"

"Not anymore. I'm getting it by myself. But I admit he's been a great help. Introducing me to people. Coming with me to meetings. But he's got a newspaper to run. You know me…once I get my teeth into something."

"Oh yeah. I know."

"Besides, I promised Joan I'm in for the long haul."

"Remember her at Holly's wedding last May?" Lori asked. "You commented how odd she looked."

"Yeah. Like her face was lopsided. And she told Trevor she was too tired to meet Elliot the day after the wedding. And you know how much Joan loved dogs. I guess she already was sick," Charlie recalled.

They both turned silent, lost in memories of Joan for a moment. Charlie absently noticed Trevor setting up his lounge by the pool. Sitting down to slip off his flip-flops. Slathering himself with sunscreen. Then following his two cousins over to the ladder behind the very high and impressive waterslide.

"I know I'm a broken record," Charlie said suddenly, "but the water in McCall is *literally* sick."

"You know I never wanted to go into that water," Lori reminded her.

"Yeah. I remember that. I read in another report yesterday about septic tanks that were never removed when the city began installing the new sewer system in the 1980s, leached into the lake. On top of that, leakage from storm drains at Roberts Park, Mill Park, and near the city boat ramp at Legacy Park, where the old mill used to be, were known to be leaking and flowing into the lake."

"Oh great! Isn't that where the kids would hang out when we came up to McCall?"

"Yep. And the land itself could very well have been contaminated by the mill and never cleaned up properly."

"So, you're going to be the one to put all this together and tell your neighbors that their beautiful lake is full of crap?"

"It might as well be me. No one else has the balls!"

Lori laughed.

"Well, it's true," Charlie insisted. "I know I'm on to something important. I know that there have been documented reports on the release of antimony, arsenic, cadmium, lead, and mercury downstream of the Stibnite mining district. These are some of the same findings in our lake. There has to be a link between our water problems and Stibnite. Not to mention Warren and Cinnabar, which are even closer to McCall and probably have a direct drainage route to the lake. That adds more to my growing list of possible contamination sites."

"Well, a word of advice, Nancy Drew. Watch your back. You're going to piss off a lot of people."

Suddenly, Charlie turned her full attention toward the pool area. Lori's gaze followed hers. They both watched Trevor laboring like a ninety-five year old man to get up each rung of the mammoth waterslide ladder. He stopped midpoint, and Charlie held her breath as she watched him whisper something to Marisa. Her heart broke to see him slowly making his way back down the ladder to the ground. He hastily retrieved his things from his lounge chair then slunk away toward the building where their rooms were.

"You see that?" Charlie said. Lori nodded. "There's your answer. At this point, I don't care who I piss off."

Trevor sought the solace of his room, where he didn't have to make excuses about what he couldn't do. He finished more class assignments. He noted it took him longer than before to complete his work. Dr. Chang explained that chemo treatments could affect his powers of concentration for a time. Just another depressing problem to contemplate. He flopped onto his bed and tried to go back to sleep. He couldn't. He wasn't really sleepy—just emotionally drained.

At breakfast, the maitre d' handed him a printout with the hotel's activities for the day. One of them was a grass-skirt-making class. *That's about all I can do these days. Go sit with the old ladies and weave a grass skirt!*

"No pity parties on this vacation," his mother had admonished as they boarded the plane in Boise. "You're alive. Getting well. Just remember that."

But it was hard not to spiral down into the dark depths of despair. A year ago he'd been right here on this same island, spending most of his daylight hours riding the waves on his boogie board. He didn't have to worry about getting tired. He didn't have to worry about getting sunburned because of his medications. He didn't have to worry about drowning in the *shallow* water!

He went into the bathroom and splashed water on his face. He studied himself in the mirror. Forcing a smile, he tried to make it go from his mouth to his eyes. It didn't work. *You're still alive*, he said silently to his reflection. *Bullies can't get to me.* But his dad had said to some guy who came to work on the house, "My son is dying of brain cancer."

Suddenly he thought about Grandma Joan. How she died without him or his mom being able to say goodbye to her. He wondered what caused her death. He felt so alone right now.

He got his cell phone from the table by his bed and called The Pet Lodge in Boise where Elliot was boarding.

"How's my boy doing?" he asked the proprietor.

"Great."

"Does he miss me?" Trevor asked.

"Yes, he does. He told me so himself."

Trevor laughed heartily. The happiness was finally in his eyes. That felt good.

He got off the phone and put away his class assignments, grabbed some sunscreen and a shirt, and then went down to the pool to find his cousins.

CHAPTER TWENTY-FOUR

In the early morning hours of Trevor's fourteenth birthday, his cell phone rang while he was still in bed, half-asleep. It was his sister Amy.

"Happy birthday, Trevy choo choos," she said, using a favorite childhood nickname for him.

"Thanks, Amy." He swung his legs over the side of the bed and sat up. He was surprised to notice a bit of color to his skin. Not so sickly white. That made him happy, too. Now that she'd awakened him, he couldn't wait to get this special day started. "How are you?"

She said, "I'm good. Just making breakfast. What are you going to do today?"

"I'm going to play golf with my mom at Kapalua Bay. With my new clubs from Make-A-Wish. Then tonight we're going to dinner at Bubba Gump Shrimp Company. You know, named after that movie *Forrest Gump*? It's a really neat place in Lahaina."

"Great."

"Hey, Amy. I am so sad about Grandma Joan. When's the funeral? My mom and I want to come."

There was a long pause. "Actually the funeral is for family only, Trevor."

"What are you talking about? We *are* family!"

"Well, the funeral is only for *close* family."

"But we were very close to her! She was my Grandma Joan. She loved me, too."

"Sorry, Trev. We're not inviting Dad, either."

"Okay, Amy. I better get going."

"Love you, Trevor."

"Love you, too."

He sat on edge of the bed feeling his insides shaking, as he remembered how just this past February, when he was at the worst of his illness, he'd worn a mask to go on the airplane to Amy's wedding in San Diego. He was mortified walking through the airport like that. Pale. Weak. Sick to his stomach the whole time. But she said he was her brother, and she needed him there. Their family wouldn't be complete without him on her wedding day. So he suffered the stress and humiliation and went: for her. For *family!*

The phone rang. It was Charlie. "Happy birthday," she chirped and then sang the birthday song to him.

"Thanks, Mom," he said, hoping he didn't sound shell-shocked.

"You ready to try out those new clubs?" she asked.

"I'm kinda scared I won't be able to hold my balance on my back swing," he confessed.

"Just remember what your golf teacher told you last summer about balancing on the good leg."

"Well, he can play with a wooden leg. 'Cause he's a great athlete. But what if I can't?"

"We can address that *if* we get to it. I can't believe it…you're fourteen."

"Yeah," he said.

"Trev, you sound like you might not be feeling well."

Now was his chance to tell his mother what Amy had said. But he didn't want to ruin her day, too. He knew she was working on special notes to express her love and admiration for Grandma Joan at the funeral. How could he be the one to tell her she was not going to get to say goodbye to a woman she loved like a mother?

"No, I'm okay. What time are we leaving?"

"The car's downstairs now."

He was quiet in the car on the way to the rainy side of the island, where Kapalua Bay Resort and Golf Club was located. They began to climb to a higher elevation. The weather changed dramatically. Soon they were in a thick layer of clouds, almost approaching a foggy mist.

"Hope we don't get rained out," Charlie said.

Trevor grunted. He was finding it hard to shake Amy's words out of his head. Until this morning, all Trevor had been thinking about was how physically daunting getting through an entire round would be on Kapalua Bay's hilly course. He had the weight of desire and expectation pressing on him, all built up since their plane landed a few days ago. But now he had this other heavier boulder pressing on his heart, given to him for his birthday by his loving sister.

The valet took their clubs from the car. "Sure hope this lifts so you guys can play," he said.

Charlie replied, "I hope so, too. It's my son's fourteenth birthday. We came all the way from Idaho."

He pointed out the way to the pro shop. No sooner did they get inside than it began pouring, a real deluge.

"Oh great!" Trevor exclaimed. "This really tops off my birthday."

"Let's just get some breakfast," Charlie suggested, after checking in with the pro.

"This kind of rain in the morning isn't unusual on our side of the island," the pro assured Trevor and Charlie. "It passes quickly. We have a great restaurant next door with a good view of the course."

They found a table by the window. The grass ran continuously uphill, broken only by ominous bunkers. In the distance the rainclouds created a foggy impression. As the hard rain subsided, the mist still clung to the treetops, giving off the eerie feeling of a rainforest.

They ordered breakfast and sat looking outside. Trevor observed, "It kind of reminds me of Grandma Joan's property in Fairbanks Ranch. So green and full of trees. You remember where she would bury all her dogs? She had those sculptures made of each one and buried them underneath their sculpture. She loved her dogs. I wish she'd been able to meet Elliot. I miss her already."

"Me, too," Charlie said. "She was a great lady."

"Mom, I have to tell you something. About when Amy called this morning."

"Oh yeah? What did she have to say?"

"That we aren't family and can't come to Grandma Joan's funeral."

Charlie blanched and clearly was too stunned to speak. She toyed with her omelet and then glanced at Trevor, who was eyeing her for a reaction. "I don't know what to say," she told him. "This really hurts. I am so sorry, Trev."

"What a nice birthday surprise, huh, Mom? Kind of put an even bigger damper on the day than the rain."

"Well, try not to let it ruin your day, honey."

"And another thing…my dad isn't invited either."

Charlie put down her fork and took a deep breath. "Oh, man. Mark my words, bud. The shit is going to hit the fan."

~

When they finally got onto the course, it seemed even more like a rainforest. Trevor joked that he half-expected to see spider monkeys and jaguars lurking. Soon, though, he was engrossed in the golfing experience. He loved the lush feel of the cushiony grass under his feet.

As he made his way from hole to hole, he felt a jolt of companionship with the golfer, Paul Azinger, about whom he recently wrote a paper for school. It was on the subject of someone famous who overcame a disability. Azinger beat cancer, lymphoma, and bounced back to win his first tournament right here.

Because it was such an arduously hilly course, Trevor was offered a special flag for handicapped people, but he refused. It was essential that he at least pretend to be normal. Toward the end of the round, with his energy sapped and forced to contemplate stopping, Trevor decided to finish one more hole. The golf gods were smiling down on him, as he sank a thirty-foot putt on an undulating par four and made his first birdie post surgery. In some ways, he opined to his mother, it must have been like Paul Azinger winning the *whole* tournament: it felt like a sign that maybe one day he would get better, and like his golf idol, would beat that bully back, too.

The return ride to their hotel to get ready for his birthday dinner with his cousins was more upbeat. That birdie gave him a new sense of himself. He felt happier than he had in a long time. More optimistic that his life might turn around. By now, the judge would have granted Trevor's request and told his dad that the custody was changing. Trevor would get to live in Boise. Go to a new school there with kids who wouldn't judge him by who he used to be. Even the conversation with Amy took a back seat for the rest of the day and extended into his last night on the island.

Chapter Twenty-Five

Their red-eye flight from Maui was about forty-five minutes from Boise Airport when Trevor woke up. He saw his mother gazing out the window into the early morning sky. She looked worried.

"You okay, Mom?"

She turned and managed a tepid smile. "Well, bud. Not really. I got a message from my attorney at the airport before taking off."

"Don't tell me I have to go back and live with my dad?"

Charlie nodded.

"Why, Mom? I thought the judge was going to help me."

"I guess he just can't make up his mind. You'll have to finish out the semester. Then he'll revisit the issue."

Trevor leaned back and shut his eyes. "When do I have to go back?" he asked.

"This morning. When we land. Your dad will be there to pick you up."

He mumbled sarcastically, "Well, that's a perfect ending to this trip."

Almost as soon as Trevor settled into his dad's Suburban for the ride up to McCall, Ballard laid into him.

"The judge showed me the letter you wrote to him."

"He did?" Trevor replied, bewildered that the jurist would divulge a private communication he wrote two weeks before, citing all of his reasons for leaving McCall and his father's custody.

"This behavior is outrageous! Disloyal. I'm taking this personally," Ballard said vehemently.

Trevor shrank from the accusatory tone in his dad's voice. Every ounce of hope that the judge respected him and his desire for privacy in their dealings was gone. He'd been betrayed.

"Dad, I just don't understand why you won't let me do this. I don't want to live in McCall anymore. My life is different now. Boise is a better place for me. It's not about you at all."

Ballard retorted with increasing venom that it was about him. It was a matter of personal honor for him to be preferred over Charlie, and if Trevor was not going to acquiesce calmly, Ballard was determined to make it impossible for his son to leave under any circumstances.

"Where are we going?" Trevor suddenly said, when his father took a detour away from the road that would take them up the mountain.

"Walmart."

Trevor hunched against the door, trying to get as far away as possible from his father's anger. It was useless. There was no place far enough.

His dad wasn't through with him. "I don't know why you'd want to live down here and go to a new school anyway," he added. "The kids are just going to laugh at you because you walk funny."

By this time, Ballard had turned into the Walmart parking lot, whipped into a parking space, and asked Trevor if he wanted to go inside with him. Trevor mumbled no.

"I'll leave the car keys so you can listen to the radio."

As his dad walked away, Trevor slumped down in the seat. Stunned by his father's belittling words, he sat there as the pain worked its way to the surface.

Charlie arrived home to find her cleaning crew just opening the front door.

"That was good timing," she said as Julie, Angie, and a third woman offered to help with her many pieces of luggage. She laughed as they eyed each other. "I promise I'm going to go to flight school to learn how to pack."

No sooner had they lugged her heavy bags across the threshold into the entry hall than they were nearly bowled over by the stench of rotting meat.

"What the f..." Charlie exclaimed, setting her bag down and looking at Julie.

"Don't blame me. I haven't been here since you left."

They all walked toward the pungent odor, and when they reached the kitchen, they saw a river of congealed blood originating from her refrigerator/freezer.

"What the hell happened?" Charlie asked, nearly gagging from the stench. She tried to turn on the lights and found they were off.

"Power loss," Julie offered.

The housekeepers got to work cleaning the mess, while Charlie phoned Idaho Power. She learned that the power was turned off one day after she and Trevor left for Hawaii. Ballard had phoned the company, said he was the owner of the Boise house and it was vacant, and therefore demanded all of the power shut off. The clerk never questioned his authority.

"Wait a minute... the bill is paid through the end of this month," Charlie protested vehemently. "It's only October twenty-first."

"Ma'am, Mr. Smith was really forceful," the woman told her. "He kept insisting that we turn all the power off."

"But the house doesn't belong to him," she explained, sounding as exasperated as she felt. "It was awarded to me as my sole and separate property three weeks ago. Mr. Smith knows that this was part of our property settlement. He didn't have the authority to have my power shut off."

"I hear your frustration," the woman said, "but there is nothing we could have done."

Charlie slammed the phone down. She no sooner walked away from her desk when the phone rang. She picked it up, thinking it was the power company calling back. It was Trevor. Somehow she gleaned through his sobs that he was in the parking lot at Walmart, and his father had verbally abused him until he was hysterical.

"I've had it with that man," she snapped. "I'll come get you right now."

"No, Mom! He already thinks we have a *plot* against him," Trevor cried. "I don't want him to know I called you."

"I don't give a damn what he thinks."

She maneuvered like an Indy driver over to Walmart and found Trevor red-faced from crying. It tore her up to think of her son this way after seeing him so happy in Hawaii only hours before.

"Trev, I'll grab your stuff and put it in my car. Come on. You're going with me."

She removed Trevor's luggage from Ballard's Suburban. She noticed his keys still in the ignition. She pushed the lock button and slammed the door. As she drove off the lot, Charlie understood that because he was supposed to be in his father's physical custody, technically she had just kidnapped her own son.

Charlie immediately phoned her attorney when she got home.

"Get him back to Ballard right now," he insisted.

"Not this time," she replied. "I don't care if it is technically kidnapping." They went back and forth for a few more minutes. Charlie started to cave.

"I'm not going," Trevor yelled. "I can't be with my dad."

Charlie took one look at Trevor's tear-stained face and regained her resolve. "This is emotional abuse of a child," she argued. "Let them throw me in jail," she railed. "I don't care anymore." She slammed down the receiver.

Joan's voice suddenly popped into her head, reminding her not to act rashly or Trevor wouldn't have her in his life. She took a deep breath, collected herself, and phoned her attorney. She told him that she'd like to speak to the Parenting Coordinator, Jean Uranga, a no-nonsense Boise attorney whom the court appointed last spring as Trevor's advocate. "I'll do whatever she recommends."

Ms. Uranga called within the hour. She chatted briefly with Charlie and then at length with Trevor to get his side of the story. In a report to the court about the incident a few days later, Uranga wrote: "The boy was alarmed when his father accused him and Charlie of 'plotting' the move for months. Trevor is clearly in a fragile emotional state at this point and is suffering as a result of actions by his father. Ballard is very verbally abusive and appears to have little empathy for Trevor's feelings."

Uranga also attempted to interact with Ballard. He was verbally abusive to her as well. All that mattered to him, she wrote in her report, was that he had a court order to have custody of Trevor. He refused to discuss what happened in the car on the way to Walmart.

She went on to recount: "He related that he had no confidence in my abilities as a parenting coordinator and stated I was untruthful, dishonest, and biased." Uranga contacted Ballard's attorney and related to him that his client was totally uncooperative.

The next day, Uranga participated in a conference call with Ballard and his attorney. At this time Ballard "acknowledged he told Trevor the children at the school in Boise would make fun of him because of the way Trevor walks."

According to Uranga, Ballard further insisted, "these problems were created because Trevor was empowered to think he could make up his own mind. Ballard demanded immediate compliance with the court order, with little regard for Trevor's concerns and feelings."

———⌒———

After all the conference calls ended, Trevor had to return to McCall, had to return to school there, and had to resume living in his father's custody. Life did not improve with his dad. Quite the opposite. The tension and rancor between them ratcheted up a notch.

According to Uranga's written report to the court: "Ballard is preventing Trevor from calling his mother and has told Trevor that he will have his mother arrested for kidnapping."

As a matter of fact, Trevor was so terrified of what his father would do to him if he were caught talking to his mother that he took to phoning her in the bathroom with the shower running so his father couldn't possibly hear him.

Uranga further wrote that while Trevor had been in his father's custody, his resolve to leave his father's house had only strengthened. She concluded, "I would support a decision awarding immediate change of primary physical custody to Charlie Smith while any further proceedings are pending."

She filed her report in court on October twenty-eighth. Three days later, Trevor once again phoned Charlie, and this time there were no tears. His tone was even scarier: flat and emotionless.

"I can't live like this any longer," he told his mother. "I'm done. If you won't help, if the courts won't help, I'll have to end this my own way."

"Trevor, start packing. I'll be there in two hours."

Once he was settled in his mother's car, with all of his belongings piled in the back and Elliot on his lap, Trevor phoned his father at his girlfriend's house.

"I'm on my way down the mountain, Dad."

"You guys better turn around right this minute!" he shouted.

"I'm never coming back to live with you full-time."

"I'm calling the police to intercept your mother's car. I'll have you dragged back up here and have your mother thrown in jail for custodial interference," he threatened.

"Bye, Dad." Trevor pushed the *end* button on his cell. "I'm scared of what he'll do to me. And to you, Mom," Trevor said.

"Me, too. But I'm with you on this one-hundred percent."

Even so, they drove looking over their shoulders until they were safely in the garage of the Winterwood Lane house. But nothing happened. No sirens. No police cars. No jail for Charlie.

Trevor kept thinking about what his mother had told him months ago when the battle to beat cancer seemed too hard: if you get up and fight, the bully will back down.

Trevor started River Glen Junior High in Boise a few days later. As he limped unsteadily into his new school, he was overwhelmed by the bigness of the building compared to Payette Lakes Middle School. So many kids doing their thing, going in every direction, laughing, playfully shoving. He tried not to get in anyone's way as he looked for his counselor's office. It wouldn't be cool to get knocked over on day one. He couldn't bear the thought that his dad might be right: *The kids will laugh at you because you walk funny.*

*Cancer Kid:
Trevor at home after
a chemo treatment,
being comforted
by Elliot.*

*Brown Tie and
Lumber Company: The
old mill on
Payette Lake in
McCall, Idaho.
Historical
photo appeared in*
McCall Magazine,
Summer/Fall 2004.

*Signs of Abuse:
Discarded debris
next to the marina,
along the banks of
Payette Lake, where
the mill once stood.
Photo taken
August 9, 2008.*

Stibnite Mine 2003: The abandoned mining site, now on the Superfund's National Priorities List, still bears signs of the toxic substances that poisoned the area. Cyanide was used in the heap leach mining process.

*Trevor with
Mark Johnson,
anchorman for
Channel 7 News,
Idaho's
NBC affiliate.*

*Mike Stewart, publisher
and owner of* **The Long
Valley Advocate,** *in his
publishing office, 2003.*

**We must become the change
we want to see in the world.**
Mohandas Karamchand Gandhi

Part Three:

MOVING FORWARD

Chapter Twenty-Six

Boise, Idaho
Boise City Hall
Fall 2006

Trevor unfolded his lanky frame and strode to the podium in the City Hall hearing room. Though nearly six feet tall now, he still had a baby face and braces on his teeth, which made him appear younger than his seventeen years.

His limp finally disappeared, although he still worried about his balance when under stress. It made him more thoughtful. More in the moment. Today his posture was purposeful. Other than the faint vertical surgery scar going up the back of his head, visible because his hair was so short and had grown back in thinner than before, he looked healthy and strong.

Charlie was so proud of him. He was a public speaker now, addressing Boise civic groups about his cancer and the ongoing struggle to learn what caused childhood cancer clusters. Over the past year and a half, he had appeared on local television news shows with her, discussing his involvement in community health affairs. He had sat for numerous interviews with reporters from the *Idaho Statesman* newspaper and other publications.

About forty minutes earlier, the Smiths were among more than a hundred interested citizens who had filed into the meeting room to fill the seats in the audience. City Council members already were seated behind a curved table on the dais, and representatives of the Atlanta Gold Mine Company and the affected state agencies were at another table in the front of the room. Among the state's representatives was Bruce Schuld of the Idaho Department of Environmental Quality, whom Charlie had met with Mike Stewart back in 2003. Try as she might, she still hadn't cornered him for a long discussion about the contamination in Stibnite and what it might mean for McCall.

The topic for discussion tonight: the pros and cons of re-opening a gold mine about sixty miles from Boise in tiny Atlanta, Idaho. Atlanta Gold Mine, Inc., planned to resume explorations using cyanide heap-leaching techniques.

As one of several pre-selected speakers, Charlie already had given her testimony in opposition to the resumption of mining in this area. She insisted that she was not against mining *per se*, merely against this particular form of mining. She used the travesty of Stibnite as an illustration. Now it was Trevor's turn at the microphone.

Mayor Dave Bieter made a point of giving special recognition to Trevor. In 2004, the mayor had presided over a ceremony in this same hearing room. At that time Bieter had handed Trevor an award for Bravery, one of several such citations given out to Boise students picked by principals from middle schools throughout the district. It was quite an honor and achievement for the teen who had limped into a new school a few months before.

As he usually did, tonight Trevor prefaced his main points with tidbits of his personal story: cancer patient, survivor, childhood cancer activist. Charlie couldn't have been happier with the way he was maturing since leaving McCall and his father's custody three years ago. There were still touch-and-go moments. Unexpected emotional reversals. Several physical setbacks. In sum, though, laughter replaced tears. Hope replaced fear. Order triumphed over chaos. Living with her in Boise provided an added benefit. It allowed Trevor to be introduced in an integral way to her growing research into environmental responsibility and toxins as they related to childhood cancer. He took to it with the intensity of someone who never lost sight of the fact that he might still be on borrowed time and had to hurry to complete his mission to change the world for the better.

A smattering of applause followed Trevor's brief but pointed remarks.

"You did great," she whispered, as he sat down next to her.

Trevor pinched her playfully on the top of the knee and smiled. "Thanks, Mom. I know *you're* not prejudiced," he teased and then quieted as another man rose to take the microphone.

This new speaker introduced himself as Jack Holden*, a former fishery biologist. A man in his mid-to-late sixties, he'd been around long enough to be able to say with certainty, "Every mine in Idaho has had problems. Serious problems that never got publicized." He added, "In fact, in 1995, Hecla Mining had 250 water-quality violations at their Grouse Creek Mine. That's in one year!" Charlie shivered at the realization that Hecla was an early owner/operator of Stibnite as well.

Predictably, the mining company representative responded to Holden's accusations by promising that they would be more careful. More modern techniques allowed for better control, they said. Grumblings of disbelief could be heard among the spectators.

Another of the reps ventured, "Look, cyanide isn't even harmful." That induced grumbling and guffaws. "I have a cold." He pointed to a glass of water on the table in front of him. "If that was cyanide in there, I could drink it right now and be okay. Hey, it might even get rid of my cold." The audience burst into spontaneous, derisive laughter at the apparent absurdity of this assertion.

Mayor Bieter quieted things down. Another few speakers quickly presented their views. One in particular brought up the common problem of abandoned toxic tailings getting into the streams and rivers. The representatives of the mining company downplayed concerns about this as well. They assured the audience there would be oversight by standardized testing for heavy metal contamination.

Charlie knew now that standardized testing was a virtual cop-out. The majority of standardized water tests the government did were easy to perform and inexpensive. None of them were set up to reveal more lethal contamination that might occur when heavy metals were exposed to air, water, and sunlight, then broke down and recombined. The published results of standard tests, whose limits were easier to meet, were oftentimes smokescreens to make the populous feel safe when it might not be safe at all.

Another protestor got up to speak who really got her attention. He broached the disquieting subject of forest fires, which everyone in the room was well aware plagued Idaho every year, and their effect on mining locations. Directing his comments and questions to Bruce Schuld, he asked how the government could explain away the dangers posed when tons of leftover tailings became part of a raging fire, like the one at Stibnite back in the mid-1990s, which could lead to even more toxic airborne substances? Couldn't the toxic substances blow to other locales? Couldn't they get deposited into other rivers and streams *miles* away?

Schuld admitted casually, "I never thought about that. But it makes sense."

It did make sense. Perfect sense. In fact, the idea sparked a fire in Charlie's mind: if the newly combined toxic substances could pollute rivers and streams far afield, why not a *lake*?

When they returned home from the hearing after nine p.m., Trevor said he still had homework to finish and went to his room. Charlie went back into the closet. Literally. She settled in for a long siege in her makeshift office, rooting first through her piles of documents about Stibnite. Then she culled out her water documents about Payette Lake. Finally she gathered all the clippings and data she had about the horrendous McCall fire of 1994.

Starting at the beginning, she spent several hours sitting on the floor organizing into new piles every document spread out around her. It all started coming together finally. The 1994 fire started in McCall. It burned all the way to Stibnite. *Only thirty-eight miles? Essentially they were the same fire. The same. That's it!* she thought. All this time, she had pictured two separate fires. But they never were.

She still could remember the remarkable lightning storm that ignited the trees three miles out of town. She'd seen the hills burst into flames from the panoramic restaurant window at the Shore Lodge where they were having dinner. From the start, everyone in town sensed it was going to be a bitch of a fire. Soon it was out of control, huge enough to deserve a name: The Blackwell Fire. Just north of the town of McCall, the Blackwell forest area covered thousands of acres. Since it was so close to where they lived, the Smiths often went riding and hiking there.

Now they were forced to endure acrid smoke and ash while the fire raged for *four months.* By the time it joined with other fires and reached Montana, where it petered out due to winter weather, the fire had consumed over three hundred thousand acres.

Almost immediately, scores of people in McCall developed medical problems: detached retinas, various malignant and benign tumors, and breathing disorders. Even so, no one second-guessed whether it was safe to continue to dwell amidst the toxic residue of the fire and the dregs left behind by the fire retardant, sprayed from above by Forest Service pilots known as Smoke Jumpers. People sat on their docks and stood in their yards, eyes skyward, marveling at the red clouds of powder streaking the sky and raining down on everything.

The town was overrun with soldiers and Forest Service personnel. With the local atmosphere vibrating with the intensity of a warzone, Charlie and Ballard existed in a state of high anxiety, especially after representatives of the Forest Service descended on them to warn that they might have to evacuate at a moment's notice, because the winds had shifted precariously.

"We just evacuated a couple hundred boy scouts from Camp Morrison. Fire got to within a mile of the water over that way."

"That's just east of here. Are they okay?" she asked.

"They're fine. But they were sleeping outside. Better to be safe than sorry."

"You see, fires this strong create their own weather," another official explained to her. "No one can know for sure what the winds are going to do from moment to moment."

At the time those words held little import for Charlie, except that everything in the house could perish from the unpredictability of the maniacal fire. Now she understood his meaning at a deeper level: Whatever was blowing around in the weather of the fire could go anywhere, even blow in directions it never had blown before.

Just tonight she found a document that referred to Stibnite as the *Sahara Desert of Idaho* because of constantly windy conditions. Add to these *naturally* occurring winds the capricious maelstroms whipped up by the wildfire, and a perfect storm for tragedy emerged: the toxic tailings from years past mixed with the new ash, swirling them together in many directions, including over the ridge toward McCall. There the noxious mixture settled onto everything in the vicinity of Payette Lake and joined with the toxic fire retardant residue, all of it freezing through the winter and eventually melting its way into the lake in the spring.

Of course, Charlie suspected none of this in 1994 during the height of the scare at her home. Friends phoned them from more inland areas around McCall to offer the use of their trucks and cars to help them save their things. She could still recall how Ballard hurried to secure their artwork while she collected their precious photographs and other family mementos. They packed up as much as they could inside their boat and their SUVs, ready to evacuate at once.

At the eleventh hour came a knock on the door. A weary Forest Service officer stood there. "No need to leave," he said. "Winds have shifted again."

They breathed a sigh of relief but remained vigilant as they settled down to do what many of their neighbors were doing: setting up a front-row seat on their dock to watch the pilots dump load after red load on the fire.

Charlie looked up from her papers and checked her watch. It was the middle of the night. She yawned and realized how stiff she was, stood up slowly, and stretched. Shoulders. Neck. Head. Everything ached. Even her hair hurt. She padded into the kitchen and brewed herself a cup of tea. It was three in the morning. Despite the hour and the pains in her body, her mind was still energized.

She retrieved some of her research on the 1994 fire and came back to the kitchen table. Soon she was lost in data about flame retardant that made her skin crawl. Forty percent of it contained sodium ferrocyanide. Used to prevent corrosion in the tanks of the airplanes dropping the solvent, like so many chemicals that alone might not be lethal, the sodium ferrocyanide turned into an even more toxic and deadly cyanide compound when exposed to water and sunlight. Fire retardant contained and even killed fires. Yet it also could kill people who came into contact with it. She read on: There also was harmful dye in fire retardant that was used to allow pilots to check their load for accuracy. Ammonium phosphate was another ingredient used in fire retardants. It was a high source of elemental nitrogen, another substance toxic to humans.

From her water reports, she knew that in 1995, one year after the fire and the same year she moved to McCall full-time, Payette Lake's primary inlet recorded elevated nitrate concentrations. All the reports indicated that the addition of this large amount of phosphate and nitrogen to the lake created a proliferation of phytoplankton growth. That led to an exhausted supply of dissolved oxygen in the lake from September to November of 1995 for the first time on record. A three-hundred-foot-deep lake's oxygen level had plummeted to zero.

Charlie went back to bed but tossed and turned until seven a.m. She phoned Paul Woods, the scientist from the USGS who continued to feed her information surreptitiously whenever he could.

"I need to know why the oxygen level of the lake plummeted to zero a year after the forest fire of 1994," she asked him.

"Simply, this loss of oxygen at the bottom is not what you want to see in a lake that is considered to be of high quality," he answered. "Look, you dump 227,000+ gallons of fire retardant on a fire and you'll put it out. But it finds its way into the lake." He added grimly, "Lakes are basically sumps of watersheds."

"That's what I was afraid you'd say. What about the high levels of mercury in the water now?"

"That could have come from forest-fire residue, too."

"Not wastes from the Cinnebar and Warren mercury mines?"

"Oh yeah. That, as well."

"Looks like Mike Stewart's right...we have a cancer *cocktail* up in Payette Lake."

"Could be."

"Still can't talk about it?"

"Pretty soon," he said pointedly.

Charlie phoned Mike as soon as she said goodbye to Paul Woods. "It's the wind, Mike!" she exclaimed. "We don't need any of the damned forks—or spoons or knives—of the Salmon River water to flow from Stibnite to Payette Lake. We have *wind*!"

"Whoa, slow down," he said. "Pass that by me one more time."

Charlie explained to her friend that she might have solved the puzzle about how Stibnite's toxicity could have impacted Payette Lake through the 1994 fire. He was impressed.

"Don't be. It was Bruce Schuld flippantly answering a question at a meeting I attended yesterday about wind, fire, and toxins that set me on the path to this."

"However you got there, I think you're on to something."

"So does Paul Woods, but you never heard me say that."

"By the way, did you ever solve that other puzzle about the federal lawsuit at Stibnite?" Mike asked.

Charlie and Mike had settled into a nice routine of checking in with one another every few weeks. Sometimes they went as much as a few months between talks. They needed some catching up.

"Still working on that," she said.

"How's the health survey going? Is that guy out of Fallon still helping you?"

Mike was referring to Floyd Sands. Charlie contacted the activist in 2005 to talk about his work in Fallon, Nevada. His daughter, Stephanie, was diagnosed with leukemia in 1999 and soon learned that she was part of a childhood cancer cluster in their town. She lost her battle to the disease in 2001. Between 1997 and 2002 there were seventeen documented cases. In 2002, public health authorities admitted that Fallon represented the worst childhood cancer cluster in American medical history. In his daughter's memory, Sands coordinated a complete health survey of the entire Fallon area that took place in 2002. He called it Stephanie's Walk.

"He sent me his questionnaire. I was in the planning stages when the folks assisting me up in McCall got cold feet and backed out," Charlie said. "Floyd told me that people have to drive their own train. Maybe the people of McCall will figure that out one day. I'll be there for them when they do. If not, I'll come up with something else."

"Well, when you do, don't forget to clue me in. I'll cover it."

Back in 2004, Mike had begun doing stories from time to time in his weekly newspaper about the Smiths' outreach and exploits, keeping their names in the news and on people's minds, even if only in Valley County.

Mike's first interview with Charlie reported her plans to pull sediment samples from Payette Lake, using a diver out of Coeur d'Alene. It was also her first self-funded foray into finding out what might be lurking in the depths of that glacial body of water. A few days after the late October outing in her thirty-foot pontoon boat under grey skies threatening snow, Mike published an article about it in *The Long Valley Advocate*. It was a detailed account of the attempt to understand if a connection existed between the rampant illness in McCall and the ongoing problems with the poor water quality. The article delved into Charlie and Trevor's pasts as residents in McCall, Trevor's battle with cancer and the Smiths' quest for answers.

Within a week of that article, Charlie's phone began ringing off the hook with people seeking her out. One of those callers was Dieuwke (Duka) Spencer, the former head of Idaho Central District Health in McCall. She said she was impressed by Charlie's perseverance. It was Spencer who had worked with Mike Stewart on an aborted attempt to learn if a flurry of breast cancer cases in Valley County in 1995 constituted a cluster.

"I want you to know that there are those in the community who are cheering you on," Dieuwke said.

Charlie replied, "I hope people are starting to come around and see why we have to expose these problems."

"It's great that you'll put yourself on the line."

"It's worth taking that chance when you've got a son battling brain cancer." Charlie reiterated how committed she still was to finding answers, despite the huge financial drain footing the bill alone. "Even so," she added, "I'm willing to put my money where my mouth is, but it's depressing not to be able to see the light at the end of the tunnel."

"Maybe this will help. There's a newly formed commission, the Comprehensive Cancer Alliance for Idaho (CCAI). They're putting together a master plan for the state of Idaho to address the causes, cures, and treatment of cancer. It's in the beginning stages right now, and I want to give you a phone number of the woman in charge. I think you'd be a great addition."

"I don't know if I'm ready to be a *state* commissioner."

"Mike thinks you are. And so do I. I've already spoken to some of the members about your work, and they're anxious to hear from you."

Charlie had made the call to Patti Moran, the head of the new commission and the director of the Idaho Cancer Control Program at the Department of Health and Welfare. Moran insisted that Charlie come on board. Charlie worried about being able to hold her own but jumped in anyway.

Before long, she felt as if she truly belonged in the same room with the other commissioners who were employees of various public health agencies in the state and in health-related jobs at local hospitals. One of them was Chris Johnson, her old nemesis from the Idaho Tumor Registry. He was just as surprised to see her on the panel. Their interaction was awkward at first, but she worked hard to win him over.

Charlie's entry onto this larger stage had caused her to take stock of herself. It felt good to be listened to and taken seriously. Over time, she became ever bolder. When the other members failed to include a childhood cancer section in their plan to look at toxins as a possible cause of this disease, she told them she would have to drop off the commission. To her surprise, they wouldn't hear of it. In fact, they not only asked her to stay on, but they created a separate Childhood Cancer Strategic Plan to be released after the completion of the General Strategic Plan. They added Trevor as a member of the Childhood Cancer panel as well. He became the first Idaho teenager to be appointed to a position like this.

As Charlie's reputation for her selfless work on behalf of children with cancer grew throughout Idaho, she eventually crossed paths with Mark Johnson, the popular news anchor on Channel 7, the Idaho NBC affiliate. He wanted to interview her, Trevor, and anyone else in McCall who might also believe that toxins were part of the cause of all the cancer and other illnesses up there.

During their preliminary discussions about the upcoming shoot, Johnson had encouraged Trevor to open up about what he'd been going through since the surgery. Trevor explained about how good he felt when his chemo port was removed, leaving him free from having drugs pumped into his system. He also revealed how depressed he became when he had to give himself shots to grow taller, the cancer treatments having stunted his body's maturation just at the time of puberty. Although Trevor appreciated Johnson's interest in him, he began to have second thoughts about going through with the commitment.

"What do you think, Mom?"

"I'm with you whatever you decide. I think Mark can handle this issue well, though. He's a compassionate man, and he knows what this disease can do. He lost his first wife to cancer when she was twenty-two."

"I didn't know that."

"And Mark only wants to help us to get the word out about cancer clusters and what a horrible impact they're having on the kids in our state."

"And that's what I want to do, too," Trevor admitted.

After getting a thumbs-up from Trevor, the anchorman had assigned a film crew to follow him around the Children's Oncology Center where he was treated and at St. Luke's Hospital where he still underwent his MRIs. They shot hours of footage for a news segment about Trevor, Charlie, and McCall that was aired in January of 2005 throughout Idaho. That TV interview led to requests from more groups wanting the Smiths to appear and speak about their struggles and their work.

And last night, in a City Hall hearing room, they both made a forceful public stand against the opening of another gold mine using the same techniques that wreaked such havoc in Stibnite.

In fact, as they were leaving the hearing, another local newscaster stopped Charlie for a comment. She reiterated her opposition to the mine and then smiled beguilingly into the camera's lens. "Let me ask you this: If cyanide is so safe, why do they kill rats with it?"

CHAPTER TWENTY-SEVEN

The bell rang. Government class was over. Trevor gathered up his books and stuffed them into his backpack. As he was walking toward the door, his teacher Mr. Carlton, called out, "Hey, Trev, do you have a minute?"

"Sure. What's up?"

"I saw your mom on the news last night," Mr. Carlton said. "She sure knows how to deliver a zinger! I heard you testified at the protest hearing, too."

"I did," Trevor said.

"Well, I think what you guys are doing is great."

"Thanks, Mr. Carlton. I think it's important trying to get our government to clean up our environment."

"Hell yeah, it is. But I think your problem is going to be big business."

"As you heard on the news, nothing scares my mom!"

Mr. Carlton laughed. "I got to be honest, Trev. It's not going to be an easy battle, but keep at it." He opened his own personal refrigerator at the back of the classroom. "You want a Coke?"

"No, thanks. I'm good."

"Okay. What the hell are you standing around for, then?" he asked playfully, adding, "Get out of here and get to lunch."

As Trevor walked down the hall toward the lunch area, he thought how much he liked Mr. Carlton. He and the grey-haired, middle-aged government teacher had an easy relationship built upon informal bantering and mutual respect. Trevor often talked to him about his extracurricular activities in the arena of cancer and children. Mr. Carlton, like most of his teachers, took an interest in this other part of his life. He wished kids his own age cared as much. Or at all.

The halls were nearly deserted by now. Everybody was either in the cafeteria or outside congregated in groups around lunch tables. Some of the seniors were heading off in their cars to eat in the nearby restaurants.

As usual, Trevor found no one to eat with him. He made his way to his truck, which was parked at the far end of the campus in a spot with a view of the athletic field. He settled into the driver's seat and opened his bag. Looked inside. A healthy lunch.

Since going back to school, he remained vigilant about eating a wholesome diet. No more Mickey D's and fries for him. No drugs or alcohol, either. He had enough of putting drugs into his system. It was another thing that separated him from a lot of teenagers and made social interaction awkward. But that was the least of his worries.

At the end of 2004, an endocrinologist had informed him that he must inject himself with growth-hormone shots five days a week. Before brain cancer, Trevor was in the ninetieth percentile for growth for his age; now he was in the fiftieth.

The doctor had explained how the cancer treatments had zapped Trevor's system at the age of thirteen, when most of puberty was supposed to take place. He wasn't maturing like he should have been: stalled growth, voice not lowering. He was afraid of taking the hormone shots because some of the literature said that it might cause cancer down the line. The last thing he wanted was to get any kind of cancer again.

At that time, his dad still had a great deal of input into Trevor's decisions. He favored taking them. "Do you want to only be five-foot-five your whole life?" his dad said to him. His mom was against synthetic hormones. She assured Trevor that she just wanted him healthy and didn't care if he ever grew another inch. He could still hear her exact words: "In my eyes, you're already a giant."

Not surprisingly, Trevor felt torn between his father's wishes for him to be tall and his own feelings about drugs that were more in line with his mom's. But he was desperate to get back to that ninetieth percentile, so he gave himself the shots for almost a year. During that time, he developed an embarrassing lumpiness in his lower abdomen where he injected the hormones. It wouldn't go away no matter how many sit-ups he did. *What am I doing to myself? I'm already a giant.* So he quit. Cold turkey. He figured he didn't need to chance a new cancer or more unsightly bulges. His dad thought he was making a foolish mistake.

Sometimes when he was alone in his truck, like today, he'd eat absently and think back to the inexorable end of his relationship with his dad. The difference in his parents' attitude toward his taking that medication and how they valued their son brought home to Trevor how little he wanted to be in his father's company any longer. Once these feelings were revealed in court documents, the latest family court judge in Boise ordered Trevor to see a psychologist with Ballard to try to patch things up. Trevor had replied with a resounding "NO WAY!"

Trevor informed the judge there was no point to joint therapy. "I wish I could have a normal relationship with my dad, but I can't: he's not normal," he said. By this time, Trevor—and the courts—knew Ballard Smith was an admitted, convicted liar. Trevor also knew his father could fool anyone he came up against, even a psychologist. If lying were a sport, his father would have won the gold medal in the Olympics for it. It was scary watching his dad develop and deliver one of his whoppers with a straight face; Trevor personally had observed him do it and outwit a previous psychologist at the start of his parents' custody proceedings.

Then there were the other lies, ones that were almost too painful to discuss. But he finally divulged the worst to the judge: When Trevor was ten, his dad accused him and Chris Gould of ordering porno movies from DirecTV after his mom found one on their television. It turned out his father was the culprit all along, but he continued to insist it was Trevor and Chris for *four days* before he finally broke down, wept, and admitted the truth.

Trevor tried to convey to the judge the extent of the anguish his father caused back then, memories of that purgatory which he still carried inside of him. He could still hear the rage in Tina Gould's voice when she shouted at his dad after he apologized for putting Chris through the wringer: "Your crocodile tears don't impress me, Ballard; you only feel bad because you got caught, not because you care about the boys. You robbed them of their innocence. I can never forgive you for that!" And she hadn't. Soon Tina and Bo Gould quit working for his parents and took their boys to Boise to live. Trevor lost his best friend until he, too, moved to Boise fulltime.

Trevor became irate every time he thought about how the family court system continually mishandled his case since 2002, until he finally concluded the legal system was not set up to get to the heart of a bully like his dad. None of the several judges presiding over the Smiths' divorce ever understood that Trevor was more an object than a person to his father. He was a possession his father could barter to make a better deal in the estate dissolution proceedings, like one of his prized paintings or antique bronzes, or the trophy house on the lake.

Eventually it dawned on Trevor that no one in the justice system could save him. If he wanted any kind of a life, he'd have to get over Ballard Smith by himself. The solution was so simple that he wondered later why it had taken him two years to come up with it. Long after the court restrained his father from coming any closer than the curb at his mom's Winterwood Lane house, it finally restrained him from phoning Charlie's home phone, too, since he harassed her unmercifully whenever she answered. One day toward the end of 2005, it occurred to Trevor that if he merely changed his cell phone number he could block the last avenue his dad had to reach him. It turned out to be pivotal.

The sound of his dad's voice on the other end of the line berating him many times a day, accusing him of disloyalty, and harassing him, used to make him buckle under with fear. No more. The sound of his sisters' voices yelling at him and accusing him of disloyalty to their father used to reduce him to debilitating bouts of depression. No more.

Ballard spent all last year dragging Charlie and Trevor into court, demanding they give him that cell phone number. "That's up to Trevor. It's not mine to give out," his mother repeatedly told the judge. Trevor merely remained infuriatingly silent. He heard that their family judge finally threw up his hands in exasperation and said to his father, "What do you want me to do, Mr. Smith? Arrest the boy?"

To satisfy the court that his father could reach him in an emergency, Trevor kept an e-mail account where Ballard could send communications and maintain some connection. He received e-mails at this address from his sisters, too. Oftentimes these messages were fraught with recriminations, accusing Trevor of being manipulated and turned against them and their father. How could he forsake his family, they wanted to know? He frequently thought back to the day of his fourteenth birthday in Maui when he still didn't know if he would live or die, and Amy callously informed him that he wasn't family. How could they have it both ways?

Some kids were walking toward him now. He instantly stopped chewing and slunk down in his seat, hoping they wouldn't notice him all alone in his truck.

They have it so easy, he thought, their footsteps getting farther away but leaving the echo of their laughter in his ears. Instead of spending time with his few friends, he still spent his time mostly going to doctors' appointments: optometrists to deal with the trouble with his eyes that continued to plague him; radiation specialists to administer biannual MRIs; ENTs for the infernal buzzing in his ear; internists of every description. A new low had assaulted him a few months ago:

his male hormone levels were nearly non-existent. His endocrinologist recommended that Trevor see an additional specialist right away—a fertility doctor.

It was almost four years since his surgery, and now this. Since being confronted with having to take growth hormone shots to get taller, he had accepted that chemotherapy tried to kill his body's internal clock. Now, it seemed, it had really done a number on his reproductive organs.

He met alone with the fertility specialist, who explained that Trevor needed testosterone. "If you ever want to have kids, you'll need to start thinking about that now," the doctor said sympathetically.

Trevor could hardly accept what he was hearing. He hadn't actually ever been on a date, and here he was forced to think about whether he wanted to be a father. The doc gave Trevor the option of doing nothing or of starting a regimen of shots not unlike the ones he had taken to grow. Although he was almost six feet tall, he still didn't have any facial hair, and there were other physical signs that he wasn't making the progress he should be. He kept thinking that maybe the testosterone would do the trick, like a magic potion. One injection and he'd morph into the teenager he so desperately wanted to be: gruff and manly, sprouting stubble he had to shave *twice* a day.

Trevor took the hormone injections for a few weeks, after which he was instructed to give a semen sample to the lab. The doctor felt that if he wanted to have children some day, he would have to freeze the samples ahead of time, since no one could assure him that in the future he'd be able to have kids naturally. All of it became a very uncomfortable and embarrassing situation.

Alone in his room, he read the semen kit instructions about "collecting" it in the morning and returning it to the lab within forty-five minutes for processing, making sure to keep it at body temperature. During the drive to the lab that next morning, he cradled the vials under his shirt to keep the samples warm. He kept thinking that maybe he was protecting his future son or daughter.

He dropped off the kit and waited to hear from someone, hoping for good news. The results took a few days to come back. He met with the fertility doctor again.

"I'm sorry to say there were no sperm in the two samples," the doctor said.

I'm shooting blanks, he thought dejectedly. "Is there anything at all that we can do?" Trevor had asked the doctor, trying to sound adult and contain his enormous sense of defeat.

The doctor treated him with deference, sounding upbeat about a pretty depressing situation. He counseled Trevor to go off of the testosterone for a couple of months and try again at a later time. "Even with that," the doctor added, "there's only about a twenty-percent chance of success."

Trevor listened and calculated the odds. Always good at math, he knew this was very bad news. He had driven home feeling more defeated by the minute. He couldn't help thinking how ironic his existence had become: his first fight was to keep life, and now he would be in the fight of his life to give life.

Just like that, Trevor's world turned bleak again. It seemed as if he never could quite get his head above water for any length of time and take a deep breath before something pulled him back down. He became increasingly anxious about shooting blanks, but he had no one with whom to discuss this. How could he go to his best friend, Chris Gould, and lay that on him? Why would Chris want to hear about that kind of problem? Trevor wouldn't, if the shoe was on the other foot.

Girls were out of the equation. How could he ask someone out on a date? It felt weird to think about anything romantic. He began to feel tied up in knots. Completely encapsulated in his own misery. He couldn't admit any of this to his mother, either. As understanding and cool as she was, this definitely was a guy thing. Bro was too busy. They weren't as close as they used to be. Trevor never even considered sharing this with his father.

What he needed was a peer group. But where was one? He realized how he had suffered through surgery, treatments, and now the aftermath of surviving without the safety net of having someone else with his same problems to share the burden. The attorney, Jean Uranga, phoned him from time to time to see how he was getting along. "Fine," he would answer, without much conviction. The fact was he didn't want to talk to anyone about his true feelings by this time. Outwardly he was doing everything in a calm manner, but inside he was a spectacular train wreck.

Little by little, Trevor retreated, sitting in his truck at Boise High like he was today, eating lunch by himself. From his spot looking at the athletic field, he had a clear view of the kids interacting. Most were in groups. Some sat off on the bleachers alone. A few didn't seem so happy. He knew all teenagers had problems, but somehow his seemed more dispiriting.

Sometimes he would eat and work on the speeches he was asked to give about kids with cancer. Civic groups like Kiwanis and the YMCA requested his presence at their events. He recently gave a stirring speech to a gathering of more than one hundred people in Emmett, Idaho, who had been affected by the Nevada nuclear tests run in the 1950s. They were part of a group called Downwinders. Many of the victims hugged him afterwards and gave him praise for his bravery. Bravery was a word frequently paired with his name. He wasn't so sure how apt a description it was. He was good at hiding the fact that these events left him feeling hollow. They didn't improve his sorry state of mind because he was scared to reveal what was actually in his true heart: how small and alone he felt when he wasn't in front of a crowd.

Trevor's once stellar marks were taking a nosedive to Bs and Cs. His mom discussed this with him. It mystified her because he still seemed so diligent. He explained that he found it hard to concentrate, to memorize, to recall what he studied. Some of his failures could be attributed to the post-cancer treatments: Dr. Chang, and others, had told him that a syndrome called "chemo brain" was real—lapses of memory and forgetfulness. *Check. Check.* Could some of his intellectual decline be a result of actual damage to his brain from the surgery itself? He wanted to find out. And he was afraid to find out. One thing he knew for sure: The high goals for a top college, that he had set for himself before getting sick, seemed a distant dream now.

Lunch period was almost over. He started to take another bite of his sandwich. His appetite was gone. He got out of his truck. Dumped what remained of his lunch into the trash and walked slowly to his next class.

Chapter Twenty-Eight

Emmett, Idaho was only about thirty miles northwest of Boise, practically a hop, skip, and a jump from the state capitol building along State Street to Highway 16. Yet it seemed light years from that hard-charging, capitol district, or many of the newly-gentrified neighborhoods along the route. Primarily still a farming community, this picturesque rural enclave was also home to a sprawling Boise Cascade mill.

Charlie was on her way there this morning to help a new friend, Tona Henderson, plan the first Idaho Downwinder's Conference at the beginning of the year. Always struggling to get the funds to keep going, Tona and the founder of the Idaho Downwinders, J. Preston Truman, had come to Charlie for help, and she agreed to underwrite the event that would take place at the Idaho Historical Museum in Boise.

Tona owned Emmett's most popular bakery, The Rumor Mill, a decades-old family business. Located on Fourth Avenue just off the main street in town, her neighbors congregated there in the morning to drink coffee, eat doughnuts, and gossip. A few years back, shooting the breeze began to include personal stories about the 1950s Nevada nuclear bomb tests controversy. It seemed that these explosions near Las Vegas resulted in radioactive plumes that wafted downwind over a number of western states, including Idaho. Emmett was hit hard by those toxic dustings, which resulted years later in scores of cancer cases.

At Charlie's initial meeting at the bakery with Tona a year earlier, the energetic woman had described the day after the first nuclear tests had taken place in Nevada. Everyone in town, and those who lived on the local dairy farms just outside of the city, woke up to find a white powdery substance covering everything. Just a kid at the time, Tona recalled how excited she was to find it snowing in summer!

The white dust intermittently fell from the sky after each detonation and continued to blanket the residents for many more years while the United States and the Soviet Union raced one another to build the most lethal bombs. The United States performed more than one hundred open-air tests in Nevada between 1951 and 1962.

"We thought we had nothing to worry about," Tona told Charlie. "Our families were assured by government authorities those flakes posed no health hazard. Some of my parents' friends drove into the hills at night to get a better look at the pink sunsets caused by radioactive dust."

As the years passed, local cancer rates soared: thyroid, brain, all types of cancer. "In my own family, we have over twenty members from Emmett who have had cancer!" Tona had exclaimed to a horrified Charlie.

"We weren't the only ones affected. Utah, Nevada, and Colorado, as well as Arizona, all got big doses of that harmful dust. It contained radioactive iodine-131. It finally came out that it all was passed on in the milk of the cows that ate the poisoned grass. Even people who lived in town had a cow in those days. It was like every one of us was exposed to 100 x-rays!

"But for decades we Idahoans didn't know any of this. Victims in other states, like Nevada, Arizona and Utah, received payments of at least $50,000 apiece for their suffering. Yet all of our Idaho counties were exposed to more iodine-131. Emmett worse than most.

"When the truth began to leak out that we'd had the wool pulled over our eyes, I jumped on it right away. Everyone in our town was anxious to tell their own stories about the fallout and how it affected their families. You can't imagine how bad it was when we all learned that our *own* state legislators knew we should have been compensated but kept it from us."

She asked Charlie rhetorically, "Why would they lie to us?" To get her own answers, Tona taught herself everything there was to know about the Nevada tests and how other states had been treated.

At that time, Tona and her husband urged everyone to stop grousing and to write their own letters of protest to local, state, and federal officials. To facilitate that, they printed up a form letter for their friends and neighbors to fill in. Then Tona joined up with J. Preston Truman from southern Idaho. "We always had a lot of heart," she explained to Charlie, "but very little money. That hurt our efforts."

With the assistance of a local Emmett reporter, Tona moved her meetings out of the bakery and consolidated them into one huge rally at a larger venue in a park across from the county courthouse, which had an area with a band shell and place for a microphone. Just about everyone in town showed up.

Tona told Charlie that she was overwhelmed that afternoon as she watched hundreds of Emmett residents get up and tell their stories about families riddled with cancer. With local and state dignitaries, along with more media, in attendance, they finally were being heard.

"I thought, Wow! At last something might get done to help my community and the rest of Idaho, after so many decades of being lied to."

Tona's spirits were further buoyed after the rally when she learned that the National Academy of Sciences (NAS) committed to come to their town to take testimony from those who were affected. They also promised to do a study and make a recommendation to Congress about whether to include Idaho in the Radiation Exposure Compensation Act (RECA).

Then the bubble of high expectations burst: Tona found out what Charlie had discovered about data collecting for McCall. With only 9,000 residents, the Emmett population was not considered dense enough to give the kind of statistical results required by the NAS. In other words, they were statistically insignificant.

As the fallout study, and then the bill introduced by Idaho's U.S. Senator Mike Crapo to add Idaho to RECA, languished in committees where they would probably die a quiet death, Tona and her co-workers lobbied for more widespread pressure.

About that time, Tona caught Charlie being interviewed on television and decided to give her a call. Tona's sincerity, fervor, and compassion won over Charlie. She agreed to join the Downwinders' efforts. She and Trevor went to their rallies. Trevor even gave a speech at one of them.

Today's working session with Tona at the bakery was to go over details for the January conference. With only a few months to go, they were in a time crunch. If they pulled it off, this event would provide the most exposure Tona and Truman's group had ever had in Idaho.

"Want a doughnut with your tea?" Tona asked, as Charlie settled down at a table near a large plate-glass window. The bakery was nearly deserted after the early morning deluge of customers.

"No thanks. Just tea."

"I don't know why I ask. You always say no."

"I gain two pounds every time I'm here just smelling the things," Charlie joked.

Tona put down their mugs on the table and grabbed a chair.

"New photos?" Charlie asked, glancing around the shop. Framed pictures of locals in their military uniforms lined the walls. Every war America ever fought seemed represented. Tona had told Charlie how proud she was of the patriotism of her patrons and her own family's military record. This was another reason she became so disillusioned when she realized how they all had been lied to. "Good eye, Charlie. We do have a few."

"Unending wars over there. Different battles here at home," Charlie commented.

"Speaking of that. Something new is brewing," she told Charlie. "Divine Strake."

Charlie smiled. "Is that a new-fangled coffee cake you just created?"

"Hardly," Tona replied with a laugh.

She went on to explain that Divine Strake was the name recently given by the military to a proposed bomb-explosion experiment in which seven hundred tons of explosives would be set off in Nevada in the exact location of the old nuclear bomb tests. Some claimed the test was designed to ascertain the effectiveness of targeted non-nuclear bombs on underground chambers, such as bunkers—or in the case of this test, mine shafts.

"I don't believe this!" Charlie exclaimed.

"Awful, isn't it? Good news is that the Shoshone Indian tribe in Nevada slapped them with a lawsuit to stop it. Slowed down the process. We're joining them. So are Downwinders in Utah, Arizona, and Nevada."

"Stop them on what grounds?" Charlie asked.

"No environmental impact study has been done to prove that it's safe to resume testing in the heart of the old above-ground, nuclear-blast site. Can you imagine what could happen? Experts claim that the contaminated dust that settled back into the ground could be churned up and sent across the winds again."

"Sure, let's just kill another generation of Westerners," Charlie groaned.

"Well, all of us Idahoan Downwinders are determined to stop this 'experiment.' We're tired of being lab rats. And we need your media connections to help us. You're so good at making important noise."

"You're not so bad, yourself," Charlie said.

"I'm not in your league, Charlie. We really need you on this."

Charlie agreed to get as much print and TV publicity for them as she could. In addition, she would continue coordinating the January conference program, arranging for prominent speakers in the field of nuclear testing and toxic exposure.

They spent the next hour finalizing these plans. As Charlie drove the thirty miles back home, she had the leisure to think about Tona's anger at being lied to by her local and federal representatives. It was a sore spot that wouldn't heal. It came up in so many of their conversations. No one liked being lied to. It rankled Tona to be told to back off, stop acting crazy, stop the worry—even though she personally witnessed her own family falling sick and suffering, often dying long before they ever should have. All of it had turned Tona's rational world upside down.

And when the lie came out, and she helped others to make noise and insist on their rights, too, things got even worse for her. That was similar to the way Charlie felt whenever she got close to a breakthrough up in McCall, and everyone said she should drop her nonsense. That she was making things up. Like Tona in Emmett, Charlie vowed to get to the bottom of the health problems in her beautiful village by the lake. One day. After learning about the Downwinders, Charlie's beliefs about her Stibnite wind theory were strengthened. She needed more proof, however. The secrets of the old mill-site contamination were still sealed away in the court in Cascade. Why was the settlement sealed if they had nothing to hide? "That's the key, Charlie, that will open the door to this town's secrets," Mike had told her. Until that happened, her former McCall friends felt free to lash out at her with impunity, calling her a headstrong troublemaker who couldn't accept that it was her son's defective genes, not a defective environment, that caused his brain cancer. What about all the other sick kids up there? Was it a town filled with children and young adults with defective genes? Hardly!

Don't worry, Joan, I'm in this for the long haul, she thought now, as she neared her home. She remembered the urgency in Joan's voice during that last conversation back in June of 2003. Joan had called Charlie a fearless fighter and said she loved that about her. *I am a fighter, Joan. Not afraid of too much either. You were right. I certainly will find out who my friends are. I've endured a lot worse than not being invited to a dinner party.*

Charlie wasn't all that spiritual, but at this moment it felt as if Joan's fighting spirit had nudged her into accepting Tona's first call, going out to see her, and then signing on to help with her important work. Joan and her daughter both had been so determined to stop nuclear proliferation in the world, giving enormous sums of money and their time to the cause. Now Charlie was involved in her own small way, too. She could hear Joan now: *Downwinders? Who woulda thunk it?*

CHAPTER TWENTY-NINE

W*hat the hell am I doing out here?* Charlie thought, as she slowed her SUV to a crawl. She had left her home in Boise just as a light dusting of snow began to cover everything. Weather reports forecast it to fall throughout the night. Even so, she had forgotten how dicey the drive up the mountain to McCall could be in January in a full-fledged snow dump.

To make matters worse, her cell phone began to ring. She fumbled for it on the passenger seat, fully expecting it to be Trevor calling to check up on her progress—again.

It was Dr. Richard Miller, the keynote speaker for the Downwinder Conference that would take place in a little more than two weeks.

"Hey, Charlie," Miller said. "Hope I haven't caught you at a bad time."

"Can you hold on a sec?" she replied, swerving to the side of the road. She wasn't the only one parked this way, although some of the angles of the other vehicles seemed to indicate they had slid off the road without meaning to. "Okay. I can talk now. I'm just outside of McCall, so if we cut out, I'll have to call you back."

"I just wanted to firm up my travel plans," he said. "Airline tickets, hotel, etc., etc."

"All under control. I've also lined up some press for you. Our top environmental reporter from the *Idaho Statesman* newspaper wants to do an interview. We've been promised a lot of daily coverage during the conference. I got a green light for TV spots for you, and also for Dr. Owen Hoffman, our other speaker."

"I know him well. This is wonderful news, Charlie."

She added, "I think you'll be perfect to appear with Mark Johnson on his Sunday talk show, *Viewpoint.* It's Idaho's answer to *Meet the Press.*"

"Sounds perfect," Miller replied. "I heard that your governor has agreed to proclaim January 'Downwinder's Month.'"

"That was quite a coup! My son Trevor helped Tona get that accomplished. As a reward for his dogged pursuit of the governor, he's been selected to read the proclamation and to give a short speech about the importance of RECA being expanded to Idaho residents."

"Good for him. I know this will be a fruitful conference."

"Hey, I don't mean to be abrupt. I'm in the middle of a whiteout, and I have to be in McCall to testify on another environmental matter very shortly. If you need more information, just give me a call at home tomorrow."

She put the car in gear and inched out onto the highway, where she proceeded at a crawl as the flakes increased in size and intensity. *No surprise there,* she thought. *I'm in Valley County, which gets the most snowfall in all of Idaho every winter.*

For nearly a year, Charlie had been communicating on a regular basis with the two keynote speakers, both experts on nuclear fallout and its ramifications. Dr. Miller had founded the technical consulting firm, Legis Corporation, in Houston, Texas in 1984, which looked into problems with companies that were involved with the chemical industry. *Under a Cloud,* a book he wrote about nuclear fallout, discussed the history of American above-ground nuclear testing and included a map of the nuclear debris clouds.

Hoffman, president of SENES Oak Ridge, Inc., Center for Risk Analysis, had an impressive resume. With more than thirty years' experience evaluating the impact of nuclear and other environmental toxins on humans, he was widely accepted as an expert on environmental risk. He also was instrumental in developing several interactive dose-and-risk calculators for the Nevada Test Site fallout.

As Richard Miller had just indicated, the lineup of speakers and the expected coverage portended a great turnout and result. If all went as expected, the Downwinders in Idaho would not only be on the map in their fight to gain RECA funds, they could very well help to kill Divine Strake altogether.

That Charlie and Trevor were now part of this fight was especially satisfying. She only hoped she didn't die in this snowstorm before she gave her testimony in McCall, or got back home to Boise.

———

Kathy Lovell, a local mother in her early thirties, warmly greeted Charlie when she arrived at the municipal McCall Golf Course clubhouse, where the town was holding a meeting concerning health violations by a local asphalt company.

"I've been praying you'd get here in one piece. I wouldn't have been surprised if you cancelled," she said. "What with the storm."

Charlie glanced around the room. It was filled to capacity and buzzing with angry citizens ready to give their piece of mind to the local DEQ officials about the asphalt company. This confrontation with the asphalt plant had begun almost two years before after some of the locals complained about a noxious odor seeping into their homes and their businesses, their hospital, and their schools.

Charlie first learned about the brouhaha from her new acquaintance, Kathy Lovell, who after watching her and Trevor on Mark Johnson's

Channel 7 segment on McCall the previous year, had sought Charlie's counsel about her own worries.

"It's not just cancer that we have to expose," she had said. Kathy's young daughter suffered from apraxia, a rare neurological disorder. "She's not the only child in this town suffering from this condition. I believe her illness has something to do with Stibnite and the mill because her tests show a high level of antimony."

With the passage of time, Kathy became increasingly irate with each new diagnosis in McCall of brain cancer, apraxia, autism, and any number of other diseases that affected young people. She vented to Charlie, who always was willing to listen. Before long, Kathy became Charlie's de facto pipeline to what was happening in McCall and who was getting sick. One time, Charlie asked her to compile a list of all of the sick people she knew, and Kathy had replied, "Why don't I just give you the McCall phonebook and cross out the few names of the people who *aren't* sick?"

Then, late last year, Kathy gave Charlie some promising news about the asphalt plant: The conflict was reaching the boiling point. An attorney from Oregon who lived in McCall part-time had entered the fray. Could she give the woman Charlie's number?

A few days later, Mary Wood phoned. She told Charlie she was a professor of law at the University of Oregon and, from this point on would be the attorney handling the case of the citizens of McCall against the asphalt plant.

"You don't know how tenacious I can be," she said. "But I know your work. And I think what you're accomplishing is amazing."

"Kathy thinks that I may be able to help the cause," Charlie replied. "I'm encouraged by your involvement, because it's been difficult to get my old friends and neighbors to drive their own train on these important issues."

"This train has already left the station," Wood assured her.

She then filled Charlie in on the particulars of the case. Not only was the alleged violation taking place near Charlie's former home, it concerned a production plant—Valley Asphalt and Paving Company, established in 1993—that Charlie never even knew existed. It had been hidden from view for years, until exposed by a new scenic road recently built across from the waste treatment plant, southwest of McCall-Donnelly Elementary School and along the Payette River.

Valley Asphalt and Paving now faced a potential fine of more than $55,000 for violating its air quality permit. The DEQ had come down hard, accusing the owners of exceeding their quota of toxic emissions. However, in a completely cynical move, the company petitioned the DEQ to simply raise the quota so that it would not be breaking the law. According to some astonished locals, the DEQ actually was considering doing this.

"What can I do from here in Boise?" Charlie had asked.

"Get us media. And lots of it. I know how good you can be at promoting the health of our children over greed. And we also would love for you to come up to McCall to testify in our big public hearing. Having your voice join ours would give our claims even more credence."

Wood went on to explain that the lawsuit she was shepherding claimed that the owners of Valley Asphalt and Paving wanted the right to burn used oil, which could come from various sources. If successful, they would force McCall residents to breathe in air infused with arsenic, lead, mercury, chromium, nickel, formaldehyde, acetaldehyde, benzene, dioxins, furans, and cadmium. And more. In fact, the DEQ had identified at least fifty-four toxins, including dangerous carcinogens.

Later she sent Charlie a copy of the document. In part she argued: "The public owns the air shed, and breathing is not a choice, like what to eat or drive. If your eyes sting, your nose burns, you lose your voice, and you have to go in your house, then close the windows, then leave... you are oppressed and denied your rights."

The complaint was filed on behalf of McCall Citizens against Asphalt Pollution. It was not limited to homeowners near the plant, since citizens from all over the McCall area complained of the asphalt smell and pollution. Many said they couldn't walk or bicycle on the new scenic Deinhard Pass where the plant was located. Several health-care professionals in McCall—including Dr. Jennifer Gray, who had misdiagnosed Trevor's brain cancer—said the odor and the chemicals that caused it penetrated the hospital, putting patients at risk.

Charlie had worked her tail off to get media coverage for the citizen's group. After braving the winter storm tonight, she arrived just in time to kick off the protest as the first speaker.

She said, *My son Trevor spent the majority of his seventeen years growing up in the McCall area. In November of 2002, Trevor, at thirteen, was diagnosed with brain cancer. At that time, Trevor and I moved to Boise, so he could be close to his treatments at St. Luke's. It has been four years now, and Trevor is cancer free.*

In that same year when Trevor was diagnosed, there were four other brain cancers diagnosed in the McCall area. According to the state epidemiologist, that number is very high for the population base here. There were also various other forms of cancers and autoimmune diseases that were diagnosed over the past several years.

I became concerned, as did others, about external factors that could perhaps be contributing to the high rate of illnesses. I started researching and looking into various environmental contaminants and the role they play in cancer. I mainly focused on mining, milling, the use of fire retardants, and the faulty water filtration system, but I overlooked the possibility that this asphalt plant could perhaps be part of the smoking gun. That was entirely due to my ignorance. I didn't realize that McCall had an asphalt plant that could possibly be emitting fifty-four toxins into our air. This toxic plume from the Valley Asphalt plant is a hazard to everyone's health. It has been proven that cancer is not simply a disease of genes gone bad, but environmental exposures are definitely a factor.

I am an active member of the Comprehensive Cancer Alliance for Idaho. Part of our vision is to make sure every Idahoan has the opportunity for proper cancer prevention and detection. How can we prevent cancer if we allow companies such as Valley Asphalt to deliberately contaminate?

I would certainly hope that DEQ recognizes the health risk to the citizens of McCall. If they were to grant this permit to Valley Asphalt, I think it would be a travesty. It's up to DEQ to support and to insure that the public needs are being met. My son Trevor could not be here tonight, but he wanted me to ask DEQ: At what point does money become more important than people's health? And don't you think you have a moral obligation to do everything in your power to keep children safe?

As Charlie neared the end of her speech, the door opened, and Dr. Jennifer Gray strode into the room. She carried a sheaf of papers. Seemed distracted. Another couple of speakers presented their views. Then Charlie heard Dr. Gray's name being called to take the floor.

This should be interesting. Charlie still wasn't completely over the way the doctor had dismissed her concerns about Trevor in the ER back in 2002 before his brain cancer diagnosis.

But the minute the woman began to speak, Charlie knew that Dr. Jennifer Gray had come onboard. Gray began with an urgent plea: "I implore the DEQ not to approve this permit." She went on to say: "I often find myself in a position as a clinician of having to use my common sense and judgment. So, specifically, if a patient who has known asthma or reactive airway disease goes outside on a particular day that the air quality is poor, I don't need to look at the DEQ site to see that… Even if you don't look at the specific toxins and potential carcinogenic or teratogenic effects, you could, for example, look at the multiple comments of residents of the area, including myself, who on certain days don't feel comfortable allowing their children to play outside… I don't want to see you coming in certainly with tumors. Also, I don't want to see you with acute asthma attacks. I've taken care of patients who have died in my ER with asthma attacks. It's a serious, serious,

serious matter…. So, as a physician and a mother in this community, I implore the DEQ not to grant this permit…"

As Gray retook her seat, she sought Charlie's eyes and smiled at her. Charlie nodded back. They were both mothers. They got it.

The next day, Charlie received an e-mail from Mary Wood. She wrote: Charlie, so great meeting you last night. I was thrilled that you were the first to go, because you really set the tone for the whole hearing. Thank you for driving up. Your testimony carried far beyond your own words and really emboldened people. It was crucial.

We'll see, she thought. But there was a bigger spring in her step as she went about tying up all the loose ends for the Downwinders Conference.

CHAPTER THIRTY

It was an inspiring spring day. Cool but not cold. Clear blue skies broken by wafting cumulus clouds. A light breeze nudged the cottonwoods to shed some of their fuzz. The white fluff that made his mother sneeze was everywhere in their neighborhood, so thick on the ground in some places it looked like snow.

It didn't faze Trevor, who was hunched over the handlebars pumping the pedals of his fourteen-speed bike as hard as he could for the last two hundred yards back to his house. Some days he liked to pretend he was Lance Armstrong on the final leg of the Tour de France. Crowds cheering him on. Flags waving. Ever since Grandma Joan sent him the autobiography of Armstrong that first Christmas after his surgery, Trevor made him one of his idols. He'd read the book numerous times over the past five years.

He continued to have problems at school, so these bike rides around the neighborhood helped him work off his frustrations. His counselor, Hildy Brown*, had met with his mom a while back. Brown told her that he'd have to get a handle on all of his absences. His mother had explained that most of the absences were for doctors' appointments. Hildy said that she personally understood and sympathized, but the school had a strict absentee policy, and she was concerned that he might not pass. Also, she had told his mom about the guitar class he dropped.

He had been so demoralized by not being able to learn how to play an instrument that appealed to him a lot. The steel strings cut through his skin. He had trouble remembering the chord progressions. He admitted to her that his level of frustration could be excessive. But so much in his life was frustrating that things like this pushed him to the edge. In any case, this led him to see a therapist, who used to be an oncologist and now specialized in kids and teens with cancer. She'd helped him sort through some of his anxiety and problems, but not all. He never told her about shooting blanks. Or that he still ate alone just about every day at school.

The doctor tried to get him to zero in on the good things that were happening to him. There were many of those, including being involved in the Idaho Childhood Cancer Strategic Plan, giving the keynote speech last January in front of three hundred of St. Luke's Hospital's most philanthropic donors, reading the Downwinder Proclamation at the very successful Downwinders Conference, and being asked to be the Youth Ambassador to the National Disease Cluster Alliance (NDCA). NDCA was Floyd Sands' new foundation, created in reaction to the way he'd been shunted aside by government authorities when he tried to get them to do something about the cancer cluster in Fallon, Nevada.

Trevor knew that anyone looking through the window of his life would see that he had a full plate of civic duties and a satisfyingly altruistic life in the limelight. He just needed to find a way to get that public life to mesh with his solitary personal life.

He parked his bike in the garage, stashed his helmet and shoes, and went inside. He freed Elliot from his crate and romped with him on the patio. A few minutes later, he went in to check the mail. Among the big stack, Trevor noticed an envelope addressed to him from NDCA. He thought it probably was a notice for their next board meeting in Arizona.

Instead, found a letter from Floyd Sands. He took it into the kitchen and sat down at the table along with a big glass of milk and some fruit.

He drained half the glass and then began to read the missive addressed to Floyd's friends and colleagues:

> *During my daughter Stephanie's 26-month struggle with leukemia, one of the hardest things for me to deal with personally was the realization that I was utterly powerless to help her in many ways. Parents of children fighting cancer are only able to provide love, comfort, reassurance, and support; we are not able to bring about a cure for our child, nor are we able to relieve their suffering...when our child is struck down by cancer we realize... how impotent, how completely unable to help our child we really are.*
>
> *It's much the same for a community experiencing a disease cluster. A year and a half into Stephanie's struggle, I learned of the Fallon Childhood Leukemia Cluster, and Stephanie's case was soon included. As time wore on, I watched and worked with the Nevada State Health Division, US CDC/ATSDR, state and local governmental agencies, and others as they conducted their various studies, public meetings, PR events, news releases, and public utterances. At the beginning, I believed that a genuine scientific study of the Fallon Cluster had been undertaken, that our governmental agencies were "on the ball" in doing the right things at the right times and for the right reasons. I witnessed the actions of the Nevada State Health Division and others as they slowly drove a wedge between the community and the Fallon leukemia families from their own neighbors and supporters. I witnessed these agencies gradually desensitize, then dehumanize, and finally demonize the Fallon leukemia children and their families...I watched as these agencies announced their utter failure in determining the causes and contributors to the Fallon cluster. I watched as these agencies fairly reveled in their failure. I watched as the Fallon Childhood Leukemia Cluster became these agencies' 109th consecutive failure at cancer cluster investigation...*

Trevor crushed the pages, dropped them onto the table, and sat there in a state of shock. Was everything he and his mother doing for nothing? Would they find the same official doors slammed in their faces, too? Would they find themselves more isolated from their communities even as they tried to help them?

"Goddammit!" he screamed again and again. He got up, knocking over his chair, and stormed out of the room, with Elliot skittering after him.

Charlie came home and found her kitchen in disarray. A half drunk glass of milk. Uneaten cut-up fruit. An overturned chair. All the lights still on. No TV coming from Trevor's room or the library. No Elliot.

Then she noticed the crumpled papers on the table. Her first thought was that Trevor must have gotten another court summons from Ballard. Once he broke off all contact with his father, the man began treating his son like an enemy, exacerbating the already awful situation.

She picked up the papers, straightened them out, and noticed the NDCA letterhead. She read Floyd's heart-wrenching memo. Tears came to her eyes. He was such a good friend and kind soul. She hated to see how he was suffering despite his successes as an advocate. From their first conversation, they had formed a bond: parents of children with cancer, and a shared goal to find out why so many small towns like Fallon and McCall had such an anomaly of children diagnosed with the disease. He counseled her about doing her own survey and commiserated when she told him how difficult the state authorities were making it for her. The Cancer Analysis Working Group in Idaho (CAWG) insisted that they would only accept her health survey results if the people questioned gave her all of their personal information, including their social-security numbers. Sands had agreed that this was just par for the course for local, state, and federal agencies, whose main job was to keep the average citizen from getting information that could expose a cancer cluster in their community.

After Floyd established the NDCA with Dee Lewis, a determined California advocate for the study of cancer clusters, Charlie joined their Board of Directors. She laughingly thought of herself and Trevor as "the players to be named later" on an otherwise impressive board, consisting of a national who's-who of environmental scientists, doctors, and lay activists, all of whom believed that now was the time to earnestly expand research into disease clusters, even if the federal government would not.

She found Trevor asleep under a quilt on the sofa in the library. Elliot was nestled around his chest and neck. He looked up at her with his big, soulful eyes as she entered the room.

"Hey, boy," she whispered.

His tail wagging woke Trevor. He groaned. "Oh, hi," he said.

"I saw Floyd's letter."

"Pretty upsetting, huh?"

She sat down in the wingback chair next to the sofa. "Par for the course. No one ever said what we're trying to do would be easy."

Trevor got up and stretched. He was even taller. Still not much of a stubble. But he'd been working out at the gym and his shoulders appeared broader. "I guess," he said.

"Want to talk about it?"

He shook his head. "So, what's for dinner?"

That night, Charlie phoned Floyd. He was happy to hear from her.

"I just wanted you to know that not everything is bleak. I'm not sure you heard, but we prevailed in the asphalt plant lawsuit. Not only were they denied the permit, they got a huge fine."

"Congratulations. Chip away at them one lawsuit at a time. We're still embroiled in lawsuits and anger here in Fallon. It's escalating. Getting really ugly, as you know from my letter."

"Another great piece of news. Divine Strake was shelved—*for good*."

"Of course, I heard about that a while back. You're on a roll, Charlie. You should step up your investigation in McCall. Finally get all those angry citizens to join in the bigger fight."

"I was thinking about that, too. They seem ripe."

"Maybe hand over your information to Mary Wood and let her do a bigger class-action suit."

"Except I wouldn't join it. I never want to step into a courtroom again if I don't have to. There must be some other way."

"Then I've got two words for you: Mark Witten."

Charlie was acquainted with Dr. Mark Witten, a portly, garrulous, middle-aged research professor of pediatric toxicology at the University of Arizona in Tucson. He was on the board of directors of NDCA with her and Trevor. Having had the pleasure of perusing his *curriculum vitae*, Charlie knew that Dr. Witten had many stellar accomplishments, including the publication of dozens of scientific papers in the area of pediatric toxins and researching cancer clusters. According to Floyd, Dr. Witten and his team were using tree-core analysis to make major breakthroughs in getting to the cause of the leukemia cancer cluster in Fallon, Nevada, and several other locations around the country.

She promised Floyd that she would contact Dr. Witten.

"Of course, I remember you," Witten said when Charlie phoned him the next week. "How could I forget such a beautiful woman?"

"And here I thought I was memorable for my intellect!"

He laughed, a sound that matched his booming, baritone speaking voice. "Floyd mentioned I might be hearing from you."

"Then you know that I still want to use Floyd's questionnaire to do a field survey of McCall's health history in the last decade. And I wanted to know if you possibly could add to that an overall study of the impact of environmental toxins on the McCall area specifically and Valley County generally?"

"Have you done any other testing of the area?"

"Sort of," she equivocated. "Back in the fall of 2004, I funded a water study of the lake. Doug Freeland, a diver out of Coeur d'Alene, did the work using my boat and rented instruments. The results of the sediment samples came back inconclusive. Freeland did the best he could, but he had another commitment, which caused a four-day delay in getting the samples to the lab."

"Water studies aren't always that reliable anyway. In fact, the tree-core preparation my partner and I do is a far better method of analysis. We have scientific papers recently published that are gaining acceptance in academic circles."

"I've heard that before—about how important it is to have other scientists validate your results."

"That's what peer review is all about. Getting your work published in a reputable journal. If the scientific community turns its back on you, you're done."

She understood. In fact, in the spring of 2004, Charlie had gone on what turned into a wild-goose chase to the University of Nevada at Reno, where she met with a team of well-respected scientists, most of whom had worked on highly publicized cancer cluster cases and at Superfund sites. At every turn in their session with Charlie, they stressed the importance of conclusions resulting from accepted scientific methods that were publishable, or she'd be wasting her money. When she queried them about the cost of such studies, the price quoted to achieve her goal was ludicrous to the extreme. "I think they thought I was Charlie Fort Knox rather than Smith! The U.S. Government couldn't even afford these guys."

"It's the U.S. Government who pays them the big bucks, Charlie. This is the essence of the problem. Unless the situation is superfund-size, or as big as the cluster in Fallon and cannot be shoved under the rug, they're not coming in to investigate and spend all that money."

"That's awful!"

"It's reality. An individual, or a small community group, has nowhere to turn because they don't have the wherewithal. That's where Paul and I come in. We are infinitely more affordable but just as reliable. We hope to change the paradigm. Already this year, we've done tree-core studies in Massachusetts, Alabama, Arizona, Kansas and New York. At this time we're involved in nine different studies. From what Floyd told me, you sound like you need our help, too. My colleague, Paul Sheppard, and I can fly out to McCall at the end of the summer to do some preliminary sampling."

CHAPTER THIRTY-ONE

I n anticipation of Witten and Sheppard's arrival in August, Trevor and Charlie began to plan on spending a few weeks in McCall. She contacted her friend, Dave Holland, to find and rent a central location where the health survey data could be dropped off and collated. A local McCall businessman, Dave was eager to help because his own son died of brain cancer in 2004 at the age of twenty-two. At that time, Charlie had introduced him to Mike Stewart, who interviewed the man for the *Long Valley Advocate*. He told Mike that he was committed to doing whatever was necessary to find out the truth about what caused his son's illness. It couldn't be genetic, he argued, since the boy's best friend was diagnosed with brain cancer at the same time. This young man's cancer was in remission at the time of Holland's interview in 2004. Just this year, though, it came back, and he committed suicide. Charlie spoke to Dr. Harris about the tragedy. He informed her that both young men had been avid Boy Scouts and had camped out often in the areas all around Valley County, including Camp Morrison, which had been threatened by the 1994 fire. And still another of those boys' scouting friends also was fighting brain cancer.

A few weeks before they were due to roll into McCall, Charlie got a frantic call from Dave Holland. The still-bereaved father told her he could no longer be involved with executing the survey. He didn't have to say aloud what she knew he was thinking: As much as he cared, he feared for his time-share business.

Then Else Fuller popped onto Charlie's radar screen.

"I wish you still lived in McCall," Charlie lamented when Else phoned. "We need someone like you up there to corral the cats and handle this survey."

"No way. I'm glad I got the hell out of Dodge! I have some unfortunate news to tell you," she said.

"What?"

"I have two tumors on my spine and need surgery."

"*Tumors?* Holy crap! Cancer?"

"The doctors seem certain they're benign. But I tell you, Charlie, you're on to something up there. How can it be a coincidence that I bought a house in McCall from a woman who got cancer and died, and now I have this? I can hardly walk from the pain."

"I'm just relieved you're not living there anymore to get more exposure. Still sharing the house in Reno with that gorgeous grandson of yours? Trevor's been following him. How's he doing with the Atlanta Braves?"

"Well, he blew his arm out, and he's on the disabled list for a few weeks. As far as sharing a house with a twenty-five-year old: it's different. But it's hard to enjoy anything when you're in such pain."

———

Charlie worked diligently, trying to put together a new group of motivated citizens in McCall to do the day-to-day work on the survey. No luck. The questionnaire was shelved. Probably for good this time.

Then Mark Witten phoned her with more unsettling developments. Paul Sheppard had an emergency in his family and wouldn't be able to make it up to McCall.

"Look, without Paul there to do the job of collecting the tree cores and notating, there's very little I could do."

"You have no idea how crushing a disappointment this is."

"Don't be discouraged, Charlie. Contamination doesn't leave a tree. We'll make plans to do the investigation next year."

She wasn't holding her breath.

⌒

Thrown into a funk, Charlie sat at her desk in the family room after that call from Dr. Witten, staring vacantly into space. Every plan for McCall seemed so unsettled. Every idea so difficult to execute from down here in Boise. Had she run her course in trying to solve the environmental dilemma of McCall? It felt awful contemplating giving up on the place.

Now what? As she often did these days when faced with a bit of extra time or a gnawing sense that she wasn't making enough headway, she turned on her computer and began going through her e-mails. Her inbox was filled, as usual, with requests for help from people in other states.

Today there was also an e-mail from NDCA with an attachment. She clicked on it. It was a long document detailing scores of hot spots cropping up nationally in small communities like McCall. Those who were suffering were generally unable to protect themselves against environmental contamination because they lived in towns too tiny to get noticed, and they often were too poor to mount a battle of any kind.

She read on, learning about an ongoing fight in Maricopa County, Arizona. The residents became worried in the late 1980s that groundwater contamination from the nearby Phoenix Goodyear Airport North might have been the cause of an alarming number of children dying of pediatric leukemia. The documented outbreak showed twice the number of cases as what would normally be expected. More than ten years after initial inquiries from the community, a public health assessment from the Agency for Toxic Substances and Disease Registry in 2000 reported that there were no <u>statistically</u> elevated incidences of total cancers or leukemia. The folks in the area kept suffering, and according to officials with NDCA, this town was now on their list for further investigation for suspected cancer clusters.

Then there was Kettleman City, California. It provided another case study for Charlie of a small town suffering because of its proximity to industry that produced toxic wastes. An alarming number of birth defects and cancer cases there prompted residents to protest a 1,600-acre landfill just 3.5 miles away—a facility that was permitted to take in household and hazardous waste, including substances that were proven to cause cancer. In a 2006 letter to the US Department of Energy, Senator Barbara Boxer of California cited concerns that the landfill was taking in radioactive soil from the rocket engineering company, Rocketdyne. Landfill operators denied that their facility impacted the nearby community and subsequently applied for a permit to expand their operations. The facility, operated by Waste Management, Inc., was too powerful, and they prevailed. For now. NDCA was taking this fight on, too.

In October 2001, in Prairie Grove, Arkansas, the Arkansas Department of Health began investigating a potential cluster of testicular cancer, with cases nearly five times the national rate. The town sat near a now-closed nuclear reactor, a low-level radioactive landfill, and a poultry plant. Results of the study were released the following year, concluding that contaminated soil at the children's elementary school did not contain levels that would harm their health. Since then, fifty families had pooled their limited resources to hire environmental attorneys, because they believed the cancers are tied to the environmental abuses of those nearby businesses.

According to the NDCA report, the East Coast of the United States appeared to be suffering as much from hot spot outbreaks as the rest of the country. In Victor, New York, the New York State Department of Health released a study that found no link between an unusually high number of brain cancer cases and contaminants in the area's groundwater. They specifically mentioned no connection between the brain-cancer cases and the contamination of groundwater by the toxic industrial solvent trichloroethene, or TCE. "This type of study cannot prove any cause-and-effect relationships," state health officials wrote in a four-page summary mailed to town residents in conjunction with the report's release. Rebuffed by the governmental agencies, those outraged citizens turned to NDCA.

Charlie got up and paced the house. She was so furious. All of these examples, and more, confirmed for her what she already knew from her own experience with McCall and the Downwinders in tiny Emmett: that small towns got short shrift with cancer registries and health agencies looking for cluster possibilities. The requirement that certain base population figures be of sufficient numbers, in order to ensure a scientific sampling of cases versus residents, was always the sticking point.

She sat down at her desk again, this time with a pen and paper handy. She began to jot ideas down for her and Trevor's next speeches. She wrote: "Like children, who are more susceptible to cancer caused by exposure to environmental toxins, small communities are often more vulnerable because of their size. Similarly, those communities often lack the regulatory oversight of larger communities when it comes to pollution from nearby industrial operations—the kind that often seek out quiet, isolated enclaves to do their business."

In addition to the cases she had just perused in the NDCA document, Charlie had more examples of her own. Mothers from small towns around the country had called her, begging for her assistance. One of these women was Stephanie Carper from Trenton, Ohio. Their neighborhood was near a nuclear plant, and now her fifteen-year-old daughter had thyroid cancer. She was one of many cases in a ten-mile radius. Stephanie formed a community group, ThyKidz, to look into the suspected cancer cluster. Like Charlie and Tona, Stephanie learned that her town was statistically irrelevant. They were getting nowhere with officials. She wanted Charlie's advice and requested she join their board of directors. Charlie demurred on the board position but said she'd continue to advise from afar. "Make as much noise as possible," she had counseled Stephanie.

A mother from Athens, Georgia, and another from a rural area in Pennsylvania had recently contacted her, asking the same questions as Stephanie from Ohio. "Be proactive. Make as much noise as possible."

Charlie spent the evening consumed with thoughts about how to make her own noise: something beyond what she and Trevor already were doing; something that would finally change the status quo.

She fell asleep quickly for once, but then endured a series of unsettling dreams that woke her up. She tried to piece together what they were about. In one vignette, she was a little girl about five. Maybe six. She was in a desert. The wind kept blowing dust into her face. Into her hair. Suddenly she was running. Chasing a colorful scarf. It was just out of reach. Then a man was chasing her. She felt scared. It wasn't a game. He was catching up. She saw that it was her father. Not the old man who died a few years ago, but her younger, handsome, Errol Flynn–look-alike dad. He was calling out to her, "Why didn't you tell me what he did to you, so I could help you?"

She threw on a robe and padded into the kitchen. It was a little before four a.m. Sat there sipping a cup of tea. Thinking. The desert felt like Barstow, where she had lived when she was four. In a trailer. Her mother's clean clothes always blew off the line. She was forever chasing the sheets into the desert. Her mother made her wear a scarf not unlike the one in her dream. She remembered now that her brother once told her that he could see the mushroom clouds from that trailer when the bomb tests were taking place in the early '50s. But her dad was telling her something important. It felt like it had to do with David Diffenderfer.

Another vignette suddenly popped into her consciousness: she was running again. This time she was running from David Diffenderfer. She wasn't sure if it was before her father dream or after. David kept saying, "It's only hide-and-seek; it's only a game," as he chased her into a trailer. It was dusty inside. But the trailer morphed into that Encino barn. Horse manure everywhere. She could smell it. Feel it rubbed on her arms. Suddenly her father was there handing her the scarf. He yelled over the howling wind, "Why didn't you tell me? I could have saved you."

Back in bed, Charlie huddled under the covers. She couldn't fall asleep, nor could she stop trying to figure out her dad's dream message. Stop running? Speak out? Get it out?

Should she finally look for David Diffendefer? Was that the message of her dream? Could she confront him after fifty years? Would cracking open the hard rock of the past be like one of the elements she frequently read about—resting quietly in its original composition, but when exposed to air and water and sunlight, it reacts and turns into a more deadly compound? Would it destroy her? Her dreams were telling her to let it air. Crack apart that rock. Her waking self had been telling her for years that it was better to let it remain intact and buried.

———

It started to rain. She got out of bed and stood at the window, watching the drops pockmark the pond. *I have to know*, she said to herself and sat down at the computer. She scoured the Internet, seeking information about statutes of limitation for reporting sexual molestation charges. She learned that in her case, the limitation probably had passed by now. That afternoon, she contacted a friend in the Boise Police Department to corroborate what she learned. She was right.

What if my dream was more complicated? What if it's not just about exposing David Diffenderfer but about exposing abuse? That felt right to her. For some time she'd been thinking about the concept of abuse. To her mind, there was a similarity between a kid being sexually molested and a kid being physically molested by toxins in the environment. In either instance, abuse strips a basic element out of their lives—trust. Abused children were forced to learn much too young that no mom, no dad, and no doctor would save them from the pain they must endure alone at the hand of their predator.

Afraid to consciously dwell on how she never deserved the horrors of sexual molestation or the psychological aftermath of repressed rage, through the years Charlie had gutted it out the only way she knew— alone. She tried to improve her life, tried to pretend what happened was a bad dream, and she made many wrong choices because the effects of the repression lingered like a hangover and clouded her thinking. Like Charlie, childhood cancer patients never did anything to deserve the horrors they faced every day after being attacked by their predator. She decided that she must never stop trying to expose *this* form of physical and emotional abuse. Created by a careless world, this "cancer bully" increasingly lurked in every neighborhood and attacked the most vulnerable among them.

Thank God no statutes of limitation exist in this arena, Charlie thought, *because if it takes the rest of my life, I'm determined to expose these predators.* But what could she do about it right now? It came to her when she glanced at an innocuous flyer lying on her desk amidst her growing pile of environmental documents and other papers. It was an announcement that September was National Childhood Cancer Awareness Month, and it suggested ways to publicize that fact.

Charlie remembered putting aside this call-to-action a few days earlier when everything else in her life seemed on the front burner. She mulled over the idea of doing a Childhood Cancer Awareness outreach.

She hoped to start with the mayor of Boise and get him to agree to introduce a childhood cancer proclamation in September. She also wanted to broach the subject with the governor's office. And the proclamations had to be read in a big public venue, not during a congressional session, or nobody would know. However, what kind of an event would be best?

Charlie convened a meeting with some local women and men who helped her from time to time. They brainstormed possible approaches and then unanimously decided to do a walk for awareness.

"It has to feature Trevor," one of the women insisted. "He's the face of childhood cancer in Idaho now."

That night Charlie and Trevor discussed it.

"I don't know, Mom. Giving a speech is one thing. This..."

"I know it'll be a bigger commitment than anything you've done before," she said. "Your name, your face on the line. But it'll be a huge honor, too."

A week later, Trevor returned from one of his bike rides around the neighborhood and said, "I'll do it. I *want* to do it. A walk is perfect, Mom. Remember when my dad said kids would laugh at me because I walk funny? I guess I'll be getting the last laugh."

They decided to call it **Trevor's Trek.**

CHAPTER THIRTY-TWO

Trevor was up at first light on the morning of the walk. He immediately hopped out of bed and pulled back the drapes to see if it was raining, as the weatherman had predicted for this momentous Saturday, September 15, 2007.

"Wrong again!" he sang out to Elliot, relieved to see sunlight peeking through thick ribbons of mostly white clouds. With his dog snuggled in the crook of his arm, Trevor lounged on top of the covers a while longer, a million happy thoughts cart-wheeling through his mind.

He couldn't believe how far he'd come since that awful day five years before when he was told he had brain cancer. Back then, he thought having cancer was an absolute death sentence, and he couldn't see how he would live to see fourteen, let alone have a chance to drive a car, or graduate high school...now there was a future on his horizon. He sometimes even allowed the thought: The sky's the limit.

He took a shower and dressed in jeans and a T-shirt. He slipped on his Trevor's Trek baseball cap and checked his watch. *Hours to go. Better let Mom sleep a while longer.*

He made breakfast for himself and Elliot then lingered at the table going over the brochure that he, his mom, and their committee had put together for the Trek. That brochure had found its way into most of the hospitals and clinics around Boise and many other cities in Idaho, along with the large, colorful posters they had commissioned.

He'd already received extensive newspaper coverage and several appearances on TV with Mark Johnson to hype the Trek. This morning he was scheduled to do two radio interviews with popular disc jockeys before heading out to the venue at St. Luke's Hospital, and he intended to use part of the information inside the vibrant pamphlet:

> *Sometimes the greatest distance traveled is accomplished in just a few steps. After Trevor Smith's surgery for brain cancer in November 2002, at the age of thirteen he couldn't even get out of bed. When he finally took his first steps, it was with someone holding onto him. During his chemotherapy and radiation treatments, he became too weak to stand up. When he took his first steps again, his balance was impaired and he had a limp (a side effect of chemotherapy). Facing a change to a new school during his treatments, he was told not to do it; the kids would laugh at him because he "walked funny." But he went to the new school anyway, deciding that if he could face up to cancer, he could face up to a few kids who might make fun of him.*
>
> *Trevor Smith is a survivor. At the age of seventeen, he has become a forceful voice for the children of Idaho who are suffering from cancer. Trevor, and all the other childhood cancer patients who will be alongside him at the first annual Trevor's Trek on Saturday, September 15, 2007, invite you to: Walk a Mile in Our Shoes.*
>
> *Remember, a few steps can turn into a mile. A mile can become a milestone by raising public awareness of the alarming rise of childhood cancer in Idaho.*

The radio interviews were at the Peak Broadcasting building across the street from Boise State University. The building housed multiple stations. Each one had an anteroom with its name lettered on the door and a glassed-in, soundproof cubicle where the deejays did their thing.

"Here's the first one," Charlie said as they came to the "Chris and John Morning Talk Show."

They went inside and sat in the cramped anteroom for a few minutes. Trevor was so nervous that it felt like waiting for a doctor's appointment.

It wasn't long before John came out to greet them.

"Hi, Trevor. Glad to have you on the show," John said. "This means a lot to me. I'm a cancer survivor, too."

Both he and Charlie followed the talk show host into the glassed-in cubicle.

Trevor's nerves edged up another notch as he adjusted the microphone up against his mouth. It made him uncomfortable. However, Chris and John were such jovial hosts that they eventually pulled him fully into their repartee. At every opportunity, the two jokesters continued to plug the walk. Just when Trevor was starting to feel really comfortable with the easy format of talking to the DJs and callers, his time on the air was up.

Before he knew it, he was ensconced in the cubicle of the second station, a country showcase. While he was on the air, Charlie wandered the halls and managed to pull off a third interview.

"You were *unbelievably* amazing," Charlie exclaimed as they walked back to the car.

"Let's not get carried away. Just plain old *amazing* will do!" Trevor shot back.

"No, really…"

Charlie's cell phone buzzed. She put it on speaker so Trevor could hear. An official at St. Luke's was calling to say that a well-known Boise philanthropist had listened to Trevor's interview on the radio. The old woman was so touched by his story and his commitment to help other children that she was changing her will to donate money to the pediatric oncology center of the Mountain States Tumor Institute.

"See! I told you people were going to be moved by you."

"Let's hope I moved them off their butts to come out and support the Trek."

———

Charlie was relieved to see that volunteers at the hospital were setting up the registration tables and putting out balloons and the Trevor's Trek baseball caps she designed to give out to the participants. In addition to hospital staff, she was fortunate to get a slew of volunteers from the local Idaho chapter of Make-A-Wish.

A few weeks into the planning of the Trek, Charlie had received a call from the local director of Make-A-Wish Foundation. The woman said she heard the Smiths were staging a walk for childhood cancer awareness, and her organization was impressed with what they'd done so far. She asked if they could become involved. Charlie supported Make-A-Wish and had great respect for their organization. She was flattered to know that such an esteemed charity wanted to partner with her and Trevor in their neophyte outing. And with so many details left undone, their offer was a welcome turning point. Once Make-A-Wish came on board as a co-sponsor, Charlie was able to use their licenses to cut through all the red tape that a beginning organization faced. In addition, they offered the use of their all-around expertise in outreach to assure that an event of the magnitude Charlie envisioned became a success.

"Mom, it looks like the only people here are volunteers. And the walk starts in a hour," Trevor whispered.

Charlie reminded him, "It's still early. Go mingle and have some fun."

———◠———

For days, Trevor had worried about no one coming to his Trek. This felt like his worst fears coming true. Even so, it wasn't as though no one was there. It just was... sparse. At the moment, a few of the early arrivers were approaching him. They wanted to hug him, congratulate him, take pictures with him. He patiently posed and chatted with all comers. He looked over toward the sign-in table and noticed that more people were registering. In fact, it was starting to look like a "happening."

Relieved, he strode toward a sloping section of the lawn where a larger group was congregating. A Hispanic woman intercepted him. With her was an adorable little girl with long, black curls who clutched a Trevor's Trek poster. The woman took it from her, unfurled it and pointed out one photo showing several young cancer patients inside footprints right next to the words: Walk a mile in our shoes.

"That's me; that's me!" the little girl exclaimed to Trevor.

"Really?" he said. He picked her up and looked at the photo with her. He couldn't believe how light and fragile she felt in his arms. *Would she be back next year?* He let her down gently, forcing the somber thoughts out of his head.

By the eleven o'clock start time of the Trek, Trevor's fears that no one would come out subsided completely: over two-hundred people were already signed in, with more arriving. A sea of Trevor's Trek hats bobbed everywhere. Healthy walkers mingled with young cancer survivors, some of whom were in wheelchairs.

By this time, Trevor was champing at the bit. The excitement in the air was electric. Contagious. Three off-duty Boise cops on cycles revved their motors at the head of the line. When they exchanged their helmets for Trevor's Trek caps, the crowd applauded.

Trevor took his place at the front of the throng. He caught sight of a banner some people were carrying with photos of bald kids dying of cancer who were too weak to attend this morning. *And I'm doing this for them*, Trevor thought, pointing his finger at the banner before taking a long stride forward, feeling the crowd behind him.

Their route began at St. Luke's Hospital and would end about one mile later at the steps of the City Hall. Even that short distance would be quite an accomplishment for most childhood cancer patients.

~

Music blasted out from speakers on the steps of City Hall when the marchers reached the end of their trek. Trevor spoke first, greeting one and all on this sunny, special day. He felt calm and in control as he thanked all those who had taken time out of their Saturday to help him publicize this essential quest. He then introduced a series of invited guests.

Patti Moran spoke about the work of CCAI and how much Trevor's input was helping to formulate the childhood-cancer portion of the state's strategic plan.

A grandmother told her story. A choked-up father told his.

Then Boise Superintendent of Schools, Dr. Stan Olsen, took the microphone to express his gratitude for this effort and to proclaim his solidarity with Trevor in his fight for childhood cancer awareness.

Trevor was especially humbled to have the superintendent there. If Mark Johnson once provided an important stepping stone in Trevor's life soon after his surgery by giving him purpose, lifting his spirits and leading him out of the abject depression he was suffering, then Stan Olsen came to represent yet another important stepping stone. They first began talking a few months ago about the need for this Trek. As they continued to meet and discuss Trevor's plans, Olsen drew Trevor out about his hopes and dreams. Sensing the depth of empathy in the former teacher, Trevor felt comfortable unburdening himself.

He confessed to the utter isolation he experienced once he re-entered school after his surgery and initial treatments. He explained how it grew even when he was giving speeches and becoming a public figure. He told Stan how dispiriting it was to know he would never be part of a normal teen world. Although he qualified for the golf team, he tired easily walking the course and never felt as if he could keep up with the others.

In class, Trevor found it difficult to concentrate and recall things he used to remember easily. Yet he felt that his teachers, who always treated him well, still couldn't truly understand the extent of his disabilities and clearly had no idea how to address them.

Olsen listened and listened and listened. And then, like a good teacher, he let Trevor come up with the solution for other teenagers like him who suffered a debilitating disease and then came back to walk in the shadows of every high school in Boise.

Their discussions led to the conclusion to pursue a new program for public schools, one they named Trevor's Trek Peer Program. Their goal: to establish a safe harbor for cancer survivors in Boise schools and to eliminate any feeling of isolation or bullying.

Dr. Olsen told Trevor that through their friendship he now believed that more childhood cancer awareness was crucial in Idaho, and it must begin with the teachers in the classroom and extend to students who weren't sick. To that end, the superintendant added another component to their proposed peer program: Trevor's Trek Mentors. Trevor was elated that Dr. Olsen wanted to reward those healthy students who volunteered to help recovering students gain acceptance by giving them community service credit.

The superintendant helped bring out Trevor's compassionate side, calling on him to counsel any student, no matter what grade, who was feeling lost or isolated upon his or her return to school after cancer treatment. Trevor now had friends of all ages who thirsted for his empathic counsel. He loved being able to provide the safety net for them that he never got.

Now today, Superintendent Olsen stood before this large crowd, publicly proclaiming his support for Trevor and Trevor's Trek.

At last, Mayor Dave Bieter took the microphone. Right from the get-go, he agreed to preside over the Trek and present the City Proclamation to Trevor. When Trevor and Charlie spoke with him in his office, he stated emphatically that he was honored to be involved in the inaugural event. In fact, he told Trevor and Charlie that he was grateful that finally someone was doing something to create the much-needed awareness of the rise of childhood cancer in Idaho.

Trevor moved to the side while Mayor Bieter read the City Proclamation naming September Childhood Cancer Awareness Month in Boise. Bieter quipped at the end of his presentation, "It's a good thing that this outstanding, accomplished young man is too young to run for public office, or I'd be out of a job!"

Trevor felt heat infuse his face. He was sure he was blushing. While certainly unnecessary, Trevor appreciated the mayor's accolades. He looked for his mom and found her at the end of the front row. She had a grin on her face a mile wide.

As his eyes scanned the crush of people, Trevor spied a man at the back who reminded him of his father. Suddenly, Ballard was front and center in Trevor's consciousness. He flashed on an intense memory of his father crying and rubbing his leg at St. Luke's Hospital, the day the doctors told Trevor he had brain cancer. It was the last time his father had touched him in kindness and concern.

During those moments of anxiety about no one showing up for the Trek, Trevor occasionally wondered about his father barging in on the ceremony. Would there be fireworks after having nothing at all to do with his dad for so long now? Would the day be ruined? Of course, Ballard must have heard about this event. It was widely publicized: on television, in every newspaper in the state, featured in the only newspaper in McCall, on posters in windows of many local businesses in the mountain hamlet. And his sisters broke their silence to e-mail him recently to say they had heard about Trevor's Trek all the way in San Diego.

Right at this instant, Trevor wanted his father to hear Mayor Bieter's compliments. He wished his dad had bothered to show up. But Ballard Smith was a no-show. *So what else is new?*

Trevor returned to the moment and forced a smile onto his face, realizing he must walk forward and take the proclamation from the mayor and say a few words of thanks.

Inside, though, he felt unnerved by the realization at how his father's negative energy, even if only in his mind, still could undermine his happiness at his happiest moment.

After Mayor Bieter so readily agreed to take part in the inaugural Trevor's Trek, Charlie decided to shoot for the moon and called Governor Butch Otter's office with a similar request. His staff agreed to come on board, too.

A few weeks before the walk, she took the state proclamation wording to the governor's office where she met with him in his inner sanctum. As always, he greeted her with charm and warmth, agreeing to do whatever was needed to name September Childhood Cancer Awareness Month for the state of Idaho.

"Charlie, I didn't know Idaho had this health problem until now. Why do you think this is happening?"

"Well, Governor Otter, I think we have some environmental issues going on here in this state that could be contributing to our children getting cancer."

His back stiffened, and his demeanor cooled. He countered defensively that there wasn't any more cancer now than before; they merely had better and earlier methods of detecting the disease.

Charlie bit her tongue to keep from telling him a parable she had read in the opening pages of the book *Living Downstream* by Dr. Sandra Steingraber. It was a story about a village on the banks of a river, where the townspeople saw a body floating by one day. They were too stunned to react, and the body swept downstream out of their reach. A few days later, another body passed by, but this time a few people were more alert and jumped in to pull the floater out of the water. They couldn't save him, however. After that, the townspeople mobilized to devise every manner of contraption for pulling the increasing number of bodies out of the river. Eventually, they invented impressive methods of saving a lot of them. But no one in the village ever asked the most important question: *Who* was throwing the bodies into the river in the first place?

Of course, Charlie's experiences in the past few years had caused her to ask that question. She never stopped asking it, and by now she could boast an impressive mountain of statistics to show who some of the perpetrators might be. Certainly she could disprove the governor's assertions.

But she also had learned the kid-gloves approach with the naysayers and the many doubters in Idaho. Thus, she backed off and took what she could get for now from the governor: his name on the Childhood Cancer Proclamation.

A few days later, Trevor followed up with a call to ask the governor if he would be willing to read the state proclamation at the Boise State Homecoming game which was to take place the same night as Trevor's

Trek. Otter loved the idea. With some close associates working on making it all come together, the Smiths managed to get the president of Boise State University, Bob Kustra, to take part in the ceremony as well.

———

The Boise State stadium was filled to capacity on that balmy September night. More than thirty-five thousand rabid fans were in their seats waiting for the start of the game. Before that, however, something else important would take place. Anxious for that magical moment to begin, Charlie stood fidgeting on the sidelines with Trevor. Soon her son would be walking out onto that famous blue turf between President Kustra and Governor Otter.

"I'm so freaking scared I feel like I'm going to barf," Trevor said.

"You beat back cancer," Charlie reminded him. "You don't have to fear a few thousand people in the stands."

Trevor smiled gratefully at her with a mouthful of white teeth that were finally free of braces. Charlie couldn't believe how handsome he was. How healthy he looked.

"It's time," an official told Trevor.

"I'm so ready," he turned and said to her.

Those words took Charlie back five years. *I'm so ready* was what he said over and over before they wheeled him away from her for brain surgery.

How different his life was now. Hers, too. Charlie watched as Trevor took his place between the two stalwart men and marched to the fifty-yard line. Trevor's voice was strong and clear as it reverberated throughout the field and trailed into the night air. Charlie felt as if the whole world could hear her son.

Trevor gave a brief but impassioned speech about his own cancer and why it was so important to acknowledge that this disease's attack on Idaho's children was growing each and every year. The audience cheered his courage. Governor Otter read the proclamation and handed it to Trevor.

Engulfed in the sustained roar of the appreciative crowd, Charlie felt the glory of the moment pass over her like a sudden gust of wind. As he returned toward the sidelines, Charlie could see so clearly back to a vision of Trevor without his hair. Trevor retching and crying out for the mercy of death to relieve his suffering. His taking those first awkward steps and stumbling. Getting stronger and still having to fight off his father. Trevor alone at school. Injecting himself with the shots that might make him a man. Planning his Trek for the benefit of others. Traveling so very far since he was her little boy on the lake. Her son. The young man, she realized now, who taught her how to grow up.

Trevor's Trek Walk for Childhood Cancer Awareness: September 15, 2007, in Boise, Idaho.

Dr. Stan Olsen, Boise School District Superintendent: Speaking at the first Trevor's Trek Walk for Childhood Cancer Awareness in Boise.

*Boise City Hall: Trevor
greets participants
at the conclusion
of Trevor's Trek,
September 15, 2007.*

*Trevor and Mayor David
Bieter: Trevor receives the
proclamation for childhood
cancer awareness from
Boise Mayor David Bieter,
September 15, 2007.*

*Trevor Speaks Out: Boise Mayor
David Bieter (right) and Trevor
(center right), with Idaho
Governor C.L. "Butch" Otter
(center left) and First Lady
Lori Otter (left), at the Boise
State University homecoming
game, just after Trevor's Trek,
September 15, 2007.*

Never doubt that a small group of thoughtful,
committed citizens can change the world. Indeed,
it is the only thing that ever has.

Margaret Mead

Part Four:

MAKING A DIFFERENCE

CHAPTER THIRTY-THREE

Summer, 2008

Trevor was in an especially upbeat mood as he maneuvered the twists and turns of the road. He and his mother were on their way to McCall. Elliot was riding shotgun with Charlie.

"These next two days are going to be great," Charlie said. "I can feel it."

"I can't believe how far we've come since you helped me run away from McCall in 2003."

"As Grandma Joan would have said: Who woulda thunk it?"

Trevor laughed. "I still miss her."

"Me, too."

"Here's Rainbow Bridge." He slowed down as they crossed it. "I think I can tell you now," Trevor said, reaching out and lowering the volume on the radio.

"This must be serious."

"It is. Right here is where I was going to kill myself. I had a plan to crash through the barrier and land on the boulders, then sink into that cold, raging water. Just go under and…"

"And what?" Charlie said quietly.

"Just…go to sleep and never wake up. I'm glad I didn't do it."

"You really had me petrified with all those phone calls. I was so helpless to do anything back then. Keeping you safe was one of my biggest fears for a long time."

"I know how much you tried. You saved my life, Mom."

"No, Trev. You saved yourself."

He turned up the radio to hear one of his favorite country songs, sped up, and started singing along. She joined in.

———

They settled into their suite at the Whitetail Lodge. Charlie put away her clothes then stepped out onto the veranda. It was a muggy August afternoon with a threat of a thunderstorm. Her room overlooked the pristine sand beach dotted with green umbrellas and the lake beyond. Still majestic. She spotted Trevor already seated at the outdoor restaurant, studying the menu.

She thought about what he'd revealed back at Rainbow Bridge. She shuddered then let go of her fears for his future. He would always struggle with the side effects of his cancer and the treatments. But he was a survivor. He never gave up.

Neither had Charlie. Despite momentary worries that she'd never make headway in McCall, she nevertheless kept up her search into the causes of the illnesses here, interviewing everyone who would talk to her. She was learning new things all the time about the history of the mill. The pieces were starting to fall into place.

Although she almost had given up hope that the two University of Arizona professors who had cancelled on her last year would ever find the time to fit McCall into their crowded fieldwork schedule, they actually were due to arrive late this very evening.

"I hounded them all year to get out here. I was like a bad rash that wouldn't go away," Charlie said when she phoned Mike

Stewart with the exciting news earlier in the week. "Will you be in town?"

"You're lucky I can't unload the newspaper. So, yeah, I'll be here."

"Then will you write one of your great stories? *And* be our guide?"

"Count me in."

"Can I treat you to dinner when we get into town?"

"Only if I can bring a friend. I want you to meet her."

"Has love found Mr. Stewart?" she kidded.

"No, no way," Mike protested with a laugh. "She's the new director of our district DEQ. She thinks the way we do. And has the courage to see it through."

"Trevor and I look forward to meeting her."

He said he'd phone the woman to see if she could make it. Five minutes later, he called Charlie to tell her that Linda Fellberg* was busy but would be glad to meet with her at the DEQ office in town the day after that.

"I'll be there," Charlie had promised. "Does she know what I'm trying to find out?"

"She knows that there was a lawsuit between the developer Doug Manchester and the owners of the mill site who sold him the land. She knows it's been sealed since the settlement. And, she wants to know what's in it, too."

"Sounds like my kind of girl."

~————~

When they met up early the next morning, Mike willingly took Charlie's car keys and agreed to be tour guide. The three of them drove to the local Best Western Hotel to collect Dr. Sheppard and Dr. Witten.

Dr. Paul Sheppard was tall and lanky with a bushy mustache. Officially called a dendrochemist, he had carved an entire career out of the study of tree core samples to ascertain the chemical history of a particular location. On first impression, he seemed shy and somewhat socially awkward. He looked like a science geek in his thick glasses but was dressed like a seasoned outdoorsman all set for a long hike. He even had a knapsack slung over his shoulder.

Mark Witten, always effusive, greeted Charlie and Trevor in his booming voice that felt like a hearty slap on the back. Mike was treated to one of Witten's ironman handshakes before the scientist claimed the front seat next to him.

From the back of the SUV where she, Trevor, and Sheppard were crammed together, Charlie could hear the garrulous professor launch into a long spiel about the success of their research projects in various small towns across the land. It was clear that Paul Sheppard found it difficult to get a word in edgewise.

Finally, Paul was able to sneak in a question about the area. Mike responded in his usual manner—with a reporter's enthusiasm for a story and his knowledge of Valley County.

Paul suggested they start with a location far enough from McCall to establish outside parameters. "Then we will move closer and closer to the spots where we might expect to see a problem. What I hope for is a noticeable relative change from at least one tree core that tells me to return for further sampling," he explained.

Mike headed to an area north of the lake on the road to Warren. He parked in a burned-out area about five miles from Warren. The group clambered up a rather steep hill, picking their way around charred trees, some just starting to sprout new growth. Keeping their footing was difficult. Charlie was steady and cautious but still slipped and slid over an uneven carpet of squishy mulch.

Nonplussed, Paul navigated the terrain with the nimbleness of a mountain goat or a teenager rather than a man in his mid-forties. As he climbed, he explained that field conditions often posed a problem for tree-coring outings. They ran the gamut from good to bad: sun, rain, snow, and heat; they had to fight off mosquitoes, ticks, snakes, poison ivy, thorny brambles, and sunburn.

Paul suddenly stopped walking. "This looks like a good spot to begin coring," he announced. Among the thicket, he picked an older tree, which presumably offered a longer history to decode, and quickly removed his tools from his knapsack.

Charlie was determined to get an up-close look at the coring about which she had heard so much for nearly a year now.

"This is an increment borer," he said, holding up a T-shaped instrument for her to inspect.

"Do you mind explaining the whole procedure?" she asked.

"Not at all," he replied with a grateful smile, as he adjusted his glasses. "Not many people actually want to watch. So, here we go…I will rotate the borer into the tree with the lever and extract a pencil-sized specimen. These borers are made of tungsten-hardened steel. They are hollow drills with cutting teeth on the outside."

"I see that now," Charlie commented.

"Once I get past the bark of the tree, it's only a matter of turning the borer with a handle like I'm doing now," Paul explained, "and allowing it to pull itself into the tree."

"It looks pretty difficult."

"Trees don't give up their secrets easily," he said with a laugh. "Here, want to try it?"

"Sure," Charlie said, calling for Trevor to try his hand at it, too. For a couple of minutes, she and Trevor took turns working the reluctant lever.

"You made this look a lot easier than it is," Trevor commented at one point.

"We're going to be here all day if Trevor and I keep this up," Charlie joked.

Paul relieved them. Before too long, he began to remove the borer, extracting a core from the tree.

"The specimen looks like a thin version of a pineapple core," Trevor observed.

Paul held it up for inspection. "What I have here," he said, "lets us see radial growth rings from pith to bark without having to cut the tree down."

"And you'll take it back to the lab, grind it down and make slides?" Trevor inquired.

"Exactly." At this point, Paul began to rifle through his knapsack and removed a wrapped straw. "I use these drinking straws for storage," he said. "I prefer the ones from McDonald's restaurants."

Charlie thought how ironic it was that McDonald's, which had figured so prominently in her life for so many years, was once more an oddly important component in this latest endeavor. "Why is that?" she asked, looking at Trevor who was smiling at her and probably thinking the same thought.

"They're individually wrapped and just the right diameter to hold increment cores, and they can be doubled up on each other to elongate them to obtain the right length, depending on the size of trees sampled," he explained.

At this point, Paul began a meticulous recording of the tree's location, using a GPS positioning system that he claimed also gave him highly precise waypoints. "I wonder how I ever survived before without GPS," he explained, as he finished adding other notes in a tiny, precise script to his much-used field book.

Paul started in on another tree, repeating his methods in the same exacting, painstaking manner. By this time, Mark had walked further afield with Mike Stewart. Charlie suspected he was still bending the reporter's ear about his research successes.

It began to rain lightly. Paul was not deterred. In fact, he didn't even seem to notice. Not even flashes of lightning and close thunder stopped his concentration. When the others, however, suggested it might be safer for everyone to leave, Paul agreed, saying he was finished with this spot anyway.

———～———

Within an hour, the air cleared. For the rest of the day, Paul extracted samples in and around McCall, coring near an abandoned industrial facility, the old mill site, around the general shoreline of Payette Lake, on the road across from the Smiths' former home, and several places bordering Pilgrim's Cove. Charlie had alerted Mark Johnson about this expedition when she was certain it would happen. Channel 7 News arrived in McCall when they were at Pilgrim's Cove, and their field reporter taped Paul doing coring and interviewed the two scientists, Charlie, and Trevor. The segment played on all of the evening news programs throughout Idaho and repeated the next day.

———～———

That night at dinner al fresco at Chapala's, a Mexican cantina, Paul showed a different side to himself. Charlie realized that he wasn't all that shy. He was just more comfortable talking about what he knew. Tonight he was eager to share his first impressions of McCall, calling it a spectacularly beautiful place. A lifelong outdoorsman himself, he appreciated all that this tiny resort community had to offer in every season. Before becoming a dendrochemist and a professor, Paul had been a forest ranger in the San Jacinto range in Southern California.

"Overall," Paul opined as they tarried after dinner in the cool mountain air, "with country as beautiful as what we're surrounded by now, it's hard to imagine anyone being sick in McCall, let alone too many people."

"That's what I always thought," Charlie agreed. "Then Trevor got sick. A friend of mine, who lives here and has a daughter with a rare disorder, once said, 'Why don't we show the McCall phone book to the officials who turn their back on us and just cross off the few names of the ones who aren't sick?' Seriously, that's how bad it's gotten."

"That's why we wanted to come here," Paul added. "With all due regard to the human side of disease, the existence of clusters or excessive illness provides us with an opportunity for the kind of environmental-biomedical research that we have developed. Fallon, Nevada's where we were able to perfect our methods. Charlie, for Fallon to have true significance scientifically, though, it would be best to have replicates of Fallon. We need other towns to study, like McCall, with too much illness as well as something unusual environmentally that might make it linkable to that illness. I look at McCall the way I saw Fallon at the beginning. Search everywhere and see what happens back at the lab later. Return and do it all again, and again, and again."

"And that's why we've gone all over the country doing the tree core studies. Small towns everywhere have the same problems as you do here in McCall," Mark intoned.

"We're all linked by these clusters," Charlie said emotionally.

"Exactly!" Mark exclaimed. "But the reporting of cancer cases is haphazard. Some states report by counties. Others have no firm reporting method in place. The frequency requirement for reporting the data varies from state to state. We come up against this time after time. The fact is, with today's technology, it's easy to learn how many cases of swine flu have cropped up within days, if not hours, in any given area."

"Why not do the same with cancer cases?" Trevor suggested. "Like my mom always says about how they have laws to expose sexual predators in neighborhoods, we should have laws to expose toxic predators."

"Like Megan's Law for cancer clusters," Charlie piped up.

"You two should pursue that angle."

"Maybe we will," Charlie said.

———

The next day Charlie and Trevor accompanied Mark and Paul as they cored trees further afield, going all the way to Cascade to look at the once-toxic area around the former Boise-Cascade mill, which was now a public park.

They parted in the afternoon. The two scientists were driving back to Boise for an early-morning flight home.

"Take care of those tree cores," Charlie implored.

Paul told her and Trevor that he would try to expedite the tests for their project, but he had to wait in a long line of chemists to use a state-of-the-art mass spectrophotometer that was located at a university in Washington State.

"It's like the military," Mark said. "Hurry up and wait."

"What kind of timeline are we talking about?" Trevor asked.

Paul said, "Six months. Maybe a year at the outside."

"I'm excited and disappointed at the same time," Charlie told Trevor as they headed back to their hotel. "I paid all that money to get them here, and I never thought it would take so long to get results."

"This time, though, we're working with people who have a proven track record. Look at what they've done for Floyd Sands in Fallon."

It was true. The two professors were very close to learning what actually had caused the leukemia cluster. She hoped they found it soon: Floyd recently was diagnosed with brain cancer.

Charlie's cell phone buzzed. "Would you grab that, Trev?"

Trevor answered. He mostly listened after saying hello.

"You up for more disappointment?" he asked.

"What now?"

"That was Linda Fellberg. She has to go out on the lake for the rest of the afternoon and test for mercury, or something. I guess all the trout are dying and everybody's worried."

"The more things change, the more things stay the same," Charlie observed.

"She did say to tell you that she knows what you want, and she will get it for you."

CHAPTER THIRTY-FOUR

It was the middle of September and a typical fall day in Boise. Brisk enough for a sweater and a hot drink, even with bright sunlight bleaching the sky a baby blue. Thomas Hammer Coffee Shop on Eighth Street was in the middle of a bustling block of stores and bistros. A stone's throw from the capitol building, it was a popular spot for those who worked in government.

Today, Charlie and Trevor were enjoying coffees at Hammer with Jerrod Hartman*, the program director of the Idaho Conservation League. In his early forties, he was dressed casually in a shirt and pullover sweater, jeans, and sneakers. Hair short. Almost military. Very clean-cut, with regular features.

He requested this meeting soon after seeing the Channel 7 interview from McCall with her, Trevor, and the two University of Arizona professors this past August. The Smiths were unable to get together with him until now. Both she and Trevor had been consumed with the planning of the Second Annual Trevor's Trek Walk, which just took place last week. The event was as successful as their inaugural one, with an additional twist: They used their platform to unveil the newly finished CCAI Childhood Cancer Strategic Plan. Charlie greatly hoped that it would be as fully received as the 2006 general CCAI Strategic Plan for the detection, prevention, and treatment of cancer.

"I'm glad to finally be able to talk to you both in person," Jerrod said. "I haven't told either of you, but I've been following your work through all of the newspaper stories and on TV."

"We're flattered," Trevor told him. "I try…we both try…to get our point across without offending too many people."

"Oh, I understand. Believe me. But that's just what is so great about what you've accomplished. Just by being out there, you've been able to make a difference in Idaho's efforts to fight toxins like mercury and heavy metals. Your testimony before environmental officials puts a face to the threats that numbers can't."

"A picture definitely is worth a thousand words," Charlie commented. "We learned that a long time ago."

Jerrod concurred. "You really crystallize the issues from the abstract to the concrete, Trevor."

They talked about Jerrod's own work fighting mercury emissions from coal-fired power plants. He told them that this industry was a major source of the mercury buildup in our nation's waterways.

"Even small amounts of mercury can cause harm," Hartman reminded them. "In eastern Oregon, the Ash Grove Cement Plant emitted 631 pounds of mercury in one year. I jumped right on that. We have tried to get them to reduce that amount by half. I'm particularly concerned about this eastern Oregon situation because Boiseans are only one hundred miles downwind from Ash Grove."

"Are you aware of the high levels of mercury in Payette Lake?" Charlie asked Jerrod.

"Linda Fellberg and I are in discussions. I've also had several meetings about it with DEQ down here, too."

"With so much mercury mining near McCall and even in Stibnite in the past, it's not surprising that the lake still has this problem," Charlie commented.

Jerrod said, "Trust me, you're going to hear even more about mercury contamination up there."

"I also heard that the residue of forest fires can elevate mercury levels in the environment," she said. "There was mercury mining at Warren and Cinnabar, too."

"There are so many possibilities from past abuses in and around McCall. Over 140 years of mining takes a toll!"

"And of course, we had that recent lawsuit against the asphalt plant there, as well," Charlie added.

"I followed that. This essentially has become a moral issue for me," Jerrod said. "At this time in our history when we know so much, unrestrained polluting is an affront to my children. To all children."

"Jerrod, how far back does your information go about the mining situation in Stibnite?" Charlie asked.

"I like to think I've done my homework about all of the mining districts that are polluters, especially the ones on the NPL and the Superfund sites. Without exception, hard-rock mines going through closure have presented many problems. Some of them declared bankruptcy and walked away. Others experienced cyanide and metal releases beyond what are acceptable levels. Yellow Pine, Cinnabar, and Stibnite fall into these categories."

"What about the earliest mines?" Trevor asked.

"You have to understand the 1872 U.S. Mining Law. It stated clearly that the best use of public lands was mining. To sweeten the pot, the law allowed the sale of patents and the leasing of public lands to private companies on a vast scale without asking for royalties or safeguards in return. This practice is going on to this day—at the 1872 price! Further, the Idaho Surface Mining Act reclamation standards are not tough enough. Nor is the scope wide enough to control what both scrupulous and unscrupulous mining companies can get away with. The sheer number of mine closures due to falling prices or bankruptcies makes it nearly impossible to keep up with what needs to be done to reclaim the land."

"But I thought that the mining companies had to purchase a bond to cover the closure problems," Charlie stated.

"State bonding doesn't always cover the real costs of closure. In most instances, the real costs far exceed what the law requires for a bond at the time the company submits its plan for operations and future closure. In addition, the bonding agreements don't always include what needs to be done beyond what is stated in the bond. For example, at one closure site the costs for capping the tailings facility and waste rock dumps far exceeded what was planned for. That constantly repeats itself at site after site. We have a situation now that is nearly out of control."

"Is that why Stibnite still looks the way it does?"

"It's a great example, yes," Jerrod said. "As late as 2002, the state of Idaho faced an estimated four-million-dollar liability for cleanup because the company had no assets available for recovery costs."

"Someone who lived there told me a bit about this history of dereliction. I've seen the situation firsthand as well. I've had a helluva time getting information about a federal lawsuit concerning Stibnite, possibly at the end of the 1990s. I was wondering if you might have heard about it?"

"Doesn't ring a bell. But you've piqued my curiosity. I'll see what I can find out."

Charlie said, "Sometimes I think I'm searching for the Holy Grail. It probably doesn't even exist."

———

"I've found your Holy Grail," Jerrod told Charlie when he reached her about two weeks later.

"Wow. So it's real!"

"Yes. But it was buried in an arcane mining journal that would not have popped up in any usual search on the Internet. When we had coffee, I thought I knew what you were referring to, but I didn't want to get your hopes up. You're going to like this."

⁓

Charlie went online and found the site to which Jerrod was referring. Tucked away in an issue of the *Northwest Mining Association Newsletter* of 2002, was the detailed explanation of *the* federal lawsuit for which Charlie had been searching. According to the Mining Association, there were actually two lawsuits between the federal government and Mobil Oil. Even though Mobil never mined the Stibnite site, they acquired it from Superior Oil Company in 1998. As is often the result in these situations, the U.S. Environmental Protection Agency (EPA) and the U.S. Forest Service (USFS) targeted the *new* owner to clean up the entire mining site.

Charlie carefully read the government's accusation concerning the adverse effects of Superior Oil Company's gold exploration and mining at the site in the early 1980s: "left behind...one million tons of arsenic-bearing spent ore disposed of on top of an existing four-million-ton tailings pile generated by tungsten and antimony."

Mobil did some minor cleanup of the site. Obviously not very much, since it was still a cesspool when Charlie went there in 2003. That's what the EPA and the Forest Service thought, too. The oil company learned in 1999 that it was still on the hook for whatever new demands might be made by the agencies of the federal government, and in fact, their site most likely was going to be listed on the Superfund National Priorities List. As the last viable company in the area, Mobil balked at what seemed like an attempt by the federal government to pick its deep pockets.

The Mining Association reported that what happened next put the federal government in check: Mobil Oil filed a "contribution action" against the United States under the Superfund Law. In it, they alleged that the federal government itself was "jointly liable and substantially responsible for the Superfund costs because of the government's status as former owner of the original waste disposal site and as current owner of the surrounding national forest lands."

Charlie learned from Mobil's suit that in the 1940s it was in fact a federal government entity, the U.S. Geological Survey, which discovered the antimony and tungsten deposits in the Yellow Pine mining district. Although that entity contracted with private companies during WWII to do the work, the federal government not only furloughed soldiers, they gave draft deferments to men who worked in those Stibnite mines.

Mobil's attorneys argued further that the federal government left more contaminated mine wastes than any private companies that came along later, and therefore was equally responsible for remediating the site.

Predictably, the government came back with what is called "a third-party defense," claiming the "1940s mining was performed by private mining companies without any contractual relationship to the government."

Taking a detour, Charlie looked up this attack method on the Internet and learned that the federal government had used the "third-party defense" successfully in the past, contesting lawsuits filed against them in California at the Iron Mountain site, in Idaho at the Blackbird cobalt mine, and in Montana at the Clarks Fork site.

Nevertheless, Mobil Oil's legal team pounced, asking in 2000 for "Summary Judgment." In effect, they were saying, "Judge, please find in favor of our client that the government was indeed jointly liable under Superfund." Their brief was filled with facts culled from government records that they claimed pointed to definite government involvement in mining and waste disposal.

On April 28, 2000, a federal judge granted Mobil's request for Summary Judgment. According to the Mining Association's discussion of this case: "It was the first time a sitting federal judge had stated his intent to impose liability on the government under Superfund at a mining site."

This was a stunning setback for the federal government. Their lawyers knew that this ruling must never be published and therefore set a precedent. To avoid this, they sat down with Mobil and hammered out a compromise.

Some compromise, thought Charlie. They let Mobil Oil completely off the hook. In addition to being released from all liability for future response costs covering the entire Stibnite tailings and spent-ore disposal area, they no longer held any responsibility for the nearly 7,000 surrounding acres, including downstream drainage. *None. Nada. Zero. Zilch!*

So there it was: the definitive explanation about why so little had been done to reclaim the area in modern times. Because the federal government was caught with its proverbial pants down, the private sector got away practically scot-free. And the little people continued to suffer.

It became clear to her how the scenario for that perfect storm happened during the 1994 McCall fire that inextricably joined her town and Stibnite. Had all those millions of tons of toxic tailings and the lethal leaching pits been eradicated down through the years, these contaminants never would have become part of the ash and fire retardant residue that blew over the summit to settle on the watershed bordering Payette Lake. Like the toxins from Cinnabar and Warren, Stibnite's toxins could very well have been the underlying cause of all the illness in McCall; at the very least they were a contributing factor.

CHAPTER THIRTY-FIVE

American Airlines Flight 76 from LAX to Dulles International Airport lifted off at nine a.m. Trevor checked his watch and let out an audible sigh. He had read a weather report earlier this morning announcing that a "hundred-year" summer storm was predicted to deluge the D.C. area by that evening. If they arrived on schedule, they would be safely in their hotel by the time it unleashed its fury.

Because Trevor was in the aisle seat more than halfway back, he couldn't see the plane bank and turn toward the Pacific Ocean before veering off and heading east. But he could feel it. All was good. *Check. Check.*

"You excited?" Charlie asked.

"Of course. Who wouldn't be? Tomorrow we'll be meeting with Senator Barbara Boxer to present our idea for new legislation."

"'Trevor's Law.'"

"At least for now. Who knows what the senators will finally call it? If it ever gets that far."

Just then, the captain's voice came on the loud speaker. Trevor fully expected to be told a few of the details of the flight. Cruising altitude. When to look out the window at the Grand Canyon. The

Rocky Mountains. Instead, the pilot said that they were returning to the airport. "We have hydraulics malfunctions."

"This isn't good," he said to his mother. "That storm."

"I know."

At first they were detained on board while the pilots and the technicians talked over the possibilities of fixing the problem quickly. The pilot blithely informed everyone that it was an O-ring. A simple fix.

"A simple fix? Not likely," Charlie commented to Trevor, as they all were ushered off the plane into the passenger lounge to await further word. "I remember after the NASA shuttle with Christa McAuliffe blew to smithereens, there was a public hearing. I watched it on TV. The panel of scientists decided it was a faulty O-ring that caused the catastrophe."

"She was the first teacher selected to go into space, right?" Trevor asked.

"That's right. Your substitute teacher, Barbara Morgan, replaced her."

"It's hard to believe that a woman from 'statistically insignificant' McCall, Idaho was the first teacher to successfully get to space."

"It's even more ironic that you and Barbara Morgan were both from McCall and selected as two of the five Heroes of the Year for Treasure Valley. 2007 was a banner year for you, Trev. Like the *Idaho Statesman* editorial board said, you showed extraordinary leadership and a positive influence."

"Yeah. That was an amazing honor. But me—Most Courageous?"

"Hey, you faced down the bullies in your life. That was pretty courageous in my book."

"I guess. I get embarrassed sometimes. Like calling our bill 'Trevor's Law.'"

"It didn't seem to put off Senator Boxer when we sent her the proposal. Didn't we hear back right away? Didn't she say she wanted to discuss it with us further—in person?"

"Yeah. I guess you're right."

"Just as long as you don't lose sight of the big picture. You are just one person trying to make a difference for many."

"Want to grab something to eat while we're waiting?" he asked.

"We just had breakfast. We can eat lunch on the plane. How about a drink, though?"

Trevor went off to get them bottles of water.

⁓

The "simple fix" apparently became increasingly complicated, and they were informed over the loudspeaker that the fix hadn't worked. They were going to have to take a different airplane. If they could find one. The more disgruntled passengers opted to leave altogether.

"We have no choice but to stick it out," Charlie said.

"Should I check about another airline? It's almost one o'clock."

"Let's wait a little longer."

About ten minutes later, the loudspeaker system came on again: They had found a plane and everyone could now board. This time Charlie and Trevor shared their row with an American Airlines off-duty pilot hitching a ride back to his home in D.C.

"I'm Dave," he said with an easy grin, sliding into the window seat.

Charlie was the sardine packed between him and Trevor. "What a way to begin a trip," Charlie commented.

"Yeah, it is. But don't worry. You're in good hands," he promised her with a smile. "You and your son on a vacation?"

"Actually, we're on a business trip." She went on to tell him that they planned to meet up with a scientist from the University of Arizona who worked on the causes of cancer clusters. The three of them were scheduled for an exploratory session the next day to discuss a proposed law with the chair of the U. S. Senate Environment and

Public Works Committee, Barbara Boxer, and Secretary Lisa Jackson, the head of the EPA.

"Well, that's very interesting," Dave replied. "I'm impressed. Have you ever heard of the Fallon, Nevada leukemia cancer cluster?"

Charlie couldn't hide how startled she was. "In fact, yes. The man I told you we're meeting tomorrow is Dr. Mark Witten. He and another scientist, Paul Sheppard, have been researching the Fallon cluster for seven years. They recently uncovered the probable cause of it. Tungsten emissions from a manufacturing plant."

"Amazing! How did you and your son get into this line of work?" he inquired.

"I had brain cancer," Trevor explained. "And we learned that my cancer might have come from environmental contamination."

"How are you doing?" Dave asked solicitously.

"Great! I'm cured. I vowed to help other kids if I lived."

"How old are you, young man?"

"Nineteen. Got cancer at thirteen."

"Well, I admire you, son," he said. "You know, I had friends stationed at the Fallon Naval Air Base. Two of them got brain cancer. Everybody stationed there got a letter from the Navy saying that because of the cluster, they didn't have to live on base. One of the guys wouldn't allow his family to come there at all. So I'm with you on this. Very important to get to the bottom of this situation. Very important."

The food-service cart arrived, interrupting them. The refreshment turned out to be only a tiny bag of peanuts. Charlie wished she and Trevor had eaten after all while waiting in the airport lounge. She found the best way to push hunger pangs aside was to get busy. She retrieved from her briefcase a ream of notes for their presentation in the morning and began going over them. As she turned each page, she silently thanked Paul Sheppard and Mark Witten for their invaluable input and guidance during the past year.

Trying to ignore the plane bouncing erratically in the intermittent turbulence, Charlie scanned previous notes jotted in the margins of the suggested legislation. They certainly seemed to have a good plan to improve the manner in which cancer cases were reported and addressed. It contained simple but sound propositions in easy-to-follow steps: 1) Define a geographical area for cluster/hot spot analyses on a zip-code basis throughout the United States, 2) Report all cancer cases at respective state cancer registries within a forty-five-day period, 3) Require all state cancer registries to utilize uniform methods of collating and reviewing all of the data entered into their registry, 4) Require state cancer registries to be audited by an agency of the U.S. Department of Health and Human Services on a yearly basis, 5) Conduct an investigation of the suspected cancer cluster by a new agency created within the U.S. Department of Health and Human Services or another appropriate venue within six months if the cancer rate exceeds the national average by over threefold, 6) Report all of these hot-spot investigations on a website along with bimonthly progress reports, and 7) If the U.S. Department of Health and Human Services does find probable cause for the cancer cluster, the U.S. Environmental Protection Agency must remediate the suspected environmental cause of the cancer cluster within a one-year period.

She jotted down a few new ideas and then clipped her papers together. She closed her eyes and dozed for a while. An increase in turbulence woke her up. She looked at her watch. Time to get ready to land. "Trev, can you put those in my briefcase?"

He got up to retrieve it from the overhead compartment. The plane suddenly dropped, then bounced. He managed to keep his footing but practically fell into his seat.

"What the hell was that?" Charlie gasped, taking the briefcase and quickly stashing her papers. She slid it under the seat in front of her.

"We're going through the clouds right into the mouth of the storm. It's right over Dulles," Dave informed her. "We're in sight of the airport now. You should see the lightning. These are some of the strongest winds I've ever felt. Make sure your seat belts are fastened, guys."

"You're kidding, right?" Charlie said.

"No. This is going to be a little rough. But just relax; we'll be okay," he added quickly.

Yeah, right! Charlie thought, as she tightened her seatbelt to the point of cutting off her circulation. If she made it any tighter, they'd have to amputate her legs when they landed. She glanced past Dave to try to catch a glimpse of the sky through the porthole. Indeed, lightning was everywhere. So close that the quickly following thunder penetrated the skin of the plane with a harsh noise that startled everyone.

"Jeez!" Trevor exclaimed. "White knuckle time."

Her son loved to fly and never expressed fright. Now he looked ashen. The fear in his eyes increased when a stewardess from the first-class cabin came over to their row and requested that Dave accompany her to the front of the plane.

Charlie thought she heard the words, "Wing...fire..."

The man in the aisle seat across from hers heard it, too. He looked like he was going to need a clean pair of shorts.

Then they hit another rough patch. The plane shook loudly. Lightning flashed all around. It felt as if they were in the middle of a forest of light, with the same shuddering thunderclaps. In less than a minute, Dave returned. He appeared more worried as he resettled into his seat. He kept glancing out the window.

"What's going on? Is it a fire in the engine?" Charlie whispered.

"I don't think so." The plane lurched again, smacked around by the winds. "They thought they smelled smoke up there."

As if on cue, the First Captain addressed everyone through the loudspeakers, telling the cabin stewards to secure their seat belts and prepare to land.

"Thank God!" Charlie exclaimed. "I can't wait to get off of this flight."

The plane angled down, but it didn't feel like any landing Charlie had ever experienced before. As the high wind shears fought with the pilot over who was in control of this pile of metal, they sped up. Charlie saw a sick expression settle on Dave's face. He obviously knew exactly what was taking place in the cockpit, and he didn't look like it made him very happy.

A few seconds before the rubber hit the road, she experienced a nauseating sensation of moving sideways then upwards. It felt like a slow-motion slog out of quicksand as their pilot struggled to coax the plane up through the clouds, the wind, and the rain to … where?

Passengers' frantic voices echoed up and down the aisle: "Oh my God! We're not landing! What the hell is this pilot doing?"

Charlie couldn't help but think about the recent disappearance of Air France Flight 447 en route to Paris from Rio de Janeiro; many thought that plane was disabled—perhaps even ripped apart—by lightning strikes in a fierce storm.

The captain interrupted her disquieting thoughts by announcing that they were going to circle around the airport and attempt to land from the north. "I'm hoping we get a headwind that way," he explained.

"How you doing?" she asked Trevor.

"I can't believe this is happening," he said. "Goddamn O-ring…" The words stopped in his mouth, silenced by the sensation of the nose pointing downward. He pulled his seatbelt even tighter.

Charlie could almost feel the determination of the pilot as they zeroed in on the runway. Once more, however, she could tell that they were speeding up. A lot! If possible, the winds were worse than before. The thunder louder.

"We're heading in too fast," Dave blurted at the same moment the plane shuddered and felt like it would break apart. "Pull up. Pull up," he kept whispering.

Charlie closed her eyes and grabbed Trevor's hand. His was ice cold. "Are we going to die?" Trevor blurted, voicing exactly what Charlie was feeling.

Dave leaned across her and patted Trevor on the knee. "Hey, listen. You lived through brain cancer. You are *not* going to die on this airplane."

In what was merely seconds but felt like hours, the pilot managed to lift the plane's nose and avert disaster—again. For the next half hour, he flew a pattern near the airport but out of the storm itself. Charlie felt like the plane was a patient vulture flying in lazy circles above the carcass of the storm-battered D.C. area.

"I know you don't want to hear this, folks, but it hasn't let up down there," the captain announced. "Now we're running low on fuel, and I think we're going to have to land somewhere nearby, wait for the storm to pass, and then make another attempt at Dulles."

The words "Pittsburgh, Pennsylvania" filtered into Charlie's ears through the loud grumblings filling the cabin. A short while later they landed and then taxied to a stop at one of American Airlines' empty gates.

"Must have hit pretty bad here, too," Dave announced, telling her about all of the debris he was seeing littering the tarmac.

Although they spent more than an hour on the ground while the plane refueled, no one was allowed to get off. Charlie pulled out her cell and phoned their hotel to update them on her time of arrival, explaining that she was diverted to Pittsburgh and would be checking in around midnight. The desk clerk assured her that they were holding the reservations, no matter what time she rolled in.

Apparently, the already-fierce storm in D.C. worsened between that call and their bedraggled arrival around one in the morning. A power outage caused the computer at the Ritz-Carlton Pentagon City to go down, losing the reservations. The Smiths' only consolation was the offer of a 2,500-square-foot executive suite *gratis* at another of their hotels in Georgetown.

The first thing they did when they got settled was order room service and finally eat lunch. It was nearly three a.m. when they called it a night.

CHAPTER THIRTY-SIX

Charlie was still groggy when nine o'clock rolled around, but she was dressed for success and seated at a mahogany table in the dining room of their vast suite about to have breakfast with Mark Witten. Arriving uneventfully in the late afternoon of the previous day, a few hours before the storm hit full force, he had enjoyed a leisurely dinner with other colleagues and a good night's sleep.

"We really should go over our presentation," he counseled.

She knew he was right. Even so, Charlie could barely concentrate. "You and Trevor start without me," she said with a groan. "Pass the coffee. I need another jolt of intense caffeine coursing through my veins to get my brain in gear."

"Well, I'm ready," Trevor said brightly. He did appear completely revived, clearly over whatever fears he had voiced the night before about facing death once more.

Charlie enjoyed her coffee while regarding her son at the head of the table: confident and businesslike, dressed in the typical Washington, D.C., button-down shirt, striped tie, and blue blazer. His hair was longer now and slicked back. He wore glasses this morning, a recent development. His eyes still bothered him. Double vision. Charlie told him the glasses gave him an intellectual air. He thought that was pretty cool.

Trevor's public commitments grew with each passing month. He still spoke to civic and charity groups about surviving brain cancer and his present work with childhood cancer outreach. He still counseled teens and kids throughout Boise who were dealing with the aftermath of cancer. One of them was a leukemia patient, a former cheerleader at her high school. An upbeat, outgoing girl, she now felt isolated and different. Trevor spent hours talking to her. When his senior prom came around, he decided to take her. She was in remission but still undergoing chemo. She had no hair and had to wear a wig, about which she was terribly self-conscious. Trevor gave her a corsage and told her she looked beautiful. It was an early night; she tired right away, and they left after only one dance. "I could have taken someone healthy," he said to Charlie later. "Stayed for hours. But I wanted to do this for her. I think she loved it."

It was that attitude that others found so special and that brought even more accolades and awards his way. Soon after the inaugural Trevor's Trek, he was selected to be the Youth Ambassador for Make-A-Wish Foundation of Idaho. He used this commitment to start a high-school outreach program called "Kids for Wish Kids."

And this morning in Washington, D.C., he was seated across the table from a noted scientist, discussing their strategy for facing a United States senator and the head of the EPA as if he did this every day.

~

The cavernous foyer of the Hart Building was abuzz with media looking for statements from senators walking purposefully from the Senate floor back to their offices. Cameramen, interviewers, lights: all of it made for a massively invigorating scene. Other people looked more jaded as they made their way throughout the building, lugging files and briefcases, looking like they had done this one too many times. Others, like Charlie and Trevor, appeared as if they were visitors in awe of their surroundings and excited to be part of the democratic process.

They easily spotted Senator Barbara Boxer's office on the first floor. It was a hive of activity, but a young receptionist clearly expected them and gave them a warm welcome. They sat on a well-worn couch no more than a few minutes before being escorted into the senator's private office.

While awaiting her arrival, Charlie browsed a vast array of memorabilia on every available table and nook, and she studied the photos on the walls. A pleasing mix of public and personal collectibles, it all provided at a glance an insight into the character of the three-term senator. It gave Charlie reason to hope that Barbara Boxer would be receptive to their ideas.

Before too long, some of Boxer's aides came in, followed by the senator. A small woman with a large persona, she greeted them with the warmth for which she was so famous, and immediately put them at ease by telling them she was as anxious as they were to have the meeting proceed flawlessly and to a good end.

In a matter of minutes, Secretary Jackson arrived as well, accompanied by a phalanx of her own aides from the EPA. They included a few administrative assistants, as well as an EPA scientist who had gone over Witten's data to familiarize himself with the professor's research and considerable credentials.

They settled into a circle of chairs and small sofas. After a few general pleasantries, Senator Boxer introduced the participants and explained the purpose of the meeting. She said she felt the Smiths' aims meshed with hers: making the country safe for children to grow up without getting cancer because of toxins in the environment and creating a more efficient method of achieving that end.

At this point, she turned to Charlie to moderate the ensuing discussion. Charlie told them about their bleary-eyed arrival at nearly one in the morning and added, "When we got to the baggage claim area, we noticed an enormous poster with the image of a little girl on it. She stared out at us with soulful eyes ringed with dark circles.

She had almost no hair on her head. Everything about her shouted 'cancer victim.'

"The poster's words said: Imagine a world without children. I'd like to ask you all to do the same thing." Charlie paused; the room went silent, but the energy level increased.

She then presented an overview of facts that led to the decision that there was a need for new legislation: Trevor's Law. She reminded them of the alarming statistic that cancer was the second-largest cause of death in children in the United States (only accidents came before it) and that its rates have increased nearly 67.1 percent in the last two generations. More alarming still, the United States had the fourth-largest incidence of childhood cancer in the world.

She also referred to a study of the review of toxic chemicals and childhood cancer published in May 2003 by the Lowell Center of Sustainable Production at the University of Massachusetts—Lowell, reading from it: "'Genetic predisposition accounts for no more than 20 percent of all childhood cancers and…the environmental attributable fraction of childhood cancers could be between 5 percent and 90 percent, depending on the type of cancer. This means that a potentially large percentage of childhood cancers is preventable.'"

She added, "Over a century of relatively uncontrolled pollution may be the root cause of the increase of childhood cancers, along with the trend that these cases appear to emerge in clusters."

Witten spoke up, adding, "The U.S. Center for Disease Control defines a cancer cluster, or hot spot, as when the disease rate is twice the national average for a particular geographical area. Unfortunately no federal laws govern how the cancer registries of the state departments of health must register new cancer cases in a timely manner. There is non-uniformity in utilizing either zip codes or counties, and there is no defined course of action once a hot spot has been defined. We hope that Trevor's Law will correct these glaring deficiencies. But first, please listen to one young man's story of how his small town got lost the way most small towns do when attempting to learn if they are part of a hot spot."

At this point, Trevor told his story. He captured their rapt attention as he recounted his ordeal and how it had turned him into an activist at such a young age.

Charlie followed once more with a quick recap of her litany of visits to the Idaho Tumor Registry and being ignored, and her education in the way cancer cases in small communities got overlooked which allowed hot spots to get bigger and more children to die unnecessarily. She credited private efforts by groups like the National Disease Cluster Alliance for picking up the ball that the federal government dropped in recognizing hot spots and trying to find the causes of them. "I'm all for private enterprise, like the NDCA," she stressed, "but the federal government is still the most well-funded entity to get the job done in a timely manner."

Charlie noticed that the senator's and Secretary Jackson's aides were diligently taking notes. The two women also appeared to be responding with a sincere openness to her and Trevor, and Mark. She had her proof when Cabinet Secretary Jackson commented emotionally after Charlie finished speaking.

"I admire your passion," she said. "I'm a mother, too."

Lisa Jackson was more than a mere mother; she also headed up one of the most powerful agencies in the federal government, the EPA. She oversaw a staff of approximately 18,000 professionals dedicated to protecting the public health and environment for all Americans.

Clearly, Charlie, Trevor, and Mark had lucked out. They had the ear of two powerful women, both devoted mothers and proven public servants, who believed, as they did, that the time had come to start cleaning up our environment instead of polluting it further.

The talk segued seamlessly from personal histories to their proposed methodology, with Mark taking over. "At the present time," he said, "our experience from investigating nine different childhood cancer clusters over the United States has shown that the problems presented today make it difficult to conduct scientific research into these hot spots with any significant degree of confidence. Consequently, we'd like to make the following recommendations for a new law."

Mark laid out the steps that Charlie had studied on the plane and by now knew by heart. An earnest discussion followed Mark's detailed presentation. Secretary Jackson and Senator Boxer sounded enthusiastic about the concept of Trevor's Law.

Both women reiterated their compassion for Charlie and Trevor because of the pain and suffering they had endured and for their commitment to helping others. They promised they would study this problem and the Smiths' proposed solutions further.

As she exited the senator's office at the end of the forty-five minute session, Charlie heard Chair Boxer say to an aide, "This has been a very positive meeting. Mark my words…we are going to make this law happen."

CHAPTER THIRTY-SEVEN

The trio departed the Hart Senate Office Building to find that the steady downpour hadn't let up one bit. If anything, it might have increased, and now it was cold and blustery, as well.

"Holy cow, it's blowing sideways," Mark said. "This certainly isn't Arizona summer weather."

"I don't even see this rain. As far as I'm concerned, the weather can stay like this," Trevor replied. "Because my personal barometer calls for nothing but clear skies for the foreseeable future."

"Well, I've got to tell you guys," Mark bellowed. "That might have been the best meeting I've ever had in D.C.!"

"It *was* my best!" Trevor retorted. "'Cause I've never been here before."

"I have a feeling from what they said, it won't be your last," Charlie told him.

As the rain pelted their umbrellas, they chatted excitedly for a few more minutes at the curb about plans for keeping up the pressure on the California senator and her aides to get their ideas incorporated into workable legislation.

"We have to get Senator Crapo on board, too," Trevor suggested.

"You're right about that," Charlie agreed. "He's our senator."

"And he's on the EPW Committee with Boxer," Trevor reminded her. "How lucky is that?"

"Let's not get ahead of ourselves," Mark said. "Face it. He's a conservative Republican, and Boxer's a liberal Democrat. Never the twain shall meet."

"But that's why this bill is so perfect," Trevor argued. "It isn't political at all. It's a hero maker for any senator who supports it. How can you go wrong with these buzzwords: cancer, children, safety?"

"Speaking about buzzwords, I just thought about Floyd," Charlie said. "Sure wish he could have been here with us. You know, today is the one-week anniversary of his death."

"He was only fifty-five," Mark murmured. "And he went so fast."

"This one's for him," Trevor said reverently.

"You got that right," Mark echoed. "I'm glad he lived long enough to know that we found the probable cause of the Fallon cluster." He noticed the time. "I should probably get going. I've had enough dodging raindrops." In fact, he had a flight to catch back to Arizona, and with the iffy weather he didn't want to get caught in a snarl of airport traffic. He hurried down the block to waylay a parked taxi and left them standing in the rain.

Trevor wanted to see the Viet Nam Memorial.

Charlie said, "I do, too. It holds a special place in my heart."

"Why, Mom?"

"Well, Trev, if it hadn't been for the Vietnam vet, Jack Wheeler, who got the whole project going, you might not be here today. You see, he was the man who Linda Smith fell in love with and left your father for."

"Cool! Let's go there now."

"I'm soaked," Charlie said. "I think we better get back to the hotel, dry off, and wait for the rain to let up before doing any sight-seeing."

She edged between two cars, leaned out toward the oncoming traffic, and pierced the air with her rowdiest taxi whistle. A cab instantly veered toward them, but at the last moment sped past, drenching her in a spray of dirty gutter water.

"Losing your touch, Mom? Better let me do it."

"Maybe you should flag down an ark instead. Where's Noah when you need him?"

~~~~~~~

Charlie was just about to open her briefcase when the doorbell to their suite sounded. She wrapped her fluffy terry bathrobe more securely around her and peered through the peephole. It was the front-desk clerk who had escorted them to their room after their middle-of-the-night arrival.

"You're back," she said, opening the door.

"I'm working a double shift," he explained. "Everything turn out okay for you and your son today?"

"Better than okay."

"That's great! The entire staff here is rooting for you. Me, especially."

When Charlie had told him why they were in town, he had confessed to her that he, too, was a survivor at the age of thirty, having had his leg amputated for bone cancer when he was fifteen. His mother died of cancer at the age of forty-five. He'd lived in the D.C. area his whole life. And he always wondered why so many people in his neighborhood came down with cancer.

He handed her his business card. "I just wanted to apologize again for the SNAFU at our sister hotel. I may not be here in the morning when you leave. Please keep in touch and let me know if I can help you with other Ritz-Carlton reservations in the future."

She said she would.

Settling on the couch, she tucked her legs under her and rifled through her briefcase. She took out an accordion file that she had not been able to get to on the harrowing plane ride to D.C. It was chock-full of information from Linda Fellberg, the official in charge of the DEQ office in McCall. Charlie already knew what a treasure trove was inside: the information about the Manchester lawsuit. It had taken Leslie nearly a year to get her hands on it and pass it on to her.

She quickly scanned the pages. "Yes! I knew she'd come through," Charlie murmured excitedly. "Trevor, get in here. You're gonna want to hear this stuff."

In essence, Linda had amassed something more important than the lawsuit complaint or even the sealed details of the settlement. She sent all the raw data upon which the lawsuit was based. Together Charlie and Trevor went through the documents detailing the history of Doug Manchester's association with the prior owners of the old mill site and the state of Idaho.

"Jeez, look what they found through testing the soil and groundwater," Trevor exclaimed, reading off a laundry list of heavy metals: arsenic, barium, cadmium, chromium, lead, mercury, and selenium.

Charlie stated, "This is good. These soil samples confirm that the site suffered ongoing contamination for years from petroleum and other industrial wastes. Well, we already suspected some of this. I've read other accounts about when Brown Tie and Lumber burned to the ground in 1940. They reported that the fire was worse because of all the petroleum and sawdust everywhere, even on the rafters. They rebuilt on the same land and obviously just kept on doing the same old, same old."

"But here's the corker," Trevor said, reading on. "'Inspectors also found volatile organic compounds, such as PCBs, benzene, chloroform, trichloroethane, naphthalene, and more. During the course of the site assessment and cleanup, a soil berm and six-foot-high chain-link fence were constructed around a containment cell to secure the property and keep people away. It said: DANGER—PCB Contamination.'"

"And with the shallow water table only eight feet below the surface and everything flowing into the lake, that spelled really bad news," Charlie commented.

As laid out in various legal documents, the toxic saturation on site was so bad that the developer's attorneys and environmental consultants contacted the City of McCall over petroleum-contaminated soil at the property line between the planned development and Mill Park, a city-owned public recreation area. They felt that should be cleaned up, too.

"Now we know why the conflict has been kept a secret," she replied, reading aloud about correspondence detailing the dispute over who was responsible for cleaning up that extra triangular piece of land north of the city park. At one point during the soil testing of this land, McCall City Manager George Sherman* reportedly ordered workers off the site and demanded that there be no soil testing done at all on the particular plot."

"I bet no one ever came back and tested there. Or at the public park nearby," Trevor offered.

"You're probably right. Idaho doesn't require developers to do an environmental analysis of their property prior to construction. It's 'Buyer Beware.' Our state government leaves it up to the property owners to decide whether testing is needed. That's a double-edged sword. How can someone be protected who lives next door to the polluted property?"

"That's right, Mom. Like everyone knows--toxins are not good neighbors. They migrate beyond property lines. They seep into the groundwater, lakes, and rivers, poisoning *everyone* nearby."

"Manchester's company ordered and paid for an extensive cleanup of his site, according to this document," she said, reading from an attorney's letter. "And it looks like he turned right around and sued the former mill landowner in an attempt to recover remediation costs and other related expenses."

"And I think that concealing the facts must have been part of their settlement," Trevor opined.

"You might be right," Charlie added grimly.

They turned to other official documents Linda Fellberg included in the hefty package. These concerned on-going contamination problems caused by businesses contiguous to the old mill property. Union Pacific and several well-known petroleum companies, like Chevron, Texaco, and Shell, once operated bulk fuel plants along Roosevelt Avenue just 250 feet from the site.

After Charlie had begun asking questions and interviewing locals, she heard this enterprise referred to as "the tank farm." Now she knew for certain that this land had been hard to sell because of the contamination of the gasoline seeping for years into the ground through small fissures in the tanks' walls.

Doug Freeland, the diver who pulled her sediment samplings in October of 2004, had told her, "If people only knew what was at the bottom of this lake, they wouldn't go in it. It looks like a city dump. And that's just what you can see with your naked eyes. Cars. Wagons. Refrigerators. Logs. Abandoned petrol tanks. You name it." A land developer eventually came along, bought the property anyway, and built condos. According to what Charlie was reading now, city officials have acknowledged that no record of environmental studies existed for that parcel before he began construction.

"Buyer Beware," Trevor intoned. "Some people are living on top of that crap now. They don't have a clue what still could be festering underneath their homes. I can see why so many people who live in our town have gotten sick."

"It's all coming together, Trev. The mill—contaminations that seeped into the lake. The tank farm—contamination that seeped into the lake. The asphalt plant—contaminated our air. That mickey-mouse filtration system they never finished—raw sewage seeping into the lake, followed by improperly treated tertiary water fed back into the lake. Stibnite. Warren. Cinnabar. The fire of 1994. Fire retardant."

"It's unending," Trevor groaned.

"But stir the various brews together, and we go right back to that cancer cocktail Mike told me about years ago."

"But I think we're further along today in narrowing down the causes because of Mark and Paul doing that tree coring last summer."

Before leaving for D.C., Paul had e-mailed them his preliminary findings: spikes in heavy metals at several sites around the lake.

"Good point, Trev. And like Paul said at dinner last summer: if he finds something, he will come back as many times as needed to learn the truth."

"But Mom, are you surprised that the biggest spikes came from the trees right where the lake empties out into the river and flows down to the Cascade Reservoir?"

"Not really. That's where everything flows together."

"You know how you always say people are being penny-wise and pound-foolish? Well, if they'd spent the money making the town safe, it'd be a real paradise instead of just looking like one."

"If Trevor's Law had been in place years ago," Charlie said, "any one of these red flags in our town would have gotten officials to come out and study the causes. On every level, there would have been a search for the truth rather than a need to turn away and deny a problem exists. Think how many young lives could have been saved. Telling the truth and taking responsibility are always the best choices in the long run."

"I'm glad we got to work with the people in Boise like Mark Johnson, the commissioners at CCAI, and Stan Olsen, who understand why we do what we do."

"You're right, Trev. You can't forget Mike Stewart and Tonya Dombrowski, either," Charlie added. "God, she talked to me a couple of times and probably lost her job over it! Then there's Paul Woods. He's stuck his neck out for us a few times, too. Handing me water reports with 'certain' pages dog-eared. And Tona Henderson. What a gal. She certainly taught me how to make noise. And all the mothers and fathers of sick kids who kept me hanging in there when I was disillusioned and ready to give up this fight. So many people behind the scenes to thank for helping us get here."

"Did you ever think we'd be doing this, Mom? Sitting in a Washington, D.C. hotel room reading lawsuits about environmental contamination? Going to meetings with senators and cabinet secretaries?"

"Yes, Trevor, I did. This is what happens when you are tenacious and never give up on your beliefs."

"But what about the people in McCall who still doubt us? You know, the ones who say why isn't *everyone* sick if there's an environmental cause to the illnesses?"

"Remember what Paul Sheppard told us he said to doubters?"

"Oh, yeah. That it's an accepted scientific fact that smoking causes cancer, but not everyone who smokes comes down with it.

"Exactly. The same goes for children exposed to toxins. We have to help the unlucky ones, Trev."

"Mom, I really want our legislation to become a law."

Charlie got up and went to the refrigerator, opened a bottle of water, and took a long drink. "You know what I really want besides this law being passed?"

Trevor grinned. "No, but I know you're gonna tell me."

"An hour of sunshine before we leave and a smooth flight home."

"You know what I *really* want, Mom?"

"What, honey?"

"Steak. Mashed potatoes. And corn. *Lots of corn.*"

Tree Core Expedition in McCall: From left to right: Charlie, Trevor, Dr. Paul Sheppard, Dr. Mark Witten (both from the University of Arizona), and Mike Stewart (publisher and owner of the **Long Valley Advocate** *newspaper in Cascade, Idaho. August 2008.*

Environmental Testing: Dr. Paul Sheppard extracts tree-core samples outside an old mining site near Warren, Idaho in August 2008. Samples from other McCall sites would come back positive for toxic substances in 2009 and lead to further testing.

*Trevor's Senior Prom 2008:
Trevor with his date,
Chelsie McGuiness, who
is also a cancer survivor.
Trevor helped launch
Trevor's Trek Peer Program
in the Boise Public School
District, a program to help
kids with cancer overcome
feelings of isolation during
and after treatment.*

*Cap and Gown: Trevor's
graduation from Boise High
School on May 27, 2008, was
a pivotal event. Five years
earlier, he thought he never
would live to see this day.*

*Cottonwood Grille
in Boise, Idaho: Bro,
Charlie, and Trevor
at Trevor's graduation
dinner.*

Trevor Smith Named Most Courageous: The **Idaho Statesman** *editorial board selected five people from Treasure Valley who showed extraordinary leadership or positive influence over the past year on important issues.*

EPILOGUE

Washington, D.C.
March 29, 2011
Environment and Public Works Oversight Hearing
Senate Hearing Room 211

Trevor waited until the harsh noise of his microphone subsided, and then he began to speak:

"I want to thank Chair Barbara Boxer, Ranking Member James Inhofe, and my great senator, Mike Crapo, for taking on the subject of childhood cancer and cancer clusters and what they mean to our public health. I would like to thank all of the senators on the Environment and Public Works Committee for allowing me to address some of those issues today. And—I am so very proud to be able to state that I am here today as a witness for *both* the Majority and Minority committee members.

"Most of you don't know me, other than I am associated with S.76, also known as Trevor's Law. By the end of my testimony my hope is that you will not only know me, but that you will remember me as the voice of every child in this great nation.

"As you have been told, I am a twenty-one-year-old brain cancer survivor. In November of 2002, at the age of thirteen, I was diagnosed with a highly malignant medullablastoma.

"Until that time, I was thriving in McCall, a small town nestled on the banks of a glacial lake in the beautiful mountains of Idaho. I really had a fairy-tale life in paradise. But the carefree days of my childhood changed abruptly and dramatically after my cancer diagnosis.

"Like a snap of the fingers, I was robbed of my childhood and my innocence. I was thrown into the antiseptic world of hospitals: an eight-hour surgery and a painful recovery, followed by fourteen grueling months of radiation and chemotherapy treatment.

"Unfortunately I wasn't the only kid in my town with this pernicious disease. In the same year of my diagnosis, there were four other brain cancers in our tiny resort community with a year-round permanent population of 1,700 residents. Over a ten-year period, there was an abnormally high number of cancer cases diagnosed there before and after I became ill.

"What happened in my community continually repeats itself throughout this entire country, year in and year out. Nationally, the statistics for childhood cancer are alarming. According to the CDC, forty-six children per day *(two classrooms full)* are being diagnosed with cancers unrelated to genetics or family history. As Trevor's Law states, "Cancer is the second-leading cause of death among children, exceeded only by accidents."

"Many of us young cancer survivors will forever face chronic health challenges resulting from the heroic medical measures used to save our lives. Children who have had cancer often experience confusion and embarrassment as they try to return to a so-called normal life and are dealing with the physical side effects related to their diagnosis and treatment. I can attest to that.

"Several years ago when cancer struck me, I fought so hard for my life. I endured countless needle pricks, blood transfusions, nausea, vomiting, and physical therapy, so I could live to see the sunrise and the snowfall. I am so grateful to be alive. Still, the aftermath from the cancer treatments that I received have affected me in many disturbing ways: I wake up every day to a constant ringing in my ear which never stops, I have trouble with my memory, and I may never be able to have children of my own. How ironic that I battled so hard to save my own life, yet now I may never be able to give life. And…Senators, I am considered one of the success stories.

"Although there has been a significant increase in the cure rate of childhood cancer, children still are getting sick at a steadily increasing rate. In small towns throughout our nation, possible cancer clusters exist. Parents are trying to get authorities to investigate these clusters and to discern what caused the disease patterns. Scientists and health activists say the government's current response to disease clusters ranges from piecemeal to nonexistent. Some people are told that their small populations render them *statistically insignificant.* There is nothing insignificant about even one child becoming part of a cancer cluster, then dying of that cancer without ever knowing why. Trevor's Law seeks to rectify that by allowing people in small communities to have their voices heard and their concerns validated about the environmental impact on their children's health.

"Environmental toxin exposure is insidious in all instances, yet it affects our children in greater proportion than adults. Children are *more vulnerable* to chemical toxins than adults because they have *faster metabolisms and less mature immune systems.*

"According to Dr. Sandra Steingraber, we are seeing more '…brain tumors in four-year-olds, ovarian cancer in adolescent girls, testicular cancer in adolescent boys. These cancers are rising rapidly, and of course *children don't smoke, drink, or hold stressful jobs.* We therefore can't really evoke lifestyle explanations. There are no good familial links that we know of. We are beginning to recognize that not only prenatal life but adolescent life is a time of great vulnerability to cancer-causing chemicals, when the connection between health and the environment becomes even more important' [Steingraber interview by Rita Dixit-Kubiak, *Seacoast Spirit*, Vol. I, No. 5].

"Toxins migrate right through geographical boundaries and across property lines. Cancer spares no ethnic group, no socio-economic group, nor any geographical area. In its wake we are left with the burden of enormous personal and social loss.

"I would also like to stress that childhood cancer doesn't only attack the victim, it greatly impacts every member of the family. Siblings often experience concern, fear, jealousy, guilt, resentment, and feelings of abandonment, which can last long term. Relationships between family members can become tense; there can be stress on a marriage, and frequently a family breaks up.

"I vowed that if I survived I would dedicate my life to helping other children with cancer who otherwise would never be heard. I truly believe I have been given a second chance at life to convey to you on their behalf the urgency and importance of addressing the proliferation of childhood cancer clusters and the methods of reporting them. For them, I strongly encourage you to support Trevor's Law.

"In closing, I would ask you to consider how much your child or grandchild's life and well-being are worth. And while you're doing that, please close your eyes for a brief moment and picture a world without children.

"Thank you."

A crush of well-wishers converged on Trevor after the rest of the witnesses finished their testimonials and took questions. He was nearly overwhelmed by how well his speech was received.

The female reporter who had requested an interview earlier joined the group. Another couple of journalists followed suit. She spoke up first, "How did it feel to be sitting right next to Erin Brockovich?"

"Amazing," he answered. "She told me that she is totally in favor of the work I've been doing. That it meshes with her current work, too."

"What's next for you, Trevor?" still another reporter piped up from the back of the pack.

"A lot of outreach. We have to get this bill enacted into law. Just because children can't vote doesn't mean they shouldn't have a voice. Today has been exhilarating. But I'm aware of how hard a fight we have ahead. We still have more hearings. Getting a bill passed out of this EPW committee. The list goes on and on." He glanced at his mom who stood off to the side watching him and listening. He smiled at her. "In fact, *our* work has just begun."

Trevor and Erin Brockovich, president of Brockovich Research & Consulting, testify before the Senate Environment and Public Works Committee during the March 29, 2011, Oversight Hearing on Disease Clusters and Environmental Health.

Trevor and Senator Barbara Boxer (D-CA). Boxer was an originating co-sponsor of S.76, Trevor's Law.

*Trevor and Senator Mike Crapo (R-ID). Crapo was
an originating co-sponsor of S.76, Trevor's Law.*

Trevor and Erin Brockovich after testifying at the Oversight Hearing.

Author's Afterword

During the research and writing of Charlie and Trevor's inspiring story, I became entwined in their lives, witnessing events as they unfolded. So it was not out of the ordinary for me to accompany them to Washington, D.C. in June 2009. I too experienced the most harrowing flight of my life and participated in the meeting with Senator Boxer and Secretary Lisa Jackson. Afterwards, I met up with the Smiths for that steak dinner in Georgetown.

As we celebrated our successful trip, I couldn't stop thinking about the change in Trevor since I first encountered him nearly seven years before. At that time, he was going through chemotherapy. I remember a frail, morose boy. He seemed younger than thirteen. He wouldn't look me in the eye when I interviewed him. Couldn't remember very many details of his life. I suggested that he write to me instead and use e-mail as our way of communicating.

At first, he addressed each message politely to "Mrs. Rosser." The content was formal and stilted, and useless. I asked him to forget that I once was a teacher and try to dig deeply into his memory bank, even if it hurt. I began to receive stream-of-consciousness replies to my pages of questions, each one more emotional than the next. Misspelled words, run-on sentences: all of it meant no more barriers to the hunt for his own truths.

His progress was also reflected by the way he addressed me: first, Mrs. Rosser; then Susan; and finally, Suzy Q. Six years later, the skinny boy with haunted eyes who saw the world as a scary place from which to escape had evolved into a thoughtful and confident young man.

That night while we enjoyed thick, juicy steaks and, yes, lots of summer corn and mashed potatoes, we all became introspective. I asked Trevor about the future and what he really wanted for himself now that he'd made such strides.

He hesitated thoughtfully and then said, "That's easy, Suzy Q. If the world became perfect, in the future no other child would ever again get cancer because of what we have done to poison our environment. But I know the world's not perfect. So I want to see a future where our local and federal governments actually care about the future of our children and the cleanup of the messes they and the private sector have created. I want to expand Trevor's Trek Foundation into an organization that makes the world understand what children who have battled cancer experience both during and after a diagnosis and treatment of cancer. I want to help create a freestanding sanctuary for children who are healthy enough to rejoin their community but are shunned and isolated when they return. This will be their own Happy Place."

I knew that his words were heartfelt. Still, they were thoughts I had heard him deliver so many times before. Tonight I didn't want a rehashed speech.

I was about to dig further when he rushed in, "But I want something else, too." He paused briefly, and his voice choked up. "I don't know how to make what I want happen." He stopped.

"Make *what* happen?" both Charlie and I urged.

"I want...no, I *need* to make sure that the voices of other children who suffer the way I have from emotional abuse at the hands of a parent are really heard in a court system. A court system that becomes more sensitive to the real damage that shows no obvious scars but goes on every day behind closed doors."

At that, he reached into his blue blazer and pulled out some official-looking papers. "It's done," he announced, pushing the documents across the table toward his mother.

He actually had gone through with it. Legally changed his name.

Trevor rushed on, "I'm nineteen. No one can stop this. I have nothing left in my power to show the world what he has done to me. My father doesn't deserve a son."

I glanced at Charlie, who appeared as stunned as I was. She had fought against this. Begged him to give this idea more time to settle in, hoping it was a passing phase. Now she was unable to talk.

"It'll be okay, Mom." He gave her a comforting smile. "This isn't your problem anymore."

Two more years have passed since that night. Trevor now lives alone. While taking classes at Boise State University, he's remained as involved as ever with the Trevor's Trek Foundation, whose current project is the establishment of a children's cancer pavilion at Julia Davis Park in the heart of Boise. It will be a sanctuary on the banks of a serene pond.

Our trip to Washington, D.C., this year was triumphant. For many months, Trevor worked hard for and finally won the support of Idaho Senator Mike Crapo who became an originating co-sponsor with Senator Barbara Boxer, making S.76, "Trevor's Law," truly bipartisan. In honor of his diligence, Trevor was selected as both a majority *and* minority witness for the Oversight Hearing, something nearly unheard of in the annals of the Senate or House of Representatives. Trevor's speech came together after several moments of angst. It was a miracle of composition and delivery. His mother and I were so proud of him.

And like the trip in 2009, we celebrated with a steak dinner. Toward the end of the evening, Trevor once again became introspective. He admitted that he still was troubled with his non-relationship with his father. In crisis, actually. Ballard was e-mailing him. He wanted to meet. Patch things up. Trevor was frightened to be in the same room with him. But he also feared the emotional repercussions of never speaking to the man again. He confessed, "If he dies without a further word between us, I don't know how I would handle it."

Charlie didn't say much. After eight years of being inside her head, I knew what she was thinking: You can change your phone number and even change your name, but it was still there. All of it. Under the surface. Roiling. Waiting. Just like all of her past was still there with her.

We parted that night, having settled nothing. Trevor reluctantly accepted that this decision was his alone. I felt bad, because I knew he wanted me to say he should meet with his father after all. But I couldn't tell him that. When Trevor defiantly proclaimed two years before that his father didn't deserve a son, he didn't understand that he also would be depriving himself of a father. Time and distance clearly had deadened the pain Ballard had caused. Was it easier now for Trevor to believe that even an abusive father was better than none? It did seem clear to me that he finally grasped the meaning of the ancient adage: Before embarking on the journey of revenge, dig two graves.

I thought about Trevor's personal conflict for a long time that night. How in the middle of all of his triumphs, he still had this dark anchor weighing him down. I realized then that all of our stories can coast, or dip precipitously, then soar and sometimes touch the stars. Yet the upheavals we endure, the damage that has been done, are like the layers of the earth—they make us who we are.

Susan Rosser
Rancho Mirage, California
May 13, 2011

Charlie, Trevor, and author Susan Rosser: Trevor's Trek in Boise, Idaho, September 15, 2007

Appendix A:

PRESS RELEASE FOR EPW
OVERSIGHT HEARING

****MEDIA ADVISORY****
US Senate Committee on Environment and Public Works
Full Committee
"Oversight Hearing on Disease Clusters
and Environmental Health"

BACKGROUND: Chairman Barbara Boxer (D-CA) will convene the Full Committee to assess the potential environmental health effects related to disease clusters. In January, Senator Boxer introduced legislation with Senator Mike Crapo (R-ID) to help determine whether there is a connection between "clusters" of cancer, birth defects and other diseases, and contaminants in the surrounding environment. The panel will hear testimony from Erin Brockovich and Trevor Schaefer, who survived after being diagnosed with brain cancer eight years ago at the age of 13. Trevor and his family have worked to raise awareness of disease clusters and their possible links to toxins in the environment. The complete witness list is below.

WHEN: TUESDAY, MARCH 29, 2011
                10:00 AM ET
LOCATION: **EPW Hearing Room**
                406 Dirksen Senate Office Building
                Washington, DC
WEBCAST: Webcast will be available at http://epw.senate.gov
                starting at 10:00 AM ET
WITNESSES: (Order subject to change)

<u>Panel I:</u>

- **Mr. Trevor Schaefer,** Youth Ambassador; and Founder, Trevor's Trek Foundation
- **Ms. Erin Brockovich,** President, Brockovich Research & Consulting
- **Dr. Richard B. Belzer, PhD,** President, Regulatory Checkbook
- **Dr. Gina Solomon, MD, MPH,** Senior Scientist, Natural Resources Defense Council

PRESS RELEASE FOR SENATOR BOXER AND SENATOR CRAPO'S INTRODUCTION OF S.76, "TREVOR'S LAW"

US Senate Committee on Environment and Public Works

Senators Boxer and Crapo Introduce Legislation to Help Communities Investigate and Address Disease Clusters and Environmental Hazards

Washington, DC – Senator Barbara Boxer (D-CA), Chairman of the Environment and Public Works Committee, introduced legislation with Senator Mike Crapo (R-ID) to help communities determine whether there is a connection between "clusters" of cancer, birth defects, and other diseases, and contaminants in the surrounding environment.

Senator Boxer said: **"Whenever there is an unusual increase in disease within a community, those families deserve to know that the federal government's top scientists and experts are accessible** and available to help, especially when the health and safety of children are at risk. I am pleased to introduce this bipartisan legislation that will enable communities to get the answers they need as quickly as possible."

Senator Crapo said: "As a two-time cancer survivor, I know that cancer can come from many sources. This legislation may provide the answers to questions that many families face when confronting disease, and it's important that we find ways to help Americans fully understand disease clusters. Through increasing federal agency coordination and accountability and providing more resources to affected communities, families will have more information and tools to maintain health and well-being."

Throughout the country, there are communities that experience unexpected increases in the incidence of birth defects, cancer and other diseases. The legislation, S.76, is designed to:

- Strengthen federal agency coordination and accountability when investigating these potential certain "clusters" of disease;
- Increase assistance to areas impacted by potential disease clusters; and
- Authorize federal agencies to form partnerships with states and academic institutions to investigate and help address disease clusters.

The legislation being introduced today is supported by the Trevor's Trek Foundation, co-founded by Charlie Smith and Susan Rosser with Trevor Schaefer, who survived after being diagnosed with brain cancer seven years ago at the age of thirteen. Trevor and his family have worked to raise awareness of disease clusters and their possible links to toxins in the environment, and to help build support for legislation to assist communities experiencing suspected disease clusters.

Partial Text of U.S. Senate Bill 76, "Trevor's Law"

(TO READ THE ENTIRE TEXT GO TO:
www.legiscan.com or www.trevorstrek.org)

111TH CONGRESS
2D SESSION

S. 76

To direct the Administrator of the Environmental
Protection Agency to investigate and address cancer and
disease clusters, including in infants and children.

IN THE SENATE OF THE UNITED STATES

Mrs. BOXER introduced the following bill; which
was read twice and referred to the Committee

A BILL
To direct the Administrator
of the Environmental Protection
Agency to investigate and address cancer and disease
clusters, including in infants and children.

*Be it enacted by the Senate and House of Representatives
of the United States of America in Congress assembled,*

SECTION 1. SHORT TITLE.
This Act may be cited as the "Strengthening Protections
for Children and Communities From
Disease Clusters Act," also known as
"Trevor's Law."

SECTION 2. FINDINGS.
Congress finds that—

(1) children are particularly at risk from environmental pollutants or toxic substances for various reasons, including because—(A) the nervous, immune digestive, and other systems of children are still developing as the children move though several stages of rapid growth and development;

(B) exposure to environmental pollutants or toxic substances can affect prenatal, infant, and childhood growth and development;

(C) children may be less able to detoxify and excrete toxins than adults;

(D) children eat proportionately more food, drink more fluids, breathe more air, and play outside more, which means children are more exposed to environmental pollutants and toxic substances than adults;

(E) children are less able to protect themselves from exposures to environmental pollutants or toxic substances;

(F) the behavior of children exposes children to different environmental pollutants and toxic substances than adults;

(G) the natural curiosity and tendency of children to explore leaves children open to health risks that adults can more easily avoid; and

(H) the developing brains, reproductive systems, and other organs of children are more susceptible to permanent disruption that can result in health problems during the lives of the children;

(2) according to the Department of Health and Human Services, birth defects are the leading cause of infant death in the first year of life, accounting for about 20 percent of infant deaths in 2006;

(3) according to the American Cancer Society, cancer is the second leading cause of death in children, exceeded only by accidents;

(4) according to the Centers for Disease Control and Prevention, an estimated 1 in 110 children in the United States have an autism spectrum disorder;

(5) scientific research on environmental, genetic, and other influences that may affect environmental health is a national priority;

(6) Federal agencies should work to address serious environmental health problems to better protect children and other individuals in communities, both large and small, across the United States...

Appendix D:

CONGRESSIONAL RECORD OF TREVOR SCHAEFER'S WRITTEN TESTIMONY AT EPW OVERSIGHT HEARING

Official Record: March 29, 2011

I want to thank Chair Barbara Boxer, Ranking Member James Inhofe, and my senator, Mike Crapo, for taking on the subject of childhood cancer and cancer clusters and what they mean to our public health. I would like to thank *all* of the senators on the Environment and Public Works Committee for the care you give in debating the environmental and health dilemmas a modern world creates and for allowing me to address some of those issues today. And—I am so *very* proud to be able to state that I am here today as a witness for **both** the Majority and Minority committee members.

Most of you don't know me other than that I am associated with **S.76**, also known as **Trevor's Law**. By the end of my testimony my hope is that you will not only know *me*, but that you will remember me as the voice of every child in this great nation.

(As you have been told) I am a twenty-one-year-old brain cancer survivor. In November of 2002 at the age of thirteen, I was diagnosed with a highly malignant *Medullablastoma*. What a word! I could barely pronounce it correctly, let alone get my mind around what it meant to my future.

Until that time, you see, I was living and thriving in McCall, a small town located on a lake nestled in the beautiful mountains of Idaho. I was enjoying a fairy tale life in paradise: boating with friends and family in the summer, snowboarding in the winter and playing football for my seventh grade football team. But the carefree days of my childhood changed abruptly and dramatically after my cancer diagnosis. My entire world came crumbling down around me. Cancer was an alien word to me, one that was synonymous with invasion and death. I had to suddenly face the realization that there was a chance I might never see my friends, my family or my home, again.

Like a snap of the fingers I was robbed of my childhood and my innocence. The antiseptic world of hospitals became my life as I went through invasive tests then endured an eight hour surgery to remove a golf ball sized tumor from the base of my brain. While I recuperated I could not even stand. I barely had the strength to open my eyes. How could it be that a mere two months prior to this I was struggling for a touchdown, and now I was struggling to stay alive? Soon after leaving the hospital I entered an even more terrifying life: I began fourteen grueling months of radiation and chemotherapy treatment.

Unfortunately I wasn't the only kid with this pernicious disease in my town. In the same year of my diagnosis there were four other brain cancers in our tiny resort community with a year-round permanent population of 1,700 residents. Over a ten year period there was an abnormally high number of cancer cases diagnosed there prior to, and after, my diagnosis. My mother was alerted to, and alarmed by, these numbers and took this information to the Cancer Data Registry. She expressed her fears that perhaps our beautiful little town was the wrong kind of paradise. Her fears were responded to in a patronizing fashion, the official telling her that even if her data proved true, our town was too small to warrant a cancer cluster study: We were not .

Just as she never let me give up my fight for life, she refused to give up the fight for the truth. That encounter at the Tumor Registry started both of us on the course that has led to *this* day in *this* room to consider the overall issue of childhood cancer clusters and how best to respond to those who believe they might be part of one. Some of those issues could be resolved through **S.76** which, among other things, will provide the most effective means of coordinating agencies and ensuring outreach to, and involvement of, community members.

What happened in my community continually repeats itself throughout this *entire* country, year in and year out. It impacts many of your neighborhoods and many of your neighbors. Nationally the statistics for childhood cancer are alarming. According to the CDC, *forty-six children per day ()* are being diagnosed with cancers *unrelated* to genetics or family history. The National Cancer Institute states that there are over 12,500 children diagnosed with cancer each year. As **S. 76** states, "cancer is the second leading cause of death among children, exceeded only by accidents."

According to Dr. Sandra Steingraber, Childhood cancers are "swiftly rising cancers… pediatric leukemia, brain tumors amongst four-year-olds, ovarian cancer amongst adolescent girls, testicular cancer amongst adolescent boys. These cancers are rising rapidly and of course **children don't smoke, drink, or hold stressful jobs**. We therefore can't really evoke lifestyle explanations. There are no good familial links that we know of. We are beginning to recognize that not only pre-natal life but adolescent life is a time of great vulnerability to cancer causing chemicals, when the connection between health and the environment becomes even more important." (Steingraber interview by Rita Dixit-Kubiak, *Seacoast Spirit*, Vol. I, No.5).

The emotional and monetary costs of childhood cancer and cancer clusters continue to mount, unraveling the very fabric of our society thread by thread. Many of us young cancer survivors will forever face chronic health challenges resulting from the heroic medical measures used to save our lives. According to Kevin Oeffinger of New York's Memorial Sloan-Kettering Cancer Center, childhood cancer patients' "health problems, which include heart disease, lung scarring, strokes and second cancers, can be caused both by their original tumors as well as the harsh treatments used to cure them." In fact, more than 73% of patients cured of pediatric cancer will develop chronic illness within thirty years of the diagnosis. (*New England Journal of Medicine*).

Senators, nothing is quite so lonely as being a child with cancer. Lying in a hospital bed and sitting in a chemo chair getting chemotherapy treatments and blood transfusions while other kids are outside playing ball and riding bikes isn't exactly the childhood I, or any of us, had in mind. Our growth and social advancement may be stunted, but in other ways we are forced to become mature beyond our years: learning to be patient and resilient, and becoming courageous warriors fighting our own battles without any armor.

Children who have had cancer often experience confusion and embarrassment as they try to return to a so-called *normal* life and are dealing with the physical side effects related to their diagnosis and treatment. I can attest to that. During my chemotherapy treatments I developed neuropathy, more commonly known as Foot-Drop. I walked with a decided limp and felt as though I could fall over at any moment. During the time of my treatment and this side-effect, I was changing schools. I was cautioned to think twice about going someplace new: *the kids would laugh at you because you walk funny.* Don't think that wasn't always in the back of my mind *every* hour I spent in school while I had this condition.

Although it has been almost nine years since my diagnosis of brain cancer, I am constantly reminded of this bully who tried with a vicious determination to take my life. Every morning I still wake up with a distinct ringing in my ear, which I have with me every second of every day, a residual effect from my brain tumor, only one of many. Before brain cancer I could have appeared before you and delivered this entire testimony from memory. The residual cognitive effects of chemotherapy make it difficult for me to do that.

Several years ago when cancer struck me I fought so hard for my life. I endured the countless needle pricks, blood transfusions, nausea, vomiting and physical therapy so I could live to see the sunrise and the snowfall. I am so grateful to be alive. Still, the aftermath from the cancer treatments that I received have affected me in a way where I may never be able to have children of my own. How ironic that I battled so hard to save my own life, succeeded, yet now I may never be able to give life.

The emotional side effects from cancer can be devastating to a once active and vibrant child. We can feel a range of emotions that include fear, depression, anxiety and symptoms similar to Post-Traumatic Stress Disorder. We may also feel lost or isolated because we no longer have stability or a sense of control over our lives. Lack of interest and poor self-esteem can last long after our final treatment is over.

I would also like to stress that childhood cancer doesn't only attack the victim, it greatly impacts every member of the family. Siblings often experience concern, fear, jealousy, guilt, resentment and feelings of abandonment, which can last long-term. Relationships between family members can become tense; there can be stress on a marriage, and frequently a family breaks up.

So many times at my treatment appointments, I would see a parent alone with several children, one of whom was the sick member of the family. My mother and I sometimes talked to these parents. Most of them had heartbreaking stories to tell of families going bankrupt, having to sell their house, or a mother losing her job because she had to stay home with her sick child. One time we learned from a frazzled mother sitting near us that her husband had just left her a few weeks before.

She'd lost her job and couldn't afford a babysitter for the rambunctious two-year- old in her arms who was *autistic*. She had no choice but to bring him along to the clinic while her older, six-year-old son lay on the couch next to her shivering under a blanket while awaiting his turn for treatment for advanced bone cancer.

Coping with a life-threatening disease like cancer is an ambiguous and unpredictable process. Although there has been a significant increase in the cure rate of childhood cancer, there needs to be more focus and research on what causes this disease and other catastrophic and chronic illnesses in children. There is an increasingly vast body of evidence showing that some chronic conditions such as birth defects, developmental disorders among children, and cancers are linked to the ubiquitous toxins that are dumped into the food children eat, the water they drink, and the air that they breathe.

In small towns throughout our nation possible cancer clusters exist. Parents are trying to get authorities to investigate these clusters and to discern what caused the disease patterns. Scientist and health activists say the government's current response to disease clusters ranges from *piecemeal to non-existent*. **S. 76** allows people in small communities to have their voices heard and their concerns validated about the environmental impact on their children. It would have been a different story for my mom all those years ago had this legislation been in place. This is true for so many communities throughout the nation.

Take **Clyde, Ohio**, for instance, where twelve-year-old Tanner was diagnosed with Leukemia in 2008. Tanner is one of *thirty-five* kids who have been diagnosed with cancer since 1996. His older sister, Tyler, is a cancer survivor and she is only seventeen. The cancer rate in this cluster is almost *six times the normal rate* for children in this part of Ohio.

And then we have **Sierra Vista, Arizona**, where *eleven* children were diagnosed with Leukemia in a five-year period. Linus was a toddler at the time of his diagnosis. Jessica was also two years old—and the list goes on.

In a community just outside Boise, Taylor was diagnosed with Hodgkin's Lymphoma at age eight, and Gracie was diagnosed with kidney cancer at age two. Zach, at age thirteen, has been fighting Leukemia since he was eleven years old, and Paige was diagnosed with thyroid cancer at the age of fourteen. And then there's my little friend Bradley who lives near my home. He is seven years old and has battled Neuroblastoma (a rare cancer of the nervous system) since he was three years old. His body is intersected with surgery scars resembling a road map. Bradley has been an amazing fighter and an inspiration to all who meet him. Lately, however, you can see that some of the spunk has gone out of his personality. He's become more aware that his little brother is bigger and taller than he is. And just a few months ago he was diagnosed with an old person's affliction—*cataracts* in both eyes. One day a few weeks back, Bradley's teacher found a note that he had scribbled. She gave it to his grandma. She shared it with us. In it, Bradley asked what it was like in heaven and said that he was afraid to die because he did not want dirt in his eyes.

From these few examples alone you can see why it is that I have been inspired to help develop and propose legislation like **S.76**. Introduced in the spirit of amity *not* enmity by **both** Chair Boxer and Senator Crapo, this truly **bi-partisan bill** is especially encouraging to a neophyte to the political system like me. Despite our charged political climate, **Trevor's Law** is proof that party affiliation need not prevent senators from putting children's health above politics.

What I especially like about **S.76** is that it could help pinpoint the causes of predatory disease at its earliest stage by bringing together agencies with the relevant expertise needed to investigate and report disease clusters in a timely manner. Through this multi-agency system, the burden could be lifted off the health community, which for now shoulders the arduous responsibility as the repository of cancer information. And it will also make the investigative process transparent and inclusive. No longer will those who reside in fear in small communities be told that they have no place at the table that they don't count because they are *statistically insignificant.* There is *nothing insignificant* about even one child becoming part of a cancer cluster then dying of that cancer without ever knowing why.

Environmental toxin exposure is insidious in all instances, yet it affects our children in greater proportion than adults. Let me reiterate, children are **more vulnerable** to chemical toxins than adults because they have faster metabolisms and less mature immune systems.

Toxins don't respect geographical boundaries or property lines. Cancer eschews all boundaries, too. This disease spares no ethnic group, no socio-economic group nor any geographical area. In its wake we are left with the burden of enormous personal and social loss.

I made a promise to myself that if I survived I would dedicate my time in this world to helping other children with cancer so they would not have to suffer the way I did. Senators, I was spared. I truly believe I have been given a second chance at life to convey to you the urgency and importance of a need to address the growing dilemma of childhood cancer clusters. On behalf of all the children with cancer who are suffering now and for those who may one day suffer, I strongly encourage your support for **Trevor's Law.**

In closing, I would ask you to consider how much your child or grandchild's life and well-being are worth? And while you're doing that, please close your eyes for a brief moment and picture a world without children.

Appendix E:

TESTIMONY OF ERIN BROCKOVICH AT EPW OVERSIGHT HEARING

Official Record: March 29, 2011

To Chairman Boxer and distinguished members of this committee, thank you for the opportunity to testify today on the issues of disease clusters and environmental health.

My name is Erin Brockovich and I am President of Brockovich Research and Consulting. As an environmental and consumer advocate I respond to requests for help in groundwater contamination complaints in all fifty states. I currently work on investigations in California, Texas, Florida, Michigan, New York, New Jersey, Alabama, Louisiana, Illinois, Mississippi and Missouri. I am also a proud mother of three wonderful children, two of whom are presently serving their country as soldiers in the United States Army; one currently deployed in Afghanistan.

Each month I receive over 40,000 visitors to my website, thousands of whom report issues ranging from environmental pollution, cancer and disease, worker injury and illness, and more. These people make up whole communities that are witnessing firsthand the harmful effects that exposure to chemicals, such as hexavalent chromium— an issue that my colleagues at EWG did a report on and this Committee discussed at an earlier hearing—have had on them and their families.

These communities—both large and small, and in every corner of the United States are sending out an SOS. From small farming towns like Cameron, Missouri to small desert towns like Midland, Texas, to the forgotten town of Leadwood, Missouri, where the lead mining tails are so large that children think they are hills and play on them. In passing by, as the children wave, it is startling to see the palms of their hands gray from the lead dust. To larger communities such as Champaign, Illinois and unfortunately yet again, Hinkley, California. This is becoming an all too common occurrence. It would appear that most of these communities are under siege by one form of pollution or another. Communities feel forgotten and betrayed by regulatory agencies and their elected representatives who in their minds have turned a blind eye to the problem.

Protecting the health of our families and our children should be a top priority for us all, yet the system for investigating, responding and reporting these concerns is inadequate. This is why I strongly support SB 76, the Strengthening Protection for Children and Communities from Disease Clusters Act, also known as Trevor's Law in honor of this brave young man, Trevor Schaefer.

Trevor's Law will bolster federal efforts to assist communities that are impacted by potential disease clusters and will identify sources of environmental pollutants and toxic substances suspected of causing developmental, reproductive, neurotoxic effects and numerous cancers and other adverse health effects.

According to the CDC in 2011, 1 in 3 people will develop cancer in his or her lifetime. 1 in 3! As an advocate for the past twenty years I have reached an undeniable conclusion; there are simply too many cancers in this country and not enough answers. And that is what these communities, who reach out to me, are trying to do; get answers to the most basic questions. Why is my child, who was perfectly healthy, now sick with leukemia? Why does my daughter have a brain tumor at the age of ten? Why is the same thing happening to my neighbor's kids? Hundreds of mothers and fathers ask me these questions every week.

Today I would like to share with you a map that I have put together over the past 6 months of communities that have come to me with concerns of what they believe to be excessive cancers in their neighborhoods and communities. The statistics are alarming. These are mothers reporting 6 children on the same block with leukemia; these are mothers reporting 15 children within blocks of one another who have glioblastomas. In some instances it is nurses reporting to mothers the large numbers of pediatric cancers they are seeing in certain communities. The work is being done ADHOC by concerned citizens.

We must gather data from the field and act. We must develop national strategies for identifying actionable information. We must take a "combined arms" approach to the battle against disease of our own making.

When I talk about this issue, I think of my son who is fighting a war in Afghanistan. If I were to suddenly find myself in the field of conflict, it would not matter how credentialed I was…environmentalist, PhD, or US Senator … I would take my lead from those who had been on the ground. Make no mistake; we are in a war here at home.

In this battle you are the commander. Your troops, your constituents, are sending a message, but we aren't listening. While this map is not scientific, it does show first hand experiences are providing us the data we need. They are reporting to me for help because they are concerned that pollution in their towns is making them sick. I will continue to work diligently to gather greater information, and report what we are seeing. This map begs me to do so. This is why I sit here today and share with you. Why aren't we looking at it?

Part of the puzzle that is missing has been the lack of action at an agency level identifying these disease clusters and involving the Americans affected by environmental pollution.

I have seen this firsthand, over and over again. In each situation where I am involved, agencies have come out and concluded there was or may have been a problem, documented it, reported it somewhere, wrote it up and moved on. These agencies are overburdened, understaffed and underfunded. No one appears to follow up on the health of these residents, even of those who live in and around the 1,280 Superfund sites listed on the National Priorities List as of November 29, 2010.

As a result, people have no faith in the state or federal agencies tasked to investigate what's making people sick in their communities and that is why they turn to me. But I cannot take the place of a disease registry or an official reporting program.

Trevor's Law, takes steps to address this problem by strengthening federal coordination between state and local authorities in investigating the potential causes of a disease cluster. This bill will empower communities to work with these agencies and therefore facilitate investigations and responses.

I am not here today to play scientist, nor am I here to sling accusations or assign blame. This is not a partisan issue. Gathering the information necessary to take action to protect human health is a long and daunting task, but it is time for us to stop turning away from these communities.

We MUST listen to and learn from these people affected by environmental pollutants. We can't just sit back in the safety of our offices and hear these stories and think well ... "that isn't possible", the reports say that can't happen. I am here to tell you that they do happen and they are happening.

Members of this committee carry the voice and the will of those who elected you. Those voices are crying out for help. Your constituents are fearful, frustrated and they need your help to get the answers they deserve! Communities want and need transparency between themselves, government and business. I cannot stress this enough. Transparency can help ensure accountability, but more importantly, it enables a healthy flow of communication between all parties.

The people in these communities don't know what to do with this information. For example, I received an email the other day from a woman, who through Facebook, had discovered that all of her old friends, family and acquaintances from the old neighborhood had numerous and similar cancer. They all lived in the same town, in close proximity to a facility known to have toxic releases. She came to me because she didn't know where else to turn and was asking for guidance. I could have recommended contacting a certain agency, but unfortunately many communities have learned that their issues will fall on deaf ears.

With reports like this, and a recent report that came out regarding the now famous situation in Hinkley, California, we are beginning to see what appear to be "holes" in our cancer reporting systems.

We have state agencies providing statistical analysis on cancer data, without adequately tracking population movement. I have personally read reports claiming insufficient evidence of cancer cases to support a "cluster" conclusion, yet the report admittedly did not reach out to former residents when sampling data. Senators, if you had a river of hexavalent chromium or benzene coming down your street, I suspect you might move … and no agency will ever know the affect that river will have had on your lives.

This is the "hole." The registry does not track, look for, or identify those who lived in an area during the worst of the contamination and had moved. What's needed is a more comprehensive system for gathering and analyzing cancer data. We need a "people's" national reporting agency.

I urge all of you, all of us, to explore and expand the use of all tools, including social media, to track and ensure all affected people are part of the solution. States must share information with the federal government, thru existing agencies and must export the actionable data.

Most people believe, because of a movie, that I am an environmental activist, and I do care a great deal about the environment but my real work and challenge is trying to overcome obstacles that jeopardize public health and safety, and to find ways to prevent them in the first place.

I am an advocate for awareness and a person's right to know. Often times we don't think about or understand what is happening, especially when we don't live in a given venue and know the day to day struggles a community is having until it affects us personally. Cancer or chronic disease has touched us all! Disease recognizes no party affiliation.

In April 2010, the President's Cancer Panel declared that the number of cancers caused by toxic chemicals is "grossly underestimated" and warned that American's face "grievous harm" from the largely unregulated chemicals that contaminate the air and water.

This is the critical issue in our time. Whether it is pollution in our water, the air or the products we use, the Government should take a stronger role in helping all Americans and identify what is going on. I understand that this may not be the most popular position in some circles but there is an irony to this confusing un-popularity ...

I was born and raised in Kansas, by a strong Republican and military man, who actually worked for industry, and the government, as an engineer. He is the very person that taught me the value of clean water, good land; good health and that we should have respect of one another. It always amuses me when someone thinks I have a certain party affiliation. I find it disturbing when some assume that environmental activists are anti-business. I always thought caring for the environment and public health was a conservative thing to do. I later learned that it was just the right thing to do.

It's important that we don't just come in, run some tests and leave. Make no mistake—the government should play a key role in identifying and responding to disease clusters and only the federal government can provide that national level of oversight and solution we need. But we can't lose sight of the most important part of any effort to identify and respond to a disease cluster—and that is the people themselves.

We need to come together on this as Republicans, Democrats, Independents, businesses and communities. We need government, business and affected communities to join as ONE for the betterment of the whole and clean up our messes. We should ask no more of ourselves than we would ask of our children. We need to work together to find solutions and learn what my children and countless other children who serve this country teach us—we must protect, nurture and defend what we love most; our families, health, land, and water ... our very environment.

Chairman Boxer and Senator Crapo, I commend and thank you for your leadership on this issue. Let us act now to help these communities who suffer.

Appendix F:

DANIEL ROSENBERG'S
BLOG POST AFTER
EPW OVERSIGHT HEARING

Meet Trevor Schaefer: Riveting testimony anchors strong Senate hearing on Disease Clusters and Environmental Health

Over the years I have worked on environmental and public health issues in Washington, DC, I have attended many, many hearings. And I have seen and heard many people testify at these hearings. Most people, whatever side or interest they are representing, do a good job. Very often they are government officials from any number of federal, state, or local agencies or elected offices. They are frequently professionals—typically lawyers, scientists, and academics—or members of trade associations. They deliver their testimony in a clear and concise manner, and are generally prepared to provide responsive and even helpful or enlightening answers.

But on a couple of occasions I have seen extraordinary, riveting testimony that completely captivated every senator or representative in attendance, as well as the staff, the public, the press, and anyone else in the hearing room. One of those times was when Jerry Ensminger testified at a hearing about the cancer cluster at Camp LeJeune in North

Carolina where he lived, and about his nine-year-old daughter who died of leukemia.

Another of those times was earlier today, when 21-year-old Trevor Schaefer delivered measured but powerful testimony about his own successful battle with brain cancer—beginning at age thirteen—and the need for Congress to take action to protect children and assist communities that are potentially affected by disease clusters.

Trevor, who travelled to the nation's capital from Boise, Idaho, spoke today at a Senate Environment and Public Works Committee Oversight hearing on Disease Clusters and Environmental Health. In a little more than five minutes, he described his personal experience receiving cancer treatment at such a young age, how his life has been affected and may be in the future, and how his experience is an important window on a widespread problem that affects people in cities and towns all across the country. My one-sentence summary doesn't begin to do it justice. I highly recommend you take a few minutes to watch the testimony for yourself (it begins at 31:15).

Trevor spoke specifically in support of legislation introduced by the committee's chair, Barbara Boxer of California (a Democrat), and her committee colleague, Michael Crapo of Idaho (a Republican), that would improve federal coordination and assistance for state and local governments, and community members that are trying to identify potential disease clusters or determine the potential causes of such clusters. It has been referred to as "Trevor's Law," and, after seeing his testimony from today's hearing, you'll know why, and you'll want to do what you can to help it reach the President's desk.

Trevor was joined on the witness panel by Erin Brockovich, yes, *the* Erin Brockovich, who described the thousands of contacts she receives every month from people all over the country who are struggling with striking numbers of illnesses in their communities, and are frustrated by the lack of an adequate response or assistance from government agencies. People know her story, and know that she cares about them. They turn to her for help when they believe the government can't or won't help. Her testimony was also excellent (it begins at 40:35).

And my colleague Dr. Gina Solomon testified about her professional work and the important societal benefits that we could reap by more effectively and systematically investigating potential disease clusters and their causes. She also discussed an Issue Paper that NRDC released yesterday with the National Disease Cluster Alliance that documents 42 disease clusters in 13 states, which have either been confirmed by government agencies or academic researchers, or are under current investigation by federal, state or local health agencies. Those 42 cases are just the tip of the iceberg. And in all of those communities, and the hundreds of others around the country, people are experiencing the same pain, suffering, anxiety, fear, and loss that Trevor described in his own testimony. You can see Gina's oral testimony here (at 57:11) and read her full written testimony here.

Gina explained why Trevor's Law is needed to help citizens confront the disease clusters in their communities, and why reform of the Toxic Substances Control Act (TSCA) is needed to ensure the safety of chemicals that are used in products and prevent creation of additional disease clusters in the future.

This was a valuable hearing on an issue that is both important, and, given all the many issues that Congress is dealing with (or at least pretending to deal with), easy to ignore. But those Senators who attended the hearing paid careful attention to all of the testimony, and they were serious, thoughtful, and constructive; things that cannot be taken for granted at congressional hearings. I think Trevor's testimony is something that will be difficult to ignore and, if you witnessed it, impossible to forget.

Scars of Courage

The word comes back; your fight begins.
In the beginning, you think cancer wins.

Darkness falls and drowns the light.
You feel the pain both day and night.

But you must play the hand you were dealt.
A sigh of reality as you tighten your belt.

Your hair grows thin, your step unsteady.
You're too young for this fight; you're just not ready.

Some lose their limbs but keep their heart.
But your soul stays strong through the hardest part.

The battle continues, but your time is near.
You realize the inevitable and lose all fear.

You tried so hard not to lose your way.
But you can't return, not tomorrow nor today.

You see your gravestone and the word "deceased,"
Fear no more, Mom; now I can rest in peace.

You threw up so many times into those bins.
I guess in the end, cancer wins.

You were taken from this world at too young of an age.
Your book of life never made it past the first page.

The dream you leave is for our leaders to listen.
Change the path of our future and protect our children.

Trevor Schaefer
Fall 2011